Journalists Are Not
The Enemy of the People

Journalists Are Not
The Enemy of the People

Correct News or Fake News
You be the Judge!

Gerald L. Hutson

LIBERTY HILL PUBLISHING

Liberty Hill Publishing
2301 Lucien Way #415
Maitland, FL 32751
407.339.4217
www.libertyhillpublishing.com

© 2020 by Gerald L. Hutson

Printed in the United States of America.

ISBN-13: 978-1-6305-0436-6

Thanks to my wife and children who sustained the last four years of putting together my book. Also my thanks to Andrea for her excellent typing and proofreading my manuscript. Without their support, it would have been difficult."

Authors Note:

The world is constantly changing, and the expressions of many journalists tend to keep the subject matter the same with their own twists on words, which when interpreted, end up having the same meaning. Over many years, journalist's stories are remembered or forgotten by the public, and at times not returning and remaining as history in the media world.

Journalists hold dear the First Amendment of the Constitution which protects your right and needs to know more than what your government is telling you. Journalists are doing their job and are not trying to tear down a nation, only trying to strengthen it by believing the fundamental premise behind the First Amendment, that our nation is stronger if its people are informed. Our founding fathers enshrined the freedom of journalists in the Constitution. Thomas Jefferson stated to John Tyler, the tenth President of the United States:

> "No experiment can be more interesting than that we are now trying, and which we trust will end in establishing the fact that man is governed by reason and truth. Our first object should therefore be to lave open to him all the avenues of truth. The most effective hither to found is freedom of the press. It is therefore, the first shut up by those who fear the investigation of their actions." (Thomas Jefferson-1804

America's founders believed that a free press was essential to democracy, and the American experience has proved them right. Journalism guards' freedoms and binds together communities of information that powers everything from elections to the economy. Freedom of the press has been fiercely defended by nearly all-American presidents regardless of politics or party affiliation, and regardless of their own complaints about coverage.

Over 167 years, through 33 presidents, and administrations, newspapers have sought to serve America and its citizens by seeking the truth and helping people understand the world. Mr. Trump's campaign against journalist should concern every patriotic American.

Donald Trump swore an oath to defend the U.S. Constitution. The First Amendment is the stated guarantee of a free press from government dictates, and an implied responsibility of journalist to be a check on the government's enormous powers.

Our democracy depends on journalist doing their jobs. It is essential that citizens get solid, accurate, and fair information they need to make a good judgement about politicians and policy decisions. Our system of free press will not work if journalists work does not shoulder the burden of serving as watchdogs, holding the government accountable, and looking at the many complex issues that confront the world.

President Donald Trump has dominated the news media throughout the world. Journalists have written about his everyday activities, but Trump has referred to professional journalist stories as "Fake News" and has called media coverage the "Enemy of the People".

Journalists need to be remembered so children growing up completing high school, college, and into family life with children, can see what happened to America's political system and how demands of a president are being followed by his administration:

President Donald Trump tweeted the following statements about the news media in the United States:

August 15, 2016 "If the disgusting and corrupt media covered me honestly and didn't put false meaning into the words I say, I would be beating Hillary by 20%. **10) David Jackson-USA Today**

February 17, 2017 "I see stories of chaos, chaos, yet it is the exact opposite, this administration is running like a fine-tuned machine, to be honest I inherited a mess, it's a mess, at home and abroad, a mess." **79) David Jackson-USA Today**

June 16, 2017 "They made up phony collusion with the Russians story, found zero proof, so now they go for obstruction of justice on the phony story. Nice. You are witnessing the single greatest WHICH HUNT in America political history led by some very bad and conflicted people." **120) Brian Bennett, Noah Bierman-Washington Bureau**

December 12, 2017 "Very little discussion of all the purposely false and defamatory stories put out by the Fake News Media. They are out of control; correct reporting means nothing to them. Major lies written, then forced to be withdrawn after they are exposed, a stain on America." **165) Rex W. Huppke-Chicago Tribune**

August 17, 2018 Trump often calls the media: "dishonest", "disgusting", "fake", "opposition party". **279) Kurtis Lee-Los Angeles Times**

October 30, 2018 Days after the shooting at the Pittsburgh Synagogue, Trump argued that "fraudulent" reporting was contributing to anger in the country and declared that the press was "the enemy of the people." **309) Catherine Lucey-Associated Press**

January 2, 2019 "HAPPY NEW YEAR TO EVERYONE, INCLUDING THE HATERS AND THE FAKE NEWS MEDIA!" **368) Anne Gearan-The Washington Post**

The many journalist that have expressed their writings in this book are acknowledged at the end of the book with references to each of their respective media sources to include all dates when articles were published. Recognition is given to each journalist and their contributing newspaper articles relating to President Donald Trump and his administration.

Table of Contents

IRAN NUCLEAR DEAL DROPPED | TEXAS SCHOOL SHOOTINGS | TENSIONS ON TRADE | RIGHT TO PARDON SELF | LEGAL ENTRY UNDER SEIGE | CRITICISM OF SEPARATING FAMILIES | TARIFFS PUT U.S. JOBS AT RISK | TRADE WAR SHOWDOWN LOOMS | TRUMP'S ATTACK ON MEDIA | TRUMP STANDS WITH SAUDI'S | TRUMP INSISTS CIA IS WRONG | TRUMP THREATENS TO CLOSE BORDERS | TRUMP SLAMS FEDERAL RESERVE CHAIRMAN | TRUMP PUSHES TO STRIP RIGHTS FROM MIGRANTS | SUPREME COURT RULES IN FAVOR OF TRAVEL BAN | TRUMP BERATES ALLIES

TRUMP BLASTS SPECIAL COUNCIL | MUELLER IMPLICATES PRESIDENT | PARTIAL SHUT DOWN | LIES TO TROOPS | BORDER WALL FUNDS | COHEN SENTENCED TO 3 YEARS | "COHEN BROKE LAW, NOT ME" | RUSSIA EFFORTS IN 2016 ELECTION | TRUMP FOUNDATION TO DISSOLVE | TRUMP ORDERS U.S. FORCES OUT OF SYRIA | MATTIS FORCED OUT | PLEA FOR WALL MONEY | MANIFORT ACCUSED | DACA DEAL FOR WALL MONEY | ROGER STONE INDICTED | TRUMP'S TAXES | TRUMP CALLS EMERGENCY, DEFIES CONGRESS | COHEN ACCUSATIONS OF TRUMP LIES | N. KOREA TALKS BREAKDOWN | MANIFORT SENTENCED | EMERGENCY DECLARATION REJECTED | TRUMP VETO'S BORDER RESOLUTION | TRUMP FIRES UNDOCUMENTED WORKERS | SHUTDOWN OVER | STONE PLEADS NOT GUILTY | U.S. TO QUIT NUKE PACT WITH RUSSIA | TRUMP REJECTS WALL DEBATE | GOLF COURSE FURTHERS U.K. RELATIONS | TRUMP'S TRANSCRIPT HIDDEN | CHINA TRADE TALKS HIT A BUMP | TRUMP ASKS FOR $8.6 BILLION FOR WALL

TRUMP TAKES AIM AT JOHN MCCAIN | MUELLER PROBE ENDS WITH REPORT | NO RUSSIA CONSPIRACY | THREAT TO CLOSE BORDER | TRUMP INFLATES WEALTH | SEEKING TRUMP TAX RETURNS | SUPOENA MUELLER REPORT | "OUR COUNTRY IS FULL" | QUESTION OF OBSTRUCTION | FAILURES AS COMMANDER IN CHIEF | ARE

TRUMP CALL FOR BAN ON VAPING CONCERNS I SUBPOENA OF
TRUMP TAX RETURNS I STANDOFF OVER WHISTLEBLOWER
ESCALATES I PRESIDENT ASKED UKRAINES LEADER FOR BIDEN
INQUIRY I TRUMP MENTIONED BIDEN TO UKRAINES I PRESIDENT
TRUMP DEFIANT WHEN PRESSED FOR UKRAINE FILES I PELOSI: NO
ONE IS ABOVE THE LAW I WITNESSES BOLSTER WHISTLE BLOWER
COMPLAINT

Chapter 1

1) July 21, 2016- "I am your voice"

On the last day of the Republican National Convention, Donald Trump accepted the GOP nomination for president and promised to restore "safety, prosperity and peace" to the country. Trump stated **"I am your voice. I will present the facts plainly and honestly. We cannot afford to be politically correct anymore."** Donald Trump targeted Hillary Clinton as the dangerous candidate who is unfit to lead. **"This is the legacy of Hillary Clinton: death, destruction and weakness. America is far less safe, and the world is far less stable, her bad instincts and her bad judgement are what caused so many disasters unfolding today."**

During the convention the crowd would often shout, 'lock her up' at times when Donald Trump would mention Hillary's name. Many times, during the campaign, Trump would link crime to illegal immigrants. Trump stated that thousands of illegal immigrants with criminal records that were ordered deported from our country, are now roaming free to threaten peaceful citizens. **"Nobody knows the system better than me, which is why I alone can fix it. We will make America proud again, we will make America safe again, and we will make America great again."**

Donald Trump said that he will end crimes in 2017, and there will be peace. He discussed all the killings, immigrants causing deaths. Chicago was criticized as being bad under their current administration. Trump said he is going to fix the budget and emphasized

Obama getting the country 19 trillion in debt. The statements by Donald Trump are quite bold and categorize him as the only single person that knows how our current system works, and only he can fix it. Throughout history, thru many presidents, our Democratic process has had many repairs and at times are fixed and the political system continues to survive. America has always been a strong nation, very proud, and safe for the American people. Donald Trump's stand on making **"America Great Again"** lacks logic to his thinking. The United States of America has always been a great nation.

2) July 22, 2016- With prejudice toward Mexicans who pays for wall?

Donald Trump's still all in on building a wall along our southern border. **"The border wall must cover the entirety of the southern border and must be sufficient to stop both vehicular and pedestrian traffic."** There was one thing that was missing from Trump's quote, making Mexico pay for it. Trump's campaign promise was that Mexico will pay for the wall. The wall only served as a reminder that instead of backing off prejudice remarks he made in June of 2015 about Mexicans in America being rapist's and engaging in criminal activities, the wall sufficed for Trump to stay all in and pamper his followers.

3) July 22, 2016-Trump's facts not true during speech

Donald Trump said: **"After four years of Hillary Clinton, what do we have? ISIS has spread across the region, and the entire world. Libya is in ruins, and our ambassador and his staff were left helpless to die at the hands of savage killers. Egypt was turned over to the radical Muslim Brotherhood, forcing the military to retake control. Iraq is in chaos; Iran is on the path of nuclear weapons."**

The Facts: To suggest that Clinton is to blame for the instability and violence in the Middle East, is an exaggeration by Donald Trump. Clinton had no role in military decisions made during the 2012 attack on the U.S. diplomatic post in Benghazi, Libya, that killed U.S. Ambassador Chris Stevens and three other Americans. Donald Trump said: **"The number of police officers killed in the line of duty has risen by almost 50 percent compared to this point last year."**

The Facts: This is not true according to the National Law Enforcement Officers Memorial Fund. The group found that the number of police officers who died as of July 20, 2016 is up slightly this year, at 67, compared to 62 through the same period last year. These fact examples are only a few in which Donald Trump states facts as if they were truly believable. The only habit that Trump has is making fact statements in his speeches without checking the history or background of what fact is being stated. This type of fact examples, which are at times not true, is something that the United States doesn't need for a person who has been nominated for the Republican Presidential candidate.

4) August 1, 2016- Immigration talk
Trump has vowed to build a wall along the length of the Southern border and use a **"deportation force"** to track down and deport anyone in the country illegally. Trump said, **"We are going to get rid of a lot of bad dudes over here."** It was not clear what he defined as 'bad dudes'.

5) August 10, 2016-Trump's behavior "erratic and reckless"
Trump said, **"I am running against the Washington insiders, just like I did in the Republican primaries, these are the people that have made U.S. a mess."** Susan Collins, Republican-Maine, said that other Republican critics in citing Trump's behavior, including his mocking of a reporter with a physical disability, his attacks on a

federal judge's **"Mexican heritage"**, and his dismissal of a Muslim couple who lost a son in Iraq. Fifty (50) national security officials signed a letter citing Trump's questioning of military alliances and **"erratic"** behavior.
"He would be the most reckless President in America history" a letter said.

6) August 10, 2016-Trump disputes actual facts

Trump said, **"Hillary wants to abolish, essentially abolish, the Second Amendment."**
The facts are that Clinton has never said she wants to eliminate the Second Amendment, even if she did, neither the President nor the Supreme Court nor a lower-level federal judge would have the power to do so. Trump also claimed never to have mocked a disabled The New York Times reporter despite a widely disseminated video clip showing him making jerking movements with his arms. Trump also claims he never said that Senator John McCain, as Arizona Republican, is not a war hero despite a prior, taped interview in which he said just that.

7) August 11, 2016-Obama is the founder of ISIS, according to Trump

President Barack Obama was accused by Donald Trump of establishing the Islamic State group that is wreaking havoc from the Middle East to European cities **"In many respects, you know they honor President Obama, he is the founder of ISIS"** Trump said during a campaign rally outside Ft. Lauderdale Florida. In the past Trump has also falsely suggested Obama is a Muslim or was born in Kenya, where Obama's father was born. The President was born in Hawaii.

8) August 11, 2016- Trump's bad joke draws criticism

Donald Trump "Second Amendment" comment drew criticism from those who saw it as a joke about assassinating Hillary Clinton. Trump said **"Hillary wants to abolish, essentially abolish, the second amendment. By the way, and if she gets to pick her judges, nothing you can do folks."** Many of Trump's followers already feel free to shout **"Kill her"** at his rallies. Al Baldasaro, who has been on the campaign trail with Trump, during a radio interview said that **"Hillary Clinton should be put in the firing line and shot for treason."**

9) August 14, 2016- Trump's comments viewed by some as advocating violence against Hillary Clinton

After several error free days Trump caused a major stir when his comments about supporters of the Second Amendment right to bear arms were viewed by some as advocating violence against Hillary Clinton. He came in for criticism again after saying that Obama was the **"founder of ISIS",** a false claim he repeated several times. **"He's almost like someone with an addiction who can't stop."** Fagan said. **"Until he gets help and admits it, he won't be able to change."**

10) August 15, 2016-Unfair media coverage, distorting says Trump and Aides

Trump and aids say reporters are distorting comments like the nominee's suggestion that **"Second Amendment people"** do something about the prospect of a Hillary Clinton Presidency, a comment critic interpreted as an incitement to violence. Critics also jumped on Trump's claim that President Obama is a **"founder" of the Islamic State."**

On Twitter Trump said: **"If the disgusting and corrupt media covered me honestly and didn't put false meaning into the words I say, I would be beating Hillary by 20%."**

11) August 18, 2016-Trump adding the best talent in politics

Hours after a prepared speech on "Law and Order" and days after a formal address on foreign policy, Donald Trump tried to revive a struggling campaign by adding aggressive aides in another staff shake-up. **"I believe we're adding some of the best talents in politics, with the experience and expertise needed to defeat Hillary Clinton."** Announcing two top staff hires.

12) August 21, 2016-Trump focused on African American lives.

Bryan York of the Washington Examiner, while acknowledging some of Trump's critics objections, thought Trump delivered a "focused" powerful and disciplined speech-focused largely on problems that disproportionately afflict black Americans, arguing that his proposals on crime, immigration, trade, jobs, education and other issues will improve African-American lives more that Hillary Clinton.

13) August 22, 2016- Trump 'wrestling' with how to remove illegals

After a year of using harsh rhetoric against Latinos-from calling Mexican immigrants' rapist to repeatedly attacking a federal judge as being unfair because his family was from Mexico.

"What he supports is to make sure we enforce the law, that we are respectful of those Americans who are looking for well-paying jobs and that we are fair and humane for those who live among us in this country" Conway said.

Trump is "wrestling" with how to remove those in the country illegally, stated Senator Jeff Sessions, R. Ala, a close advisor to Trump on immigration matters.

14) August 23, 2016- Trump's immigration shift

In a meeting with Hispanic activists, Trump indicated he was open to considering allowing those who have not committed crimes, beyond their immigration offenses, to obtain some form of legal status.

During the GOP primary, Trump vowed to use a **"deportation force"** to round up and deport millions of people living in the country illegally. **The first thing we're gonna do, when I win is, we're gonna get rid of all the bad ones. We've got gang members, we have killers, we have a lot of bad people that have to get out of this country. We're gonna get them out."**

15) August 24, 2016-As a minority, "what the hell do you have to lose?"

"Give me a chance" Trump begs at every speech, **"What the hell do you have to lose"** If you are a minority in America, you are probably living a life of desperate misery and hopeless poverty, Trump says. So why not take a risk by voting for Trump? **"When Mexico sends its people, they're not sending their best. They're not sending you... They're sending people that have lots of problems, and they're bringing those problems with (them). They're bringing crime, they're rapist. And some, I assume are good people."**

Afraid to walk down your street at night? You won't under a President Trump. Afraid of rapes and robberies and the scourge of drugs in your neighborhood? Just beep the Donald.

"I do feel sometimes like this campaign has entered into an alternative universe," Clinton said.

16) August 25, 2016-Trump courting black vote

Trump has been speaking rhetorically to African American audiences, while physically in front of crowds of white folk. In Dimondale, Michigan he delivered this line personally to black voters at home: **"You're living in poverty, your schools are no good, you have no jobs. Fifty-eight percent of your youth is unemployed. What the hell do you have to lose?"**

17) August 26, 2016- Trump changes view on immigration

During a Fox Town Hall, Trump seemed to deftly maneuver the crowd to the view that longtime immigrants who were otherwise law abiding should be allowed to stay in the country, a far cry from his past vow to create a "deportation force" to kick out all eleven million immigrants, including the families. **"We have the person, 20 years, been an upstanding person, the family is great, do we throw them out or do we work with them?** Trump asked the audience. **"No citizenship let me go a step further: They'll pay back taxes. They have to pay taxes. There's no amnesty as such. There's no amnesty, but we will work with them."** The details of Trump's Immigration Policy remain a work in progress. In a CNN interview, Trump seemed to cast doubt on his own softening, suggesting that immigrants would first need to leave the country before they could return and reap the benefits of any legalization program. Advocates of immigration reform have proposed a way to allow some immigrants to come forward, pay back taxes and fines, and begin a path toward legalization and in some cases, citizenship.

18) August 29, 2016- Vagueness on deportation

Trump has seemed open to not deporting immigrants in the U.S. illegally who don't have criminal records. What Trump has made clear in recent days is that he would deport immigrants in the country illegally who have committed certain crimes. He also said that he would not create a path to legal status or citizenship for the immigrants and that they would have to leave the country and return in a lawful way to achieve legal status.

19) September 1, 2016- Mexico will not pay for the wall

Mexico City-Showcasing his flair for the dramatic, Donald Trump flew his unpredictable campaign to Mexico in a hastily arranged summit with the country's President, insisted on building a border wall and ending illegal immigration. **"We didn't discuss payment of the wall"** adding that such a conversation would come **"at a later date."** But after the news conference, Peña Nieto contradicted that claim, tweeting that he began meeting with Trump by clarifying that Mexico would not pay for such a wall. **"At the beginning of the conversation with Trump, I made it clear that Mexico will not pay for the wall: "Mexicans who live in the U.S. contribute to prosperity there. They are people who are honest and hardworking. They respect the law and deserve the respect of everyone."**

20) September 2, 2016- Trump urges cuts to legal immigration

Trump urging cuts to legal immigration that would alter U.S. Under his plan, the U.S. would move away from the current immigration system, which emphasizes family unification, and allocates fewer VISAS, based on a person's ability to contribute to the U.S. economy. Because the overall numbers would be lower under Trump's plan **"we would be an older, increasingly whiter country and one that's not going to be able to be supported as well"** said William Frey, a leading demographer based at Brookings Institution. **"The only way we're going to have continued growth in our younger population and our labor force is continued immigration"** to offset the aging of the nation's native-born white population.

21) September 3, 2016- Trump vows to fix 'wrongs' facing African Americans.

Donald Trump swayed to songs of prayer, read scripture and wore a traditional prayer shawl on a visit to a predominately black church in Detroit as he called for a **"civil rights agenda of our time"** and vowed to fix the **"many wrongs"** facing African Americans. **"I am here to listen to you,"** Trump told the congregation at Great Faith Ministries International. **"I am here to learn." "I want to help you build and rebuild Detroit", "I fully understand that the African-American community has suffered from discrimination, and there are many wrongs that should be made right."** He also said the nation needs a **"civil rights agenda of our time"** with better education and good jobs.

22) September 10, 2016-Trumps words, categorically false

Donald Trump delivered his big immigration speech in Phoenix, uttering this inflammatory claim: **"Hillary Clinton has pledged amnesty in her 100 days, and her plan will provide Obamacare, Social Security, and Medicare for illegal immigrants, breaking the federal budget."** Suffice to say that every word was categorically false. Clinton hasn't proposed "amnesty". Undocumented aliens aren't eligible for Social Security, Medicare, or Obamacare period. Trump's statement is not merely falsehood, but an inflammatory hurtful one in convincing low information voters that their tax money is being misused.

23) September 18, 2016- Trumps "Birther controversy" false

During the 2008 campaign, Trump said, Hillary Clinton "started the birther controversy. I finished it." He now said he believes that **"President Barack Obama was born in the United States, period."** Trump's claim that Clinton started birtherism is an easily refutable lie. Trump spent years loudly questioning Obama's origin and eligibility for the presidency even after the matter was settled.

24) September 21, 2016- Trump cannot keep track of his lies
After five years of peddling lies and innuendo about the circumstances of President Barack Obama's birth, Trump vowed to the facts and acknowledged for the first time that Obama was born in the United States, although he refused to apologize for his efforts to delegitimize the nation's first black President. **"Hillary Clinton and her campaign of 2008 started the birther controversy. I finished it. I finished it. You know what I mean, President Barack Obama was born in the United States, period."** Trump will fail in the end; he won't be able to keep track of all his lies.

25) September 24, 2016- False claims by Trump before debate
"The rise of ISIS is the direct result of policy decisions made by Obama and Clinton." This is false. The terrorist group emerged as a direct result of the U.S. invasion of Iraq. **"92 million Americans are not part of the economy, a silent nation of jobless Americans."** This is a phony statistic. Trump is counting retirees, students, stay at home parents and the disabled people who say they are not seeking jobs. **"Fifty-eight percent of African-American youth is unemployed."** Another false fact. Trump basically triples the official rate by counting students and people in training programs as "unemployed" even though they are not seeking jobs. **"Since 2013 alone, the Obama administration has allowed 300,000 criminal aliens to return back into the United States communities."** The official estimate of "criminal aliens" released is about one quarter of Trump's number, which lumps together people not considered criminal aliens.
"Hillary Clinton plans to admit 620,000 Syrian refugees." There is no such plan. This is a made-up figure. **"People are pouring in pouring in, and their doing tremendous damage if you look at the crime, if you look at the economy."** This is doubly wrong. Illegal immigration flows are at their lowest level in two decades. And there is documented correlation between illegal immigration

and crime. **"Hillary Clinton started talks to give $400 million, in cash to Iran."**
Clinton had nothing to do with this transaction. **"NAFTA was signed by Bill Clinton."** No, the NAFTA agreement was negotiated and signed by President George H.W. Bush. **"Trump University got an 'A' rating from the Better Business Bureau (BBB)."** Actually, the BBB rated Trump University a D-minus, its second lowest grade.

26) October 1, 2016- Trump compliments Putin as a strong leader

While U.S.-Russia relations nose-dive over failed diplomacy in Syria, Trump has complemented Putin, calling him a strong leader and even encouraging him to track down Clinton's e-mails, though Trump later said he was being sarcastic. "You guys love Russia" Kaine said, "You both have said Vladimir Putin is a better leader than the President." **"I can say this: If we get a long and Russia went out with us and knocked the hell out of ISIS, that's ok with me folks."**

27) October 2, 2016- Trump may not have paid Taxes for 18 years.

Based on a tax document, Trump declared a $916 million loss on his 1995 income, a deduction so large it would have allowed him to legally avoid paying federal income taxes for 18 years. In its story, the Times said it hired tax experts who reported that "rules that are especially advantageous to wealthy filers would have allowed Mr. Trump to use his $916 million loss to cancel out an equivalent amount of taxable income over an 18-year period, although Mr. Trump's taxable income in subsequent years is as yet unknown, a $916 million loss in 1995 would have been large enough to wipe out more than $50 million a year taxable income over 18 years.

28) October 4, 2016- N.Y Attorney General halts fundraising of Trump Foundation

The Washington Post reported that Trump's foundation which has subsisted entirely on other people's donations since 2008-had failed to register with the state as a charity soliciting money. The post identified cases in which Trump appeared to have used the charity's money to buy portraits of himself and to settle lawsuits involving his for-profit businesses. In addition, Trump's foundation gave a $25,000 gift to a campaign committee supporting Florida Attorney General Pam Bondi, a Republican. Nonprofits such as the Trump Foundation are prohibited from giving political gifts.

29) November 19, 2016- Trump University settlement: $25 Million

"Today's $25 million settlement agreement is a stunning reversal by Donald Trump and a major victory for the over 6,000 victims of his fraudulent University." Trump had publicly vowed not to settle the lawsuits and suggested at one point during his Presidential campaign that he might reopen the school, which closed in 2010. **"I could have settled this case numerous times, but I don't want to settle cases when we're right. I don't believe in it. And when you start settling cases you know what happens? Everybody sues you because you get known as a settler. One thing about me, I am not known as a settler."** However, an analysis by USA Today of more than 4,000 lawsuits involving Trump and his companies over the years shows that it is true.

30) November 19, 2016- Trump appoints Michael Flynn and Jeff Sessions

President-Elect Donald Trump turned to two loyalists for key appointments as he prepares to put his stamp on the White House offer a vicious election cycle. Trump named retired Army Lieutenant General Michael Flynn as National Security Advisor and Alabama

Senator Jeff Sessions as Attorney General. In a statement Trump said Sessions **"is greatly admired by legal scholars and virtually everyone who knows him."** And Flynn **"is one of the country's foremost experts on military and intelligence matters."** Flynn and Sessions have in common their absolute support for the real estate billionaire. Flynn 57 is highly regarded in the military and intelligence communities. He's been a critical force in shaping Trump's work view that the United States is at war with "radical Islamic terrorism." Democrats raised immediate alarm bells, in particular about Flynn, who would be entrusted with coordinating the nation's foreign policy approach across all government agencies.

31) November 28, 2016- I won the popular vote, "millions voted illegally"

The president-elect himself launched a Twitter offensive that spanned more than 12 hours, casting a shadow over the legitimacy of an election that he actually won. **"I won the popular vote if you deduct the millions who voted illegally." "Serious voter fraud in Virginia, New Hampshire, and California."**

32) November 28, 2016- Trump picks have harmful views

Trump made a big deal about "draining the swamp" while the media focused on Hillary's emails ensuring him victory. Instead, Mike Flynn, as a General, fired from leading DIA, appointed a Trumps National Security Advisor and Jeff Sessions, who was passed over for judicial appointment for being a racist, given the position of Attorney General. Not only are Flynn and Sessions part of the "Washington Establishment," but both have very extreme views that will harm our country-Flynn lost his job as DIA because of his unrealistic and virulent anti-Muslim views that threatened our relationships with friendly Muslim countries in the pursuit of terrorists. Sessions off-repeated racist's comments about a KKK lynching of a black man and his voting record in the Senate means that investigations into police shootings and voter suppression will end. He's going with insiders and deplorable's who will turn back the clock.

33) November 29, 2016- Trumps fragile ego hits back on facts
In a weekend Tweetstorm, Trump asserted, **"In addition to winning the Electoral College in a landslide, I won the popular vote if you deduct the millions of people who voted illegally."** There is no evidence of this. Every objective analysis has concluded this was a clean election. Trump is Trump, his fragile ego requires that he hit back. Facts and truth be damned.

34) December 1, 2016- "I will be leaving my great business"
Donald Trump said he will separate himself from his global business interests while serving as President. **"I will be holding a major news conference in New York City with my children to discuss the fact that I will be leaving my great business in total order to fully focus on running the country in order to make America Great Again."** Congressional Democrats and government analysts have questioned how Trump could conduct the Presidency without violating conflict-of-interest guidelines involving his various global businesses.
"While I am not mandated to do this under the law, I feel it is virtually important, as President, to in no way have a conflict-of-interest with my various businesses."

35) December 2, 2016- Trump picks Secretary of Defense
President-elect Donald Trump has chosen retired Marine General James Mattis to be Secretary of Defense. **"For Mattis, the biggest risk for him personally is that he will have a National Security Advisor in the form of Mike Flynn who management style and extreme views may arch Mattis' eyebrows and cause conflict over time."**

36) December 5, 2016-Trump to slap tariff's on companies that outsource

Just days after praising a deal providing tax breaks to a company (Carrier) for keeping jobs in the U.S. Trump renewed his threat to slap tariffs on the products of companies that outsource in the future. **"There will be a tax soon of 35% for companies that go overseas and try to sell goods back across the border."** **"Any business that leaves our country for another country, fires its employees, builds a new factory or plant in the other country, and thinks it will sell its products back into the U.S. without retribution or consequence is wrong."**

37) December 8, 2016- Trump lied without reservation

Trump peddled bogus information and profited from that spread by others. Of the 20 most read phony election-related stories circulated, 17 made him look good or Hillary Clinton look bad. The top two: The Popes endorsement of Trump and Clinton's selling of arms to the Islamic state neither of which contained a particle of truth. What made Trump different was his conviction that most people are happy to be fed nonsense as long as it is palatable. Trump lied without reservation or limit, about topics big and small, and he got away with it.

38) December 8, 2016- Trump softens his hardline on Dreamers

Chicago will always be a sanctuary city where immigrants can access and live without fear of police harassment. Trump heard my passion about people pursuing the American dream. Trump is already softening his hardline position, **"We're going to work something out that's going to make people happy and proud. They got brought here at a very young age, they've worked here, and they've gone to school here. Some were very good students.**

Some have wonderful jobs. And they're in never-never land because they don't know what's going to happen."

39) December 8, 2016- EPA Administrator hostile toward clean air and water

"Pruitt could be the most hostile EPA Administrator toward clean air and safe drinking water in history", said Ken Cook President of the Environmental Working Group. "Pruitt has brazenly used his office as a vehicle for the agenda of big polluters and he could do immense damage as the administrator of the EPA. Trump campaigned as an unflinching crusader for fossil fuels. He has called climate change a "hoax perpetrated by the Chinese" and pledged to scrap the global climate treaty the United States signed in Paris with 195 other nations.

Note: Dow Jones Close: 19,614.81, NASDAQ Close: 5,417.36 December 2, 2016 S&P 500 Close: 2,246.15

40) December 10, 2016-CIA concludes Russia intervened to help Donald Trump win

The CIA has concluded in a secret assessment that Russia intervened in the 2016 election to help Donald Trump win the Presidency, rather than just to undermine confidence in the U.S. electoral system. Intelligence agents have identified individuals with connections to the Russian government, according to U.S. officials those described were actors known to the intelligence as part of a wider operation to boost Trump and hurt Clinton's chances. "It is the assessment of the intelligence community that Russia's goal here was to favor one candidate over the other, to help Trump get elected." Trump has consistently dismissed the intelligence community findings about Russian hacking. **"I don't' believe they interfered."**

41) December 11, 2016- Trump doesn't believe Russia interfered

Donald Trump's Presidential transition team challenged the veracity of U.S. intelligence assessment that Russia was trying to tip the November election to the Republican. The CIA has now concluded with "high confidence" that Moscow was not only interfering with the election, but that its actions were intended to help Trump. In a recent interview, Trump said he doesn't believe Russia interfered in the election. He called the steady stream of allegations tying Russian hacking to his campaign **"not a talking point, a laughing point, why not get along with Russia? And they can help us fight ISIS-and they're effective and smart."**

42) December 12, 2016-Trump called the CIA assessment "ridiculous"

A secret CIA analysis found that the Russian government's hacking of Democratic Party emails was a deliberate effort to damage Democratic nominee Hillary Clinton and boost Trump's chances. The Trump transition team mockingly compared the CIA assessment to the agency's historic misjudgment on Iraq's weapons of mass destruction. Trump called the assessment **"ridiculous"** and suggested it was an excuse Democrats put forward to rationalize their loss. **"I don't believe it; I think the Democrats are putting it out because they suffered one of the greatest defeats in the history of (U.S) politics."**

43) December 13, 2016-Fantastic team Flynn, Mattis, and Tillerson, as viewed by the Kremlin

Rex Tillerson, Michael Flynn and General James Mattis are viewed by the Kremlin as a fantastic team. "This is a fantastic team" Sergey Markov, a consultant to Putin's staff said by phone from the Russian capital. "These are people that Russia can do business with." Russia is banking on better relations with the incoming

Trump administration to help it end a stretch of international isolation and emerge from its longest recession in two decades. Trump who's pledged to work with Russia to defeat ISIS in Syria and Iraq, represents the best chance Putin has had as President to forge a productive partnership. The three appointments taken together would constitute a "dream team" for U.S.-Russia relations, according to Carter Page, a former foreign policy advisor to Trump who's came under criticism himself for his ties to Russia.

44) December 15, 2016- Michael Flynn "inappropriately shared" classified information without permission

A secret U.S. military investigation in 2010 determined that Michael Flynn, Trumps National Security Advisor, "inappropriately shared" classified information with foreign military officers in Afghanistan. Although Flynn lacked authorization to share the classified material, he was not reprimanded or disciplined. At the Republican National Convention, Flynn called on Clinton to drop out of the race for putting "our nation's security at extremely high risk with her carless use of a private email server." He egged on the partisan crowd in chants of "lock her up", adding: "If I, a guy who knows this business, if I did a tenth, a tenth of what she did, I would be in jail today."

45) December 16, 2016- Vladimir Putin personally authorized hacking

The Obama administration suggested that Russian President Vladimir Putin personally authorized the hacking of Democratic officials email accounts in the run-up to the presidential election and said it was "fact" that such actions helped Donald Trump's campaign. The White House also assailed Trump himself saying he must have known of Russia's interference. "Only Russia's senior most officials could have authorized these activities" said a White

House spokesman, reporting the words from an October U.S. intelligence assessment.

46) December 16, 2016- Kremlin flatly rejected claim of Putin's involvement

The Kremlin flatly rejected the claim of Putin's involvement, with Putin spokesman Dmitry Peskov dismissing it as "laughable nonsense". Trump and his supporters insist the Democrats outrage about Russia is really an attempt to undermine the validity of his election victory.

47) December 17, 2016- It doesn't happen without Putin's approval

Obama declined to state explicitly that Putin knew about the email hacking that roiled the presidential race, but he left no doubt who he felt was responsible. "Not much happens in Russia without Vladimir Putin that this happened at the highest levels of the government." Trump has dismissed the CIA's assessment and talk about Russian hacking as **"ridiculous"** while arguing both Democrats and the CIA are trying to undermine the legitimacy of the victory.

48) December 17, 2016- President Obama blames the highest level of Russia for hacking

Obama says U.S. could retaliate for hacking; Obama blames the "highest level" of the Russian government for hacks. President Barack Obama put Russia's Vladimir Putin on notice that the U.S. could use offensive cyber muscle to retaliate for interference in the U.S. Presidential election, his strongest suggestion to date that Putin had been well aware of campaign email hacking. Obama strongly defended his administration's response. U.S. intelligence assessment's say it was aimed at least in part on helping Donald Trump defeat Hillary Clinton, and some Democrats say it may well have tipped the results in his favor.

49) December 19, 2016- Electoral College should know about Russia hacking

"It's very much unknown whether there was collusion" John Podesta said. Without pointing a finger directly at Trump, Podesta said any ties between the Russia hacking and the President-elect's campaign should be revealed to members of the Electoral College before they confirm the election results.

50) January 3, 2017-GOP agenda-Gut Affordable Care Act, slash corporate taxes, undo Obama-EPA environmental regulations

The Republicans controlled Congress opened with Trump provided with ample room to gut the Affordable Care Act, slash corporate tax rates and undo Obama-era environmental regulations. Votes are expected on legislation to begin repealing the Affordable Care Act. With 20 million Americans now benefiting from the Affordable Care Act, the GOP's gutting of it comes with an asterisk.

51) January 3, 2017-North Korean's weapon programs "won't happen"

President-elect Donald Trump contended that North Korea would not be able to develop a nuclear weapon capable of reaching the United States, and berated China for not doing enough to help stop North Korean's weapon programs. **"It won't happen"** Trump tweeted.

52) January 5, 2017-Dismantling "Obamacare" is #1 on Donald Trump's list

Vice President-elect Mike Pence stood firm in telling Republicans that dismantling "Obamacare" is No. 1 on Donald Trump's list "were going to be in the promise keeping business." Repealing and replacing Obama's law will be the President-elects "first order of business."

53) January 5, 2017-Who to believe who hacked? Trump challenges Intel agencies.

Russia not only meddled in the election, but did so to help Trump win, according to the intelligence agencies assessment. But the administration has so far released only limited information to support that conclusion. The President-elect has seized on some American's skepticism of U.S. intelligence in general, citing high profile missteps that led to the Iraq war.

54) January 6, 2017- Intelligence assessment, Russia helped Trump win

The country's top intelligence official testified to Congress that Russia meddling in the 2016 presidential campaign went well beyond hacking to include disinformation and the dissemination of "fake news"-an effort he said that continues to this day. "Whatever crack, fissure they could find in our tapestry, they would exploit it."

55) January 7, 2017- Putin personally ordered Intelligence operation to help Donald Trump wi

Russian President Vladimir Putin personally ordered an intelligence operation against the U.S. presidential campaign and ultimately sought to help Donald Trump win the White House, according to a new **U.S. Intelligence Report** shortly after the President-elect appeared to dismiss its key findings. The report depicts the Russian operation as unprecedented, saying that an aggressive mix of digital thefts and leaks, fake news and propaganda represented **"a significant escalation level of activity and scope of effort against a U.S. election campaign."**

56) January 7, 2017-Trump praised Intelligence, but doubts hacking

President-elect Donald Trump said he had a "constructive" meeting with intelligence officials, and though he praised them, he still questioned assertions that Russia hacked Democrats in an effort to influence last year's election. **"There was absolutely no effect on the outcome of the election."**

57) January 7, 2017-Declassified report alleged Russia hacking during 2016 campaign

The Director of National Intelligence released a 25-page declassified version of its report into alleged Russian hacking during the 2016 campaign. **"We assess Russian President Vladimir Putin ordered an influence campaign in 2016 aimed at the U.S. presidential election. Russia's goals were to undermine public faith in the U.S. democratic process, denigrate Secretary (Hillary) Clinton and harm her electability and potential presidency. We further assess Putin and the Russian government developed a clear preference for President Trump."**

58) January 9, 2017- Trump touted Russia as a potential ally

Obama announced a raft of punishments in late December, including sanctions and orders for a few dozen Russian operatives to leave the U.S. Trump touted Russia as a potential ally, saying **"only stupid people or 'fools' think improving relations is a bad thing." "When I am President, Russia will respect us far more than they do now and both countries will perhaps, work together to solve great and pressing problems and issues of the world."**

59) January 12, 2017- Instead of divesting, Trump creates trust

Instead of divesting his hotels, golf courses, office buildings and other deals, Trump will create a trust for his Trump Organization holdings and turn over management to his sons, Donald Jr. and Eric. Trump will have nothing to do with any decisions involving the company, and **it will avoid any foreign deals while he is**

**President. "I could actually run my business and run govern-
ment at the same time." "I don't like the way that looks, but I
would be able to do that if I wanted to."**

60) January 12, 2017- Trump: "sick people put that crap together"

President-elect Donald Trump amplified his already heated war
with the intelligence community, accusing agent of disseminating
a salacious and unsubstantiated report about him while comparing
the leak to Nazi tactics. Trump said it was **"sick people who put
that crap together." "It was disgraceful-disgraceful that the
intelligence agencies allowed any information that turned out
to be so false and fake out. That's something that Nazi Germany
would have done and did do."**

61) January 18, 2017- Putin accuses Obama of trying to undermine Donald Trump

President Vladimir Putin took a parting shot at Obama administration accusing it of trying to undermine Donald Trump's legitimacy
with false allegation and "binding the President-elect hand and foot
to prevent him from fulfilling his election promises." "People who
order such fakes against the U.S. President-elect, fabricate them
and use them in political struggle are worse than prostitutes.

Chapter 2

62) January 20, 2017- Mr. Trump takes oath of office with associates under investigation

American law enforcement and intelligence agencies are examining intercepted communications and financial transactions as part of a broad investigation into possible links between Russian officials and associates of President-elect Donald J. Trump, including his former campaign chairman Paul Manafort **current and former senior American officials said. "Mr. Trump will take the oath of office with his associates under investigation and after the intelligence agencies concluded that the Russian government had worked to help elect him."**

63) January 21, 2017- "The wealth, strength and confidence of our country has disappeared

His 16-minute speech, the shortest since President Jimmy Carter's inauguration in 1977- lacked specific policy. In its place was a sense of anger at what he defined as a ruling class that has raided America for its own benefit. He talked of crime, gangs, drugs, poverty, jobs lost to foreign countries and a way of life destroyed by globalism. **"This American carnage stops right here and stops right now." "We are one nation, and their pain is our pain, their dreams are our dreams and their success is our success."** He described a country of shuttered and rusted factories, rampant crime, neighborhoods infested with gangs and drugs. He described the damage to the middle-class families by policies that he said took their wealth and spread it abroad. **"The forgotten men and women of our country will be forgotten no longer. Everyone is listening to you now." "We've made other countries rich while the wealth, strength and confidence of our country has disappeared over the horizon."**

64) January 23, 2017- Trump has no plans to release tax returns

Trump has no plans to release his tax returns, a marked shift from his pledge during the campaign to make them public once an audit was completed, "the White House response is that he's not going to release his tax returns." "We litigated this all through the election, people didn't care, they voted for him, and let me make this perfectly clear: Most Americans are very focused on what their tax returns will look like while President Trump is in office, not what his looks like," said Conway.

65) January 24, 2017- Trump to impose major border tax

President Trump pledged to cut regulations by 75% and impose a major "border tax" on goods manufactured abroad and sold in the United States. Trump said that businesses spend more time on paperwork complying with government regulations than on making things. **"We want to start making our products again. "**He said the border tax would help discourage companies from firing people in the U.S. making products overseas and then moving them back into the country to sell. **"They're going to have to pay a border tax-a substantial border tax."**

66) January 25, 2017- Trump: "We don't want to hurt those kids"

Immigration hawks are pressuring President Donald Trump to stick to his pledge to end legal protection for some 750,000 immigrants who came to the U.S. illegally as children. Trump promised in the campaign trail to "terminate immediately" a program started by President Barack Obama to temporarily protect these young people from deportation and offer them two-year renewable work permits. Trump called it an executive **"amnesty" that defied federal law and the constitution."** Trump believes that children brought by their parents did not break immigration willfully and should be treated differently than adults who came here illegally. "We don't want to hurt those kids." Trump has tried to emphasize more popular aspects of his immigration enforcement agenda-tightening the border and deporting those with criminal records, as Obama did. "His priority is first and foremost focused on people who pose a threat to people in our country, to criminals", said White House Press Secretary Sean Spicer. Immigrant advocates note that Trump has yet to define what categories of criminal violations would constitute grounds for swift deportation.

67) January 25, 2017- Illegal people caused Trump to lose popular vote

White House spokesman Sean Spicer said that President Trump continues to have concerns that 3 to 5 million people voted illegally. Trump claimed that people who are in the country illegally caused him to lose the popular vote to Hillary Clinton by almost 3 million. Trump echoed a twitter: **"In addition to winning the Electoral College in a landslide, I won the popular vote if you deduct the millions of people who voted illegally."**

68) January 26, 2017- Trump pledges to toughen immigration enforcement

President Donald Trump pledge to toughen immigration enforcement, signed orders to start construction of wall, expand authority to deport thousands, increase the number of detention cells and punish cities and states that refuse to cooperate. **"The day is over**

when they can stay in our country and wreak havoc, we are going to get them out and we're going to get them out fast."

69) January 26, 2017- Trump asks for major investigation into voter fraud

President Trump tweeted **"I will be asking for a major investigation into Voter Fraud, including those registered to vote in two states, those registered to vote who are dead (and many for a long time). Depending on results, we will strengthen up voting procedures."** Trump has claimed that up to 5 million illegal voters caused him to lose the popular vote to Hillary Clinton. Law makers and election officials including Republicans said there is no evidence of widespread fraud.

70) January 27, 2017- Trump insists that Mexico will pay for border wall

President Donald Trump insisted that Mexico will pay to build a Southwest border wall. Mexican President Enrique Peña canceled a planned meeting with Trump because Trump said there was no point for the Mexican leader to come if he was not willing to pick up the tab for the wall. Peña Nieto has vowed that his country will not pay for the wall, which Mexico opposes. "The world has taken advantage of us for many years, it's not going to happen anymore."

71) January 30, 2017- Trump's barring citizens of seven countries from entering the U.S.

Protesters marched, chanted and waved signs across the nation as angry advocates pressed their demand for an end to President Trump's executive order barring citizens of seven Muslim-majority countries from entering the U.S. The executive order suspends entry of all refugees from Syria indefinitely and bars entry for three months to residents from the predominantly Muslim countries of Iran, Iraq, Libya, Somalia, Sudan, Syria, and Yemen.

72) February 3, 2017- Republican controlled Congress scrapped Obama-EPA rules on environment and guns

The Republican-controlled congress scrapped Obama –EPA rules on environment and guns, counting on a new ally in the White House, President Donald Trump, to reverse years of regulations. The Senate gave final approval to a measure eliminating a rule to prevent coal mining debris from being dumped into nearby streams, while the White House approved a separate resolution **"doing away with extended background checks for gun purchases by some Social Security recipients with mental disabilities. After the 2012 school massacre in Newtown Connecticut, Obama directed the Justice Department to provide guidance to agencies regarding information they are obligated to report to the background check system. Democrats said Republicans are doing the bidding of the National Rifle Association."**

73) February 6, 2017- Trump attacks federal judge who voided travel ban

President Trump continued to attack a federal judge who voided his travel ban from seven majority Muslim nations. **"Just cannot believe a judge would put our country in such peril, if something happens blame him and the court system. People are pouring in. Bad!"** Trump took to social media after Vice President Pence predicted that a higher court would uphold the measure in the name of security. Trump criticized the judge **"The opinion of this so called judge, which essentially took law enforcement away from our country is ridiculous and will be overturned."** Republicans also criticized Trump's use of the term "so-called".

74) February 10, 2017- Trump: See you in court

A federal appeals court refused to reinstate President Donald Trump's executive order barring travelers from seven predominantly Muslim Nations from entering the U.S. The three judges unanimously said the administration had not shown an urgent need to have the order go into effect immediately. "The government has pointed to no evidence that any alien from any of the countries named in the order has perpetrated a terrorist attack in the United States." Trump has lost no time in responding to the court's ruling on Twitter: **"See you in court! The security of our nation is at stake! "We're going to win the case,"** Trump said.

75) February 14, 2017- Obama's "regulations will be overturned"

The House and Senate are churning out a steady stream of bills handpicked collection of discrete measures aimed at dismantling the regulatory agenda that President Barack Obama put in place during his waning days ins office. Many of the proposals came from a wish list compiled by the powerful Koch brothers' network, designed to loosen federal rules on the energy industry, Wall Street and other businesses aligned to the industrialists. **"A top priority of the National Rifle Association, for example, would halt a rule requiring background checks for gun buyers who have a mental health condition for which they receive Social Security disability benefits."** "With President Trump's signature, everyone at these regulations will be overturned," said Rep. Kevin McCarthy, R-California. "That's how to protect American workers and businesses, defend the Constitution, and turn words into action." But Democrats and advocacy groups warn the new measures will wipe out important safeguards.

76) February 14, 2017- Michael Flynn resigns

Michael Flynn resigned following reports that he had misled Vice President Mike Pence and other officials about his contacts with Russia. In a resignation letter, Flynn said he held numerous calls with the Russian Ambassador to the U.S. during the transition and gave "incomplete information" about those discussions to Vice

President Mike Pence. The Vice President apparently relying on information from Flynn, initially said the National Security Advisor had not discussed sanctions with the Russian envoy, though Flynn later conceded the issue may have come up.

77) February 15, 2017- Trump kept quiet about Michael Flynn for nearly three weeks
Just six days into his presidency, Donald Trump was informed his National Security Advisor had misled his Vice President about contacts with Russia. Trump kept his No. 2 in the dark and waited nearly three weeks before ousting the aide, Michael Flynn, citing a slow but steady corrosion of trust.

78) February 16, 2017- Trump denies 'conspiracy theories'
President Trump's ties to Russia are back in the spotlight after his National Security Advisor, Michael Flynn, was forced to resign. Trump's long-standing ties to Russia is why his policy is noticeably weaker on Russia then on anything else. Trump said that he would consider lifting U.S. sanctions on Russia for allegedly backing a separatist rebellion in Eastern Ukraine and meddling in the U.S. presidential election to help Trump win in return for a new nuclear arms reduction accord. In addition, Trump and Russian President Vladimir Putin agreed in a phone call to collaborate in the fight against Islamic state and to seek ways to restore trade and economic ties. President Donald Trump talks about driving hard bargains, and here he's offering concessions right off the top. Trump denied in his tweets "Conspiracy theories" about his ties to Russia. In 2008, Trump's son, Donald Jr., told investors in Moscow that the Trump Organization trademarks the Donald Trump name in Russia and planned to build housing and hotels in Moscow, St. Petersburg and Sochi and sell licenses to other developers. **"Russians make up a pretty disproportionate cross section of a lot of our assets, we see a lot of money pouring in from Russia,"** Trump said.

79) February 17, 2017- Trump: "I inherited a mess, at home and abroad, a mess"

President Trump defended his weeks-old administration as a "fined tuned machine," I am lambasted the "mess" he inherited from his predecessor and lambasted the "fake news" media. The President said he asked his former Security Advisor, Michael Flynn, to resign because he misled Vice President Pence about his calls to the Russian Ambassador to the United States. But Trump said he didn't believe Flynn did anything wrong making these calls on the faulted leakers for providing contents of the intercepted calls to the media. **"I see stories of chaos, chaos, yet it is the exact opposite, this administration is running like a fine-tuned machine, to be honest, I inherited a mess, it's a mess, at home and abroad, a mess."**

80) February 25, 2017- "Russia is fake news," I own nothing in Russia

"I owe nothing in Russia, I have no loans in Russia, I don't have any deals in Russia, Russia is fake news put out by the media." Trump and his family have been up to their eyeballs in Russian cash for decades. Father and son used to brag about Russian money. In 2008, Donald Trump Jr. told a real estate conference that **"Russians makeup a pretty disproportionate cross-section of a lot of our assets, we see a lot of money pouring in from Russia."** After staging the 2013 Miss Universe Pageant in Moscow, Trump boasted that most of Russia's financial elite attended a swank party he threw. **"Almost all of the oligarchs were in the room."** It's important to understand that politically independent Russia oligarchs do not exist. One way or another, Putin owns them all. During a Republican debate, Trump even claimed a personal relationship with Vladimir Putin. **"I got to know him very well because we both were on '60 Minutes'. We were stablemates."** Now Trump says the two have never met.

81) February 28, 2017- Trump: "Fake news the enemy of the people"

President Donald Trump turned his speech before a conservative convention into a full-throated attack on journalism, saying some reporter's makeup unnamed sources for **"fake news"** and again describing them as **"the enemy"** of the American people. **"A few days ago I called the fake news the enemy of the people, and they are –they are the enemy of the people."** While praising some reporters as honest and pledging fealty to the First Amendments, Trump claimed that **"the fake news media doesn't tell the truth and we're going to do something about it."**

82) March 1, 2017- Trump pledges to target people in U.S. illegally

President Donald Trump calls on Congress to replace Obamacare, pass massive tax relief for middle class. **"The time has come for a new program of national re-building."** He pledged to vigorously target people living in the U.S. illegally who **"threaten our communities and prey on our citizens,"** but he said, **"real and positive immigration reform is possible."** Making a direct appeal for bipartisanship, Trump turned to the Democrats and said, **"why not join forces to finally get the job done and get it done right."** Trump was vague in his call for tax reform, another Republican priority. The President also urged Congress to pass a trillion-infra-structure package financed through both public and private capital.

83) March 3, 2017- Jeff Sessions takes himself away from Russia investigation

Attorney General Jeff Sessions will recuse himself from investigations relating to the 2016 presidential campaign, which would include any Russia interference in the electoral process. "They said that since I had involvement with the campaign, I should not be involved in any campaign investigations." He concurred with their assessment and would thus recuse from any existing or future investigation involving Donald Trump's 2016 campaign. It was revealed that Sessions twice met with Russian Ambassador Sergey Kislyak during the campaign and did not disclose that fact to Congress during his confirmation hearing.

84) March 6, 2017- Justice rebukes President publicly over wiretap claim

FBI Director James Comey sought a public rebuke from the Justice Department of President Trump's claim that President Obama ordered the surveillance of Trump's phones before the election. Comey's request capped off a weekend in which Trump made a series of unsubstantiated claims about illegal wiretapping. Obama denied wiretapping Trump and former Director of National Intelligence James Clapper said he knew of no effort to seek wiretaps against Trump during his tenure. Trump tweeted **"had my 'wires tapped' in Trump Tower just before the victory. Nothing found. This is McCarthyism! Is it legal for a sitting President to be 'wiretapping' a race for President prior to an election? Turned down by court order. A NEW LOW!"**

85) March 10, 2017-Trump fired Flynn, claims unaware of his Russia contacts

President Donald Trump was not aware that his former National Security Advisor, Michael Flynn, had worked to further the interest of the government of Turkey before appointing him. Pence said that he did not know about Flynn's paid work. Flynn has drawn scrutiny from the FBI for his contacts with Russian officials. Trump fired Flynn for misleading Vice President Pence and other administration about his contacts with Russia's Ambassador to the U.S., Sergey Kislyak.

86) March 10, 2017- House Speaker Ryan: The time is here to repeal and replace Obamacare

"This is the closest we will ever get to repealing and replacing Obamacare," House Speaker Paul Ryan said. "The time is here. The time is now. This is the moment." Senate Minority Leader Charles Schumer said "This bill is one big mess, done quickly in the night. It's no wonder Leader McConnell and Speaker Ryan don't want a lot of debate. They're embarrassed." Senator Tom Cotton, Representative-Arkansas, he's urged House leaders to "start over" in the hill, "Get it right, don't get it fast."

87) March 11, 2017- Trump to do away with science behind climate change

President Trump isn't just keeping campaign promise to roll back climate change regulations. He's moving ahead to do away with the science behind the effort. Trump is to propose millions of dollars in cuts to EPA, NASA and others that study global warming. Environmental activist said rolling back rules designed to protect health and ecology is bad enough but gutting the fact-finding and academic analysis behind the rules poses far-reaching consequences. "If the Trump administration pulls the plug on this, the world goes dark," said David Doniger, Director of the Climate and Clean Air Program at the National Resources Defense Council. Trump has called climate change a hoax perpetrated by China.

88) March 13, 2017- "This is serious stuff" McCain said about Obama wiretapping Trump

"I think the President has one or two choices: either retract or to provide the information that the American people deserve, because it is his predecessor who violated the law, President Obama violated the law, we have a serious issue here, to say the least." President Trump continued his tweets but offered no evidence. "I do believe on issues such as this, accusing a former President of the United

States of something which is not only illegal, but just unheard of, this is serious stuff" McCain said.

89) March 16, 2017- Major budget cuts to education, environment and health, but 2.6 billion for border wall

The proposal, dubbed the "America First" budget by the White House, would increase defense spending and offset the spending with cuts to non-defense spending, the steepest of which would come from education, environmental protection, health and human services and foreign aid. Some agencies would be disbanded altogether, including those primarily responsible for supporting public broadcasting, legal aid and the arts. Community development block grants, learning centers and low-income heating assistance, would be eliminated. Programs supporting first time home buyers, state and local affordable housing initiatives and neighborhood revitalization would be zeroed out. There would be 2.6 billion for the proposed border wall and $314 million for immigration enforcement agents.

90) March 19, 2017-Global Supply chains face huge challenges caused by increased border tariffs

The supply chain for parts and vehicles made in the U.S., Canada and Mexico is among the most closely integrated in the world. For instance, a piece of steel might be taxed when it enters the U.S. to be made into a screw. The screw would be shipped to Mexico to fasten the box for electronic controls. That box then comes to Michigan to be attached to a V-8 engine. Then the engine goes to Mexico where it is installed in a pickup that is shipped to a dealership in Atlanta. The result: a single part that has been taxed multiple times, with each time increasing the cost of an engine made in Detroit and a vehicle sold in Georgia. Parts plants in the U.S. also make many components for vehicles built in Mexico. 40.3 percent of the content of vehicles built in Mexico in 2015 came from the

U.S.-built vehicles average 11.7 percent Mexican content. Tens of thousands of American manufacturing jobs depend on parts used in Mexican plants. Companies that rely on global supply chains would face huge business challenges caused by increased tariffs and increased cost of goods, which would in turn, likely result in reductions in employment, reduced capital investments and higher prices for consumers.

91) March 19, 2017- Comey debunks Trumps wiretapping claims

In a double-barreled assault as the White House, FBI Director James Comey knocked back President Donald Trump's claim of wiretapping by the Obama administration and disclosed that the FBI is investigating possible "coordination" between Donald Trump's presidential campaign and Russian authorities. "I have no information that supports those tweets and we have looked carefully inside the FBI," adding that the Justice Department and its components also had "no information to support" Trump's accusation. The FBI is investigating the "nature of any links between individuals associated with the Trump campaign and the Russian government and whether there was any coordination between the campaign and Russia's efforts," Comey said. Trump used Twitter to denounce the FBI investigation, as well as separate probes by the GOP-led House and Senate intelligence committees as "FAKE NEWS" adding "The Democrats made up and pushed the Russian story as an excuse for running a terrible campaign." Comey and Rogers said they stood by a report by the U.S. intelligence community that said Russian President Vladimir Putin had approved an intelligence operation in an effort to hurt Democratic Nominee Hillary Clinton and to help Trump.

92) March 25, 2017- Trump: Obamacare law was imploding "and soon would explode"

President Donald Trump and Republican leaders yanked their bill to repeal "Obamacare" off the House floor when it became clear it would fail. Democrats said Americans can "breathe a sigh of relief." Trump said former President Barack Obama's law was imploding **"and soon would explode."** Trump predicted the country would eventually need to revisit, **"We will end up with a truly great healthcare bill in the future after this mess that is Obamacare explodes."**

93) March 28, 2017- Trump to dismantle Obama's EPA climate effort

President Trump will order the Environmental Protection Agency to dismantle his predecessor's landmark climate effort, backing away from an aggressive plan to cut emissions at power plants that had been the leadership on confronting global warming. Trump threatens to cede the role America had established in leading the global environmental fight, and further cements the Trump administration's alliance with a fossil fuel industry that has long resisted climate action. The directive takes aim at the Clan Power Plan, which mandates a substantial reduction of utility plant emissions by 2030. The plants account for nearly a third of the greenhouse gas released in the United States. "The President has made it very clear that he is not going to pursue climate or environmental issues that put the U.S. economy at risk."

94) March 28, 2017-Trump reverses more Obama-EPA regulations

President rolled back more Obama-EPA regulations, signing four bills that reverse rules on education, land use and federal purchasing. Previous bills have reversed Obama regulations barring Social Security recipients with mental impairments from buying guns, restricting the dumping of mining waste in streams and rivers, and requiring energy companies to disclose how much they are paying foreign governments. Half of all bills signed by Trump have been these regulations-killing regulations. One being measuring performance of school and teacher training under the Every Student Succeeds Act, a law Obama signed in 2015 with bipartisan support.

95) March 29, 2017-Trump panicked about the Russia probe

You know things are looking grim for President Donald Trump when he starts tweeting about Hillary Clinton again. **"Why isn't the White House Intelligence Committee looking into the Bill and Hillary deal that allowed big Uranium to go to Russia, Russian speech?"** It is because she is not President, did not hold back her tax returns, did not constantly cheer for Vladimir Putin, did not hire a host of pre-Putin flunkies and did not have aides who lied about contact with Russian officials. The trump administration sought to block former acting Attorney General Sally Yates from testifying to Congress in the House investigation of links between Russian officials and Donald Trump's Presidential campaign. The Justice Department notified her possible testimony to be barred from discussion in a congressional hearing because the topics are covered by the presidential communication privilege. That would strike many as a ham-handed attempt to interfere with the investigation.

96) March 30, 2017- Probe into Russian involvement in 2016 U.S. Presidential election

The Senate Intelligence Committee's probe into Russian involvement in the 2016 U.S. Presidential election will be one of the biggest investigations in years and already involved an unprecedented level of cooperation between Congress and U.S. spy agencies. The Senate committee would carry out a full, unfettered investigation of Russian efforts to influence the presidential election and any ties to Donald Trump's campaign. The committee will go wherever the intelligence leads us. The committee refused to endorse White House statements that investigators will find that there was no collusion between the campaign and the Russians. A report by U.S. Intelligence agencies found that senior Russian officials, including Putin, wanted to undermine the U.S. Democratic process, hurt Democratic nominee Hillary Clinton and help Trump.

Chapter 3

97) April 6, 2017- Trump denounced Syria over chemical weapons attack

Trump denounced Syria over chemical weapons attack. Trump did not provide any specifics about what he might do. The photos of women and children killed in the attack. **"What happened is unacceptable to me."** The attack **"crossed a lot of lines for me."** Assad violated an agreement in 2013 to destroy his chemical weapons stockpile. **"Assad was saying 'I can get away with anything now'."** Haley warns U.S. may act against Syria if U.N. fails to do so.

98) April 7, 2017- U.S. strikes Syria with cruise missiles

The Pentagon launched dozens of cruise missiles against an airfield in central Syria in retaliation for a gruesome poison gas attack that U.S. officials said was carried out by President Bashar Assad's forces. Trump cast the U.S. assault as vital to deter future use of poison gas and called in other nations to join in seeking **"to end the slaughter and bloodshed in Syria." "Assad choked out the lives of innocent men, women and children."** Trump said.

99) April 10, 2017-There are grounds for impeachment

There are now four grounds to impeach Donald Trump. The fifth appears to be on its way. **First:** In taking the oath of office, a President promises to "faithfully execute the laws and the

constitution". That's Article II Section 2. But Trump is unfaith-
fully executing his duties as President by accusing his predecessor
President Barack Obama, of undertaking an illegal and impeachable act, with absolutely no evidence to support his accusation.
Second: Article I, Section 9 of the Constitution forbids government officials from taking things of value from foreign governments. But Trump is making big money off his Trump International
Hotel. **Third:** The 1st Amendment to the Constitution bars any law
"respecting an establishment of religion or prohibiting the free
exercise thereof." But Trumps ban on travel into the United States
from six Muslim countries which he initiated, advocated for, and
oversees-violates that provision. **Fourth:** The 1st Amendment also
bars "abridging the freedom of press." But Trumps labeling the
press **"the enemy of the people"** and choosing who he invites to
news conferences based on whether they've given him favorable
coverage, violates that provision. A **fifth** possible ground if the
evidence is there: Article II Section 3 of the Constitution defined
"treason against the United States" as "adhering to their enemies,
giving them aid and comfort." Evidence is mounting that Trump
and his aides colluded with Russian operatives to win the 2016
presidential election. Presidents can be impeached for what the
Constitution call "high crimes and misdemeanors."

100) April 12, 2017- Putin denounces Russia involvement in the poison gas attack in Syria

The White House and Russian President Vladimir Putin exchanged
heated charges over the poison gas attack in Syria, stoking fresh
tensions as Secretary of State Rex Tillerson made demands that
Russia withdraw support for the Syrian government. The Trump
administration released a declassified intelligence report that provided evidence that Russia's explanation for the deadly chemical
attack was false and that Moscow engaged in a deliberate cover up
to protect its embattled ally Syrian President Bashar Assad. The

White House said, "I think it's clear that the Russians are trying to cover up what happened there."

101) April 12, 2017- FBI obtains order to monitor Carter Page's communications

The FBI obtained a secret court order to monitor the communication of an advisor to presidential candidate Donald Trump, part of an investigation into possible links between Russia and the campaign. The FBI and the Justice Department obtained the warrant targeting Carter Page's communication after convincing a Foreign Intelligence Surveillance Court Judge that there was probable cause to believe Page was acting as an agent of a foreign power, this case Russia. This is the clearest evidence that the FBU had reason to believe during the 2016 presidential campaign that a Trump campaign advisor was in touch with Russian agents. Such contacts are now at the center of an investigation into whether the campaign coordinated with the Russian government to swing the election in Trumps favor.

102) April 22, 2017- Trump: <u>"Not after the dreamers, we are after the criminals."</u>

Young immigrants brought to the U.S. as children and living here illegally can 'rest easy', President Donald Trump said they will not be targets for deportation under his immigration policies. Trump said his administration is "not after the dreamers, we are after the criminals." Trump strongly criticized President Barack Obama for "illegal executive amnesty", including actions to spare from deportation young people who were brought to the country as children and now are here illegally. Trump said that when it comes to them, "this is a case of heart."

103) April 24, 2017- Trump least productive in first 100 days

It's no surprise that Trump would continue to break new ground once he moved into the Oval Office-though not always in a good way. The courts have blocked his signature immigration ban. Congress has balked at delivering on his promise to repeal the Affordable Care Act. The FBI is investigating Russia meddling in the election, an issue that forced the resignation of his National Security Advisor and likely to cast a shadow over the administration for months or more. Presidential historians and White House veterans say Trump has had more of the least-productive first 100 days in office of any modern President. His opening months have had an exhausting pace as he seems to career from controversy to controversy-many of them generated not by outside developments but by internal conflict and provocative tweets.

104) April 26, 2017- Trumps tax plan could add trillions to deficit

Republicans who slapped the growing national debt under former President Barack Obama are open to President Donald Trump's tax plan, even though it could add trillions of dollars to the deficit over the next decade. The Trump administration stuck with its assertion that tax reform could push economic growth about 3 percent. Commerce Secretary Wilbur Ross said the combination of changes on taxes, trade and regulations being pushed by the administration would accelerate the pace of economic growth.

105) April 27, 2017- Trump's tax plan will provide biggest windfall to the wealthy

Tax proposals from the Trump administration would benefit the U.S. households, small and large businesses and make filing taxes simpler, but it will provide the biggest windfall to the wealthy. The Tax Policy Center has estimated that the top 1% of households would see a 14% increase in after-tax income, while low- and middle-class Americans would see gains of 1.2% to 1.8%. Trump's plan would eliminate 3.8% tax on the interest, dividends and capital gains of higher-income households that help fund the Affordable Care Act that the President has so far failed to repeal and replace as promised.

106) April 28, 2017- Tax plan could reap big benefits for Trump

President Trump's one-page plan to dramatically overhaul the U.S. tax code could reap big benefits for one taxpayer in particular: Donald Trump. His push to lower the corporate tax rate could slash taxes on hundreds of limited liabilities, companies that make up his real estate and licensing empire. The billionaire and his family also stand to benefit from his plans to lower the income tax rate for the wealthiest Americans and to abolish the federal estate tax and the so-called alternative minimum tax. Tax experts say Trump also could benefit personally from other aspects of his tax plan. A leaked 2005 tax return shows the alternative minimum tax increased Trump's taxes by $31 million that year.

107) May 10, 2017- Trump fires FBI Director James Comey

President Donald Trump fired FBI Director James Comey, stunning Washington with a decision that he said was needed to allow a "new beginning" at the FBI. The firing came as the FBI investigates whether any of Trump's associates colluded with efforts by Russian intelligence agencies to influence the 2016 election. Republicans insisted that both the FBI and congressional investigations of Russia's actions would continue without White House interference. Calls from senior Democrats were for an independent prosecutor to oversee the criminal probe. In statements leading Democratic lawmakers warned the dismissal could lead to a White House effort to shut down the FBI investigation into potential collusion.

108) May 12, 2017- Trump: "I was going to fire Comey regardless of recommendation"

In a reversal President Trump revealed he planned to fire FBI Director James Comey even before meeting with top ranking Justice Department officials and soliciting their recommendations on his performance. Calling Comey, a "showboat" and "grandstander", **"I was going to fire regardless of (their) recommendation."** This contradicts the White House assertions, and the termination letter Trump sent to Comey, that the dismissal was based on recommendations of Attorney General Jeff Sessions and Deputy Attorney General Rod Rosenstein. Democrats have already decried the timing of Comey's firing as a way to short circuit the ongoing counterintelligence probe. If Trump had made the decision to fire Comey regardless of the Justice Department's opinions, then why did he ask Rosenstein for a memo? Trump said **"the FBI has been in turmoil, you know that, I know that. Everybody knows that. You take a look at the FBI a year ago, it was in virtual turmoil, less than a year ago, it hasn't recovered from that."**

109) May 17, 2017- In written memo Comey revealed that Trump asked him to shut down investigation into Michael Flynn

An associate revealed that Comey had written a memo in which he described Trump asking him to shut down an FBI investigation into former National Security Advisor Michael Flynn. Comey was abruptly fired May 9. Soon after the firing, a Comey associate told the AP that Comey recounted being asked by Trump at a January dinner if he would pledge his loyalty.

110) May 18, 2017- Former FBI Director Robert Mueller to take over investigation of Russian meddling in the 2016 election

The Justice Department in Wednesday's special council, former FBI Director Robert Mueller, to take over the investigation of Russian meddling in the 2016 election and possible collusion between Russian agents and associates of Donald Trump. Deputy Attorney General Rod Rosenstein said a special council is necessary in order for the "America people to have full confidence in the outcome" of the investigation.

111) May 19, 2017- Rosenstein knew President Donald Trump wanted to fire James Comey

The number 2 official of the Justice Department told senators that he knew President Donald Trump wanted to fire James Comey before he wrote the letter criticizing the FBI Director. "He knew that Comey was going to be removed prior to him writing the memo," Senator Claire McCaskill told reporters. Dick Durbin said Rosenstein named Robert Mueller as special counsel to make sure the "American people know that this would be handled fairly and justly." Comey wrote his own memo detailing a private conversation he had with Trump when the President tasked him to end an investigation into Michael Flynn, just after Flynn had been pushed out as National Security Advisor for lying about his conversations with the Russian Ambassador. Democrats and some Republicans insisted that the congressional panels would not take a backseat to Mueller's work.

112) May 19, 2017- Trump denied asking James Comey to drop investigation into Michael Flynn

President Trump denied asking ex-FBI Director James Comey to drop his investigation into former National Security Advisor Michael Flynn and described Democratic talk of possible impeachment as **"totally ridiculous."** Comey kept detailed notes of is past meetings with Trump. Trump said, **"I respect the move to appoint a special council for the Russia investigation, the entire thing has been a witch-hunt."**

113) May 20, 2017- Firing James Comey eased the pressure on Trump

President Donald Trump told Russian diplomats his firing of **"nut job"** James Comey had eased the pressure on him. The White House has said the firing was unrelated to the FBI's Russia investigation. Comey has told associates, Trump asked for his loyalty. In the Oval Office weeks later, Comey told associates, the President asked him to shut down on investigation into former National Security Advisor Michael Flynn. Trump noted the Russia investigation as he told Russia Foreign Minister Sergey Lavrov and Ambassador to the U.S. Sergey Kislyak: **"I just fired the head of the FBI. He was crazy, a real nut job, I faced great pressure because of Russia. That's taken care of."**

114) May 23, 2017- Trump asked two top Intelligence Chiefs to deny Russian collusion

President Donald Trump asked two top Intelligence Chiefs in March to deny publicly that there had been collusion between the Russians and his campaign. Citing current and former officials, the National Intelligence Director, Daniel Coats, and the Director of the National Security Agency, Adm. Michael S. Rogers, both refused Trumps request, judging it inappropriate.

115) June 2, 2017- Russian hackers are acting on their own per Vladimir Putin

After months of categorically denying Russian involvement in cyber-attacks during last year's U.S. presidential election, Russian President Vladimir Putin said that although the Kremlin has never used state-sponsored cyberattacks to meddle in other countries elections, some "patriotically minded" volunteer hackers may have been on their own to defend Russian interest. "Hackers can be anywhere and pop out from anywhere in the world." Like Trump, Putin has dismissed media reports accusing the Trump administration of colluding with Russia to influence the U.S. election as "fake news".

116) June 3, 2017- Russia probe grows wider-Special counsel's investigation now includes Manafort.

The special counsel investigating possible ties between President Donald Trump's campaign and Russia's government has taken over a separate criminal probe involving former Trump campaign chairman Paul Manafort. The Justice Department's criminal investigation into Manafort, who was forced to resign as Trump campaign chairman amid questions over his business dealings years ago in Ukraine, predated the 2016 election and the counterintelligence probe that in July began investigating possible collusion between Moscow and associates of Trump.

117) June 8, 2017- Comey recounts Trump's demand for "loyalty"

Former FBI Director James Comey feared from his first meeting with President Donald Trump that the Commander in Chief was trying to forge a "patronage relationship" between the two of them was intruding on the FBI role as an independent investigative agency. Comey recounts Trumps demand for "loyalty" and his request that the bureau drop at least part of its investigation of former National Security Advisor Michael Flynn. His detailed account of awkward and often tense conversations over five months, however, makes clear that he felt the President was attempting to inappropriately intercede on behalf of Flynn and influence the FBI's investigation into whether associates of Trumps were involved in Russian efforts to influence the election.

118) June 9, 2017- Comey: Trump fired me "because of the Russia investigation"

In an explosive hearing, former FBI Director James Comey told Congress that he believed President Donald Trump fired him to impede the FBI's Russia investigation and described the President's claims that the FBI was poorly led and in disarray as "lies, plain and simple", **"it's my judgement that I was fired because of the Russia investigation," "I was fired in some way to change-or endeavor to change-the way the Russia investigation was being conducted."** Comey also said that he decided to write memos for the FBI after his private meetings and phone calls with Trump because he didn't trust the President to tell the truth. **"I was honestly concerned that he might lie about the nature of our meetings."**

119) June 10, 2017- Trump denies ever asking Comey for his "loyalty"

Punching back a day after his fired FBI Directors damaging testimony, President Donald Trump accused James Comey of lying to Congress and said he was "100 percent" willing to testify under oath about their conversations. He asserted that nothing in Comey's testimony to the Senate pointed to collusion with Russia or obstruction of justice. **"Yesterday showed no collusion, no obstructions."** He further denied ever asking Comey for his **"loyalty"** contradicting Comey's detailed sworn testimony about a private dinner the two men had in the White House. Comey said he refused on all points, told Senators of the detailed memos he had written after his conversations with Trump and said he hoped those conversations were taped because he is confident of their veracity.

120) June 16, 2017- Trump: "You are witnessing the single greatest witch-hunt"

Trump slipped back into his Twitter persona, returning to the fracas that aides have been trying to get him to avoid. Trump refused to let his outside counsel do the talking for him. **"They made up a phony collusion with the Russians story, found zero proof, so now they go for obstruction of justice on the phony story. Nice." "You are witnessing the single greatest WITCH HUNT in America political history led by some very bad and conflicted people."** The lure of speaking to 32 million follower on Twitter and fighting back against allegations, Trump sees as fundamentally unfair, may be too much to resist, even as advisors and Republican strategists warn that his provocative comments may be perpetuating the cycle of leaks and accusations that launched the investigation in the first place.

121) June 28, 2017- Will Republican deliver on promise to repeal and replace Obamacare

Senator Republican leaders abruptly shelved their long-sought health care overhaul asserting they can still salvage it but raising new doubts about whether President Donald Trump and the Republicans will ever deliver on their promises to repeal and replace "Obamacare". Trump immediately invited Senate Republicans to the White House and he delivered to them: **"This will be great if we get it done, and if we don't get it done it's just going to be something that we're not going to like, and that's ok, and I understand that very well."**

122) June 28, 2017- Trump signs order to revise and rescind Obama's clean water rule

The Trump administration moved to roll back and Obama administration policy that protected more than half the nation's streams from pollution but drew attacks from farmers, fossil fuel companies, and property-rights groups as federal overreach. President Donald Trump issued an executive order instructing the Environmental Protection Agency and the U.S. Army Corps of Engineers to rescind or reverse the Obama rule, which environmentalist say is essential to protecting water for human consumption and wildlife. The Dow Chemical company wanted to ban a widely used pesticide after health studies showed it can harm children's brains. Twenty days later the EPA Administrator Scott Pruitt denied a petition to ban Dow's Chlorpyrifos pesticide from being sprayed on food, despite a review by his agency's scientist that concluded ingesting even miniscule amounts of the chemical can interfere with brain development of fetuses and infants.

123) July 4, 2017- EPA oversteps its authority
A federal appeals court in Washington ruled that the head of the Environmental Protection Agency overstepped his authority in trying to delay implementation of a new rule requiring oil and gas companies to monitor and reduce methane leaks. The U.S. Court of Appeals for the District of Columbia Circuit ordered the EPA to move forward with the Obama era requirement that aims to reduce planet warming emissions from oil and gas operations. "This ruling declares EPA's action illegal and slams the brakes on Trump Administrations brazen efforts to put the interests of corporate polluters ahead of protecting the public and the environment," said David Doniger, Director of Climate and Clean Air Program for the Natural resources Defense Council.

124) July 5, 2017- North Korea's missile could reach U.S. mainland
North Korea's successful launch of a missile that for the first time could reach the U.S. mainland ratchets up pressure on President Trump and other world leaders to resolve a growing nuclear crisis with no easy solution. Trump has repeatedly called on China to

rein in its neighbor and close ally. China suggested a compromise: North Korea would stop missile tests if the United States and South Korea scaled back exercises in the region. U.S. Secretary of State Rex Tillerson confirmed the intercontinental ballistic missile launch and called it a "now escalation" of the threat. He vowed to bring additional international pressure on the regime.

125) July 7, 2017- Trump declined to hold Russia solely responsible for meddling in the 2016 presidential campaign

On the eve of his first face-to-face meeting as President with Russia's Vladimir Putin, Donald Trump declined to hold the Kremlin solely responsible for meddling in the 2016 U.S. presidential campaign, insisting that others may have interfered as well. Breaking with the norms of presidential foreign visits, Trump in his comments strongly criticized his predecessor President Barack Obama by name, as he stood alongside the Polish President for a news conference. In a speech, Trump continued to "directly undermine" U.S. interests. "This is not putting America first, but continuing to propagate his own personal fiction at the country's expense, President Trump must have the courage to raise the issue of Russia interference in our elections directly from President Putin, otherwise the Kremlin will conclude he is weak to stand up to them," said Representative Adam Schiff, top Democratic on the House intelligence committee.

126) July 10, 2017- Trump touts proposed partnership with Russia on cybersecurity

President Donald Trump's touting of a proposed partnership with Russia on cyber security drew withering reviews from law makers, including several from his own party, while the president aids were left struggling to answer questions about just how hard Trump pressed Russian President Vladimir Putin on Moscow's meddling in last year's U.S. presidential election. Almost as soon as the Trump-Putin talks ended after more than two hours of discussion with the U.S. side staying out of camera range, Russia's Foreign Minister Sergey Lavrov happily informed reporters **that Trump had accepted Putin's denial of interference in the campaign. Putin reinforced that narrative saying that Trump had seemed "satisfied" with his protestations of innocence.** Trumps tweets touted his talk with Putin about creating an "impenetrable cyber security unit" to combat abusers like hacking and online propaganda.

127) July 11, 2017- Trump Jr. acknowledges meeting with Russian lawyer

A meeting between President Donald Trump's eldest son and a Russian lawyer during the presidential campaign occurred at the behest of a Moscow-based pop star with family ties to Trump's businesses, according to a participant in the talks. Donald Trump Jr. acknowledged that he made time for the meeting hoping to get information about Democrat Hillary Clinton. Trump Jr. took the meeting with the understanding that he would be presented with damaging information about his father's political opponent and that the material could have emanated from the Kremlin.

128) July 12, 2017- Russian lawyers had documents and in format that would incriminate Hillary Clinton

Well-connected Russians were reaching out to Donald Trump's campaign last summer, using the offer of damaging information against Hillary Clinton to gain access to the top levels of his organization, emails released by Donald Trump Jr. show Trump Jr. met in June 2016 with Natalia Veselnitskaya, a Russian lawyer, after being told in emails from a friend that she was a Russian government attorney who had "official documents and information that would "incriminate" Clinton and be very useful to your father." Her information was part of Russia and its government support for

Mr. Trump according to the emails. "If it's what you say I love it." Trump Jr. responded to the emails from his friend Rob Goldstone, a music promoter with business dealings in Russia. Goldstone's pitch was enough to secure a meeting at New York's Trump Tower attended not only by Trump Jr., but also by Jared Kushner, Donald Trump's son-in-law and advisor, and Paul Manafort, Trump's campaign chairman at the time.

129) July 13, 2017-Trump Jr. calls Russian meeting 'opposition research'

Donald Trump Jr. casts his willingness to hear potential Russian dirt about Hillary Clinton as standard opposition research into a political rival. But opposition research normally involves slogging through public records, pouring over candidate statements, and tracking a politician's every public appearance, hoping to uncover damaging material, not high-ranking campaign aides with someone they believed represented a hostile foreign government.

130) July 13, 2017-Trump about Putin "It doesn't make sense not to have some kind of relationship"

In an interview, Trump spoke for the first time about his lengthy sit-down last week with Russian President Vladimir Putin at the G-20. **"I think we get along very, very well. We are a tremendous powerful nuclear power, and so are they. It doesn't make sense not to have some kind of relationship."** Trump insisted contrary to the evidence of his son's emails and the conclusion of the U.S. intelligence community that Putin would have preferred to see Clinton win the 2016 election. Judging from his tweets, Trump has spent much of this week stewing in frustration over media coverage of his son's meeting.

131) July 19, 2017- Trump: "Let Obamacare fail, we're not going to own it"

President Donald Trump declared it's time to **"let Obamacare fail"** after the latest GOP healthcare plan crashed and burned in the Senate, a stunning failure for the President, Republican leader Mitch McConnell and a party that has vowed for years to abolish the law. Trump for the third time in a row, denying the votes to move forward with a plan for a straight-up repeal of "Obamacare". This time it was three GOP women, Susan Collins of Maine, Lisa Murkowski of Alaska and Shelly Moore Capito of West Virginia who delivered the death blow. **"I think we're probably in that position where we'll just let Obamacare fail, we're not going to own it, I'm not going to own it. I can't tell you that the Republicans are not going to own it. We'll let Obamacare fail and then the Democrats were going to come to us and they're going to say, 'How do we fix it?"**

132) July 20, 2017- Trump and Pence open White House's voter fraud task force

President Donald Trump and Vice President Pence opened the first meeting of the White House's voter fraud task force with a vigorous defense of the commission's mission, even as critics questioned its transparency, impartiality and data-collection efforts. Critics, however, have said the commission appears to have been stacked with members who supported Trump's unfounded claims that millions of fraudulent votes were cast in the 2016 election. Trump, who trailed in the popular vote by nearly 3 million votes, blamed that loss on immigrants in this country illegally who voted.

133) July 23, 2017-Trump: President has the "complete power to pardon"

A combative President Trump, reflecting growing pressure from the FBI's investigation of possible Russian ties to his campaign, issued a tweet storm claiming a President has the **"complete power to pardon".** While legal experts say the extent of a president pardon himself is not clear cut, Trump begs to differ: **"While all agree the U.S. President has the complete power to pardon, why think of that when only crime so far is LEAKS against us. FAKE NEWS."**

134) July 26, 2017- House vote on Russia ties Trump's hands

The overwhelming vote by the GOP-controlled House to impose new Russia sanctions sends a strong and defiant message to President Donald Trump-all the more remarkable because it came from his own party. The new bill orders up a regimen of tougher sanctions in reprisal for Russia's meddling in the 2016 U.S. elections. More importantly, it prevents Trump from unilaterally easing punitive measures, something he has admitted he may do. Trump's unorthodox approaches cause Congress to act on its own.

135) July 27, 2017- Trump announced ban on transgender's serving in the military

President Donald Trump blindsided his own Defense Department and Congress when he announced via Twitter a ban on transgender people serving in the military. Banning transgendered people from the military now has popped into play, even though Trump pledged to stand by the LGBT community during his presidential campaign. Trump is intent on reversing former President Barrack Obama's June 2016 decision to lift the ban on transgender people serving in the military-done after a year of study.

136) July 29, 2017- Last ditch effort to dismantle Obamacare fails

The Senate crash of the seven-year Republican drive to scrap the Obama healthcare law incited GOP finger-pointing but left the party with the wounded leaders and no evident pathway forward on an issue that won't go away. In a cliffhanger, the GOP-run Senate voted 51-49 to reject majority leader Mitch McConnell's last-ditch attempt to sustain their drive to dismantle President Barrack Obamas healthcare overhaul with a starkly trimmed-down bill. **"They should have approved healthcare last night"**, Trump said. Trump reiterated his threat to **"let Obamacare implode, 3 Republicans and 48 Democrats let the American people down."**

137) July 29, 2017- Second North Korea missile firing could reach Chicago

North Korea test fired its second intercontinental ballistic missile, which flew longer and higher than the first, according to its wary neighbors, leading analysts to conclude that a wide swath of the U.S., including Chicago and Los Angeles, is now within range of Pyongyang's weapons. Analyst had estimated that the North's first ICBM could have reached Alaska, and that the latest missile appeared to extend that range significantly. President Donald Trump has said he will not allow North Korea to obtain an ICBM that can deliver a nuclear warhead.

138) August 1, 2017- President personally wrote Trump Jr. statement.

Flying home from Germany on July 8, 2017, aboard Air Force One, Trump personally dictated a statement in which Trump Jr. said he and the Russian lawyer had **"primarily discussed a program about the adoption of Russian children"** when they met in June 2016, according to multiple people with knowledge of the deliberations. Over the next three days, multiple accounts of the meeting were provided to the media as public pressure mounted, with Trump Jr. ultimately acknowledging that he had accepted the meeting after receiving an email promising damaging information about Hilary Clinton as part of a Russian government effort to help his father's campaign. Trump has said that the Russia probe is **"the**

greatest witch hunt in political history," calling it an elaborate hoax created by the Democrats to explain Clinton losing an election she should have won.

139) August 4, 2017-Focus on Trump Jr.'s meeting with Russian lawyer

Special Counsel Robert Mueller has convened a criminal grand jury to investigate Russian interference in the 2016 election and is focusing on Donald Trump Jr.'s meeting last year with a Russian lawyer who promised damaging information about the Democrats, according to a person familiar with the probe.

140) August 9, 2017- North Korea threatened ballistic strike of U.S. territory Guam

North Korea threatened a ballistic missile strike on the U.S. territory of Guam, the latest incendiary exchange between the rogue nation and President Trump, who vowed **"fire and fury like the world has never seen."** Trump said that North Korea leader Kim Jong Un **"has been very threatening beyond a normal state, and as I said, they will be met with fire and fury and frankly power, the likes of which this world has never seen before."**

141) August 11, 2017- Trump: No intentions of firing Robert Mueller

President Donald Trump said he has no intentions of firing Robert Mueller, the special counsel investigating his campaign and administration ties to Russia, a probe he has repeatedly attacked as a "witch hunt." **"I haven't given it any thought, you say 'oh I'm going to dismiss him'. No I'm not dismissing anybody. I mean, I want them to get on with the task."**

142) August 25, 2017-Trump threatens to shut down unless Congress funds his border wall

President Trump's threat to shut down the federal government unless Congress funds his controversial border wall could hurt Republicans, prompting GOP leaders to try to avert the potentially damaging action. Congressional leaders said Trump is sparking an unnecessary and probably unwinnable battle with the Senate, where Democrats vowed to block money for what their leaders denounced as an "ineffective, immoral and expansive" barrier. Trump promised a crowd of supporters in Phoenix: **"If we have to close down our government, we're building that wall."** The President made it clear that he would blame "obstructimist Democrats" for a government shutdown, but Democrats said he's the one pushing the unpopular idea.

143) August 28, 2017-Trump pursues business in Russia while running for President

While Donald Trump was running for President in late 2015 and early 2016, his company was pursuing a plan to develop a massive Trump Tower in Moscow, according to several people familiar with the proposed and new records reviewed by Trump Organization lawyers. As part of the discussions, a Russian born real estate developer urged Trump to come to Moscow to tout the proposal and suggested he could get President Vladimir Putin to say "great things" about Trump, according to several people who have been briefed on his correspondence. The developer, Felix Sater in a November 2015 email that he and Trump Organization leaders would soon be celebrating both one of the biggest residential projects in real estate history and Donald Trump's election as President, according to two of the people with knowledge of the exchange. Sater wrote to Trump Organization Executive Vice President Michael Cohen **"something to the effect of, can you believe two guys from Brooklyn are going to elect a president?"** The details of a deal, which have not previously been disclosed, provide evidence that Trump's business was actively pursuing significant commercial interests in Russia at the same time he was campaigning to be President, and in a position to determine U.S. Russia relations. The new details from the emails, which are scheduled to be turned over to congressional investigators, also point to the likelihood of additional contacts between Russia connected individuals and Trump associates during the presidential bid.

144) August 31, 2017-Nationwide leaders pleaded with President Trump to protect DREAMERS from deportation

More than 1,850 leaders nationwide pleaded with President Trump to preserve an Obama administration program that protects DREAMERS from deportation. Trump is considering ending the Deferred Action for Childhood Arrivals program. It has granted deportation protection to nearly 800,000 undocumented immigrants brought to this country as children. Eight governors, five state attorney generals, more than 130 mayors, 230 state legislators, and a slew of faith leaders, judges, police chiefs and sheriffs signed a statement to the President. In the letter, the group highlights the economic contributions DREAMERS have made to their communities since the program was created in 2012. They said the U.S. economy would lose $460 billion over the next decade if DACA were terminated.

145) September 4, 2017-U.S. responds to North Korea claim of H-Bomb

Responding to North Korea's claimed test of a hydrogen bomb, President Donald Trump indicated military action was an option and threatened to halt all trade with countries doing business with Pyongyang, a veiled warning to China, and faulted South Korea for its "talk of appeasement." Defense Secretary Jim Mattis followed with a blunt warning, saying the U.S. will answer any threat from the North with a "massive military response, a response both effective and overwhelming."

Chapter 4

146) September 5, 2017-Six-month delay of DACA to give Congress time to pass legislation

A plan President Donald Trump is expected to announce today for young immigrants brought to the country illegally as children was embraced by some top Republicans and denounced by others as the beginning of a "civil war" within the party. Trump was preparing to announce an end to Deferred Action for Childhood Arrivals program, but with a six-month delay intended to give Congress time to pass legislation that would address the status of the hundreds of thousands of immigrants covered by the program. It remains unclear exactly how a six month delay would work in practice, including whether the government would continue to process applications under the program, which has given nearly 800,000 young immigrants a reprieve from deportation and the ability to work legally in the form of two year renewable permits.

147) September 6, 2017- Trump ends Obama's DACA, six months to resolve

President Donald Trump took action to strip away protections from deportation for roughly 800,000 people brought into the country illegally as children, giving Congress six months to write a law to resolve their plight. Trump's long-awaited decision to get rid of the Obama-era program for so-called Dreamers fir a pattern of his young presidency: He offered little guidance on what he wanted done and left it to polarize Congress to fill in the details. If Congress fails, and the people covered under the DACA are put in jeopardy of being deported to countries they know little if at all, both Trump and some supporters have suggested it will be the fault of the lawmakers.

148) September 14, 2017- House and Senate reach agreement on DACA with Trump

The top House and Senate Democrats said they had reached agreement with President Donald Trump to protect thousands of younger immigrants from deportation and fund some border security enhancements, not including Trump's long sought border wall. **"We agreed to enshrine the protections of DACA into law quickly, and to work out a package of boarder security, excluding the wall, that's acceptable to both sides,"** Pelosi and Schumer said in a joint statement. **"This is a positive step toward the Presidents strong commitment to bipartisan solutions for the issues most important to all Americans,"** the White House said.

149) September 15, 2017-Trump said he is 'fairly close' to dal to protect DREAMERS

President Trump said he's **"fairly close"** to deal with Congress that would protect young undocumented immigrants who come into the country illegally as children. But even as Trump signaled progress on a grand bargain on immigration, he also disputed claims by Democratic leaders that he had agreed to drop his insistence that Congress eventually pay for a wall along the length of the Mexican border. **"The wall will come later, we're right now renovating large sections of wall, massive sections, making it brand new."**

150) September 16, 2017-Federal Judge blocked sanctuary cities having to cooperate with immigration agents

In a ruling with national impact, a federal judge in Chicago blocked the Trump administration's rules requiring sanctuary cities to cooperate with immigration agents in order to get a public safety grant. U.S. Attorney General Jeff Sessions exceeded his authority in imposing new standards governing Edward Byrne Memorial Justice Assistance Grants across the country. U.S. District Judge Harry Leinenweber said Mayor Rahm Emanuel's administration has shown that the city could suffer "irreparable harm" in its relationship with the immigrant community if it were to comply with the U.S. Department of Justice new standards. The preliminary injunction granted by Leinenweber applies to districts nationwide.

151) September 28, 2017- First major revamp of tax code

Promising big tax cuts and a booming economy, President Donald Trump and congressional Republicans unveiled the first major revamp of the nation's tax code, a sweeping $6 trillion tax cut that would deeply reduce levies for corporations, simplify everyone's brackets and nearly double the standard deduction used by most American's. Trump declared repeatedly the plan would provide badly needed tax relief for the middle class, but there are too many gaps in the proposal to know how it actually would affect individual tax payers and families, how it would be paid for and how much it might add to the soaring $20 trillion national debt.

152) September 28, 2017-Trump's political agenda of what the EPA does as: junk science

At the Environmental Protection Agency, long time civil servants, some with doctorates in environmental work, say they have been frozen out because their voluminous administrative records are out of sync with a Trump political agenda that holds much of what they do; a junk science. EPA climate change advisor, who had 25 years with the agency resigned in a letter to Scott Pruitt, "We understand that our positions might not always prevail, but please take the time to listen to expert voices that might differ from yours and your immediate staff.

153) October 8, 2017-NRA endorsed Trump with more than $30 million

The pro-gun community had reason to suspicious of Donald Trump. He wrote in favor of an assault weapons ban and a **"slightly longer"** waiting period before gun purchases in a 2000 book and accused Republicans of walking **"the NRA line"**. Even as he rebranded himself a "2nd amendment maven" in 2013, he sounded conflicted, suggesting he favored expanded background checks. Now, after the worst mass shooting in modern history, Trump faces a gut-check moment. He could come under pressure, even from within his typically pro-gun party, to support legislation restricting gun use, however limited, in this case, a ban on so-called bump-fire stocks, like the Las Vegas shooter used, which turn semi-automatic weapons into virtual machine guns. **In a four-section paragraph on guns, Trump wrote that he supported President Bill Clinton's assault weapons ban along with a brief waiting period for gun buyers. The NRA helped to elect Trump, spending more than $30 million and endorsing him.** Trump returned the favor with some of the strongest pro-gun rhetoric ever delivered by a presidential candidate. He told an NRA audience that Democratic rival Hilary Clinton wanted to destroy the second amendment and that terrorist attacks in Paris and San Bernardino would have been stopped if more victims were armed. **"We'll talk about gun laws as time goes by"** Trump said. White House officials insist that President Donald Trump is not likely to endorse broader gun controls in the wake of the Las Vegas mass shooting.

154) October 13, 2017-Trump on devastated Puerto Rico: feds won't help 'forever'

President Donald Trump lashed out at hurricane-devastated Puerto Rico insisting in tweets that the federal government can't keep sending help "forever" and suggesting the U.S. territory was to blame for its financial struggles. San Juan Mayor Carmen Yulĭn Cruz, with whom Trump has had a running war of words, tweeted that the president's comments were "unbecoming" to a commander in chief and "seem more to come from a 'Hater in Chief'.

155) October 25, 2017-Top Republicans, Flake and Corker, slam Trump's behavior, question fitness for office

President Donald Trump endured one of the most searing rebukes of a chief executive by members of his own party in modern history, with one Republican senator accusing him of "debasing" the nation and another declaring he would rather retire than be "complicit" in the "compromise of our moral authority." "The debasement of our nation will be what he'll be remembered most for, and that's regretful," Corker said. Flake lamented the "reckless, outrageous and undignified" behavior emanating from the "top of our government." Trump tweeted that Corker **"couldn't get elected dog catcher."** Corker said he has tried to work with Trump but couldn't go no further. "I think that he's proven himself unable to rise to the occasion, world leaders are very aware that much of what he says is untrue."

156) October 31, 2017- Former Trump aides indicted for fraud, conspiracy and money laundering

The special counsel investigation Russia's role in the 2016 presidential race announced criminal charges against three former campaign aides to Donald Trump, including his former campaign chief, marking a new phase in the FBI probe of the president's inner circle. George Papadopoulos, a former foreign policy advisor to the Trump campaign, is cooperating with prosecutors led by special counsel Robert Mueller. Paul Manafort, who was Trumps campaign chief, and Richard Gates III, who was Manafort's top deputy and helped run Trumps inauguration, were separately accused of a total of 12 counts of fraud, conspiracy and money laundering in a financial scheme that ran from 2006-2017.

157) November 1, 2017-According to Trump, Papadopoulos "has already proven to be a liar"

President Donald Trump said that former campaign aide thrust into the center of special counsel Robert Mueller's Russia probe "has already proven to be a liar." Trump said: **"Few people knew the young, low level volunteer named George, who has already proven to be a liar. Check the DEMS."** Papadopoulos was approached by people claiming ties to Russia and offering "dirt" on Hillary Clinton in the form of thousands of emails. Papadopoulos pleaded guilty to lying to the FBI agents about the conversations and has been cooperating with investigators.

158) November 4, 2017-Trump launches criminal probes of former rival Hillary Clinton

President Donald Trump repeatedly called on the Justice Department and FBI to investigation his Democratic political opponents, a breach of the traditional executive branch boundaries designed to prevent the criminal justice system from becoming politicized. Trump urged federal law enforcement to "do what is right and proper" by launching criminal probes of former presidential rival Hillary Clinton and her party, a surprising use of his bully pulpit considering he acknowledged a day earlier that presidents are not supposed to intervene in such decisions.

159) November 12, 2017-Trump: "I believe very much in our intelligence agents"

President Donald Trump says he believes Russian President Vladimir Putin believes it when he says Moscow did not interfere in the 2016 U.S. presidential election. <u>"I believe that he feels that he and Russia did not meddle in the election,"</u> Trump said of Putting, <u>"as to whether I believe it, I'm with our agencies, as currently led by fine people, I believe very much in our intelligence agencies."</u> The U.S. intelligence community has concluded that Russia interfered in the election to help the Republican defeat Democrat Hillary Clinton. Trump reiterated his view that he is critical for the U.S. to get along with Russia and seemed to suggest that it was time to remove sanctions Congress has slapped on Russia in retaliation for its election meddling efforts. <u>"It's now time to get back to healing a world that is shattered and broken"</u> said Trump. <u>"Those are very important things."</u>

160) November 16, 2017-Half dozen Democrats file to impeach Trump

A half dozen Democrats introduced articles of impeachment against President Donald Trump, accusing him of obstruction of justice and other offenses, in a long shot effort that stands little chance in the Republican led House. The large majority of Democrats seem intent on nothing to do with the effort either as law makers await the results of special counsel Robert Mueller's investigation into ties between the Trump campaign and Russia. Democratic leaders have argued that the impeachment campaign riles up Trump's GOP base, a critical block in next year's midterm elections.

161) November 21, 2017-Federal Judge permanently blocks Trump's sanctuary city order

A federal judge permanently blocked President Donald Trump's executive order to cut funding from cities that limit cooperation with U.S. immigration authorities. U.S. District Court Judge William Orrick rejected the administration's arguments in a ruling that put a temporary hold on the executive order targeting so called sanctuary cities.

162) December 2, 2017-Flynn admits lying to FBI

The investigation into Russian meddling in last year's election spread to the White House for the first time as President Donald Trump's former National Security Advisor, Michael Flynn, pleaded guilty to lying to the FBI about his contacts with the Russian ambassador and agreed to help investigators as they focus on other presidential aides.

163) December 4, 2017- President's tweet disputes Comey's sworn testimony

At a crucial juncture in Special Counsel Robert Mueller's wide-ranging Russia investigation, President Donald Trump embarked on a risky gambit, going on record to directly dispute his former FBI Chief's sworn contention that the president had sought to derail an investigation into fired National Security Advisor Michael Flynn. The president tweeted: **"I never asked Comey to stop investigating Flynn, just more Fake News covering another Comey lie."**

164) December 5, 2017-Trump can't be charged his lawyer says

As the Special Counsel investigation inches deeper into the White House, President Donald Trump has repeatedly insisted that he had done nothing wrong, denying any collusion with Russia and decrying the allegations as a **"hoax."** Trump's lawyer said it's impossible for the president to obstruct justice under the law. The reason? He's too powerful. Trump "cannot obstruct justice because he is the chief law enforcement officer under (Article II of the

Constitution) and every right to express his view of any case," John Dowd, a lawyer for the president said.

165) December 12, 2017-Trump: "Media out of control, correct reporting means nothing to Them.

The President of the United States is a liar. So, it is staggering hypocrisy that President Donald Trump tweeted his most recent media critique: **"Very little discussion of all the purposely false and defamatory stories put out by the Fake News media. They are out of control, correct reporting means nothing to them. Major lies written, then forced to be withdrawn after they are exposed, a stain on America."** Journalist who lie or fabricate do not remain journalist for long.

166) December 13, 2017- Trump attacks female senator as "lightweight and a total flunky"

President Donald Trump attacked Senator Kirsten Gillibrand, a New York Democrat, in a tweet widely criticized as being sexually suggestive, sparking outrage at a time when the nation is reeling from a wave of accusations about improper behavior by powerful men, including Trump himself. Trump referred to Gillibrand as **"lightweight and a total flunky"** and that he was a New York real estate developer, she **"would come to my office 'begging' for campaign contributions and would do anything for them."** Gillibrand called Trump's tweet "a sexist smear attempt to silence my voice. You can't silence me or the millions of women who have gotten off the sidelines to speak out about the unfitness and shame you have brought to the Oval Office."

167) December 16, 2017-Trump: "Well it's a shame what's happened with the FBI"

President Donald Trump gave a distinctly mixed message to the FBI saying **"people are very, very angry"** about what they see as a political bias in the bureau but vowing unqualified support for law enforcement. **"Well it's a shame what's happened with the FBI."** Trump has described the agency as **"in tattlers, were going to rebuild the FBI. It will be bigger and better than ever."** Trump reported his claims that Clinton got off easy in the FBI investigation into her use of private email server while she was Secretary of State. He called the decision not to prosecute the Democratic presidential nominee as evidence of a **"rigged system."**

168) December 18, 2017- Trump: "No, No I'm not" firing Mueller

Amid increasing Republican attacks on Robert Mueller over the scope and impartiality of his investigation of Russian campaign meddling, President Donald Trump denied that he had any intention of firing the Special Counsel **"no, no, I'm not."**

169) December 19, 2017-Trump lists threats to security

President Donald Trump described the U.S. immigration system as a threat to National Security saying the **"wrong people"** are being admitted, even as he touched lightly on Russia's menace in a speech coinciding with release of the first comprehensive security strategy paper. **"We cannot secure our nation if we do not secure our borders,"** renewing his call to build a wall across the U.S. border with Mexico, shut down a long standing visa lottery that boosts the number of immigrants from Asia, Africa, and Eastern Europe, and what he calls "chain migration", by which U.S. citizens are allowed to sponsor some relatives to immigrate to the country. The president wants congress to revamp the immigration system to select people based on job skills, education and financial security. He called the current system **"a policy where the wrong people are allowed into our country and the right people are rejected."**

170) December 21, 2017- Young immigrants' fate on hold

A promised year's end deal to protect young immigrants brought to the country illegally as children from deportation collapsed as Republicans in Congress, fresh off passage of their tax plan, prepared to punt nearly all remaining agenda items into the New Year. Senator Dick Durbin of Illinois had a simple message to the young immigrants, known as Dreamers, "I'm sorry." Nearly 800,000 immigrants who were protected under President Barack Obama's Deferred Action for Childhood Arrivals program are at risk of deportation now that President Donald Trump has announced the end of the program in March 2018. Durbin and others continued to hold out hope that Congress could act on a version of DACA in January.

171) December 27, 2017-Trump pledges overhaul of healthcare in 2018

President Trump began his post-Christmas break by launching Twitter blasts on two issues likely to dominate his second year in office: healthcare and investigation into alleged Russian interference in the 2016 election. Trump predicted that Democrats and Republicans would come together to overhaul President Obama's healthcare law in the coming year. **"Based on the fact that the very unfair and unpopular individual mandate has been terminated as part of our tax bill, which essentially repeals (overtime) Obamacare, the Democrats and Republicans will eventually come together and develop a great new healthcare plan!"** Trump tweeted.

172) December 30, 2017-Trump says he can 'do what I want' with DOJ

President Trump said he thinks the investigation into Russian interference in the 2016 presidential election makes the U.S. **"look very bad." "I think that Bob Mueller will be fair, and everybody**

<u>**knows that there was no collusion.**</u>" While being questioned by The New York Times, the president deflected a question about a Justice Department investigation into Hillary Clinton's emails, he insisted, <u>**"I have absolute right to do what I want to do with the Justice Department"**</u> when discussing media coverage on his presidency, Trump predicted another election victory in 2020 and claimed the press had to cover him more favorably to help ratings. <u>**"Six months before the election, they'll be loving me because they're saying, please, please, don't lose Donald Trump."**</u>

173) January 4, 2018-Trump disbands his controversial voter fraud commission

President Donald Trump discontinued his commission to investigate voter fraud after more than a dozen states refused to comply with the commissions demand for all the voter data with names, social security numbers, and voting history including party affiliations. Many who reviewed the commission as critics, saw the commission as part of a campaign to make it harder for poor and minority voters to get access to the ballot box and to back up Trump's claims of voter fraud.

174) January 6, 2018- Trump's Russia denials continue

Trump continues with his denials that his presidential campaign "colluded" with Russia. <u>**"I actually think it's turning to the Democrats because there was collusion on behalf of the Democrats. There was collusion with the Russians and the Democrats. A lot of collusion."**</u> Another statement that Trump made was, <u>**"Crooked Hillary, she's the one that conspired with Vladimir Putin!"**</u>

175) January 9, 2018-Mueller seeks Trump interview

The issue was raised by Mueller about interviewing Trump. Trumps lawyers, who oversee the White House portion of the special counsel investigation, attended the meeting. Mueller and Trumps legal team discussed the terms and what would be asked in an interview. Trumps legal team hope to obtain from the Mueller's team what questions would be asked to the president. According to many prosecutors, it is unlikely Mueller would agree for the president to submit written answers to questions to avoid an interview in person.

176) January 14, 2018- Trump slams countries with Vulgar language

President Donald Trump was speaking to lawmakers when he slammed their desire to restore protections for refugees from Haiti, El Salvador and some African countries. **"Why are we having all these people from "shithole" countries come here?"** This was due to an immigration deal that would include protections for people from Haiti and other nations in Africa. Trump stated a preference for immigrants from countries like Norway, which is one of the world's whitest countries. Trump denied that he used such language, although Senate Minority Whip Dick Durbin and other witnesses confirmed the words Trump used.

177) January 14, 2018- Look what I did the first 100 days!

Trump didn't wait for the completion of his first 100 days before saying that his achievements surpassed anything in history. Trump bragged that he has signed more than 80 pieces of legislation into law. Those 80 pieces of legislation served little consequence. He signed laws naming federal buildings after people, appointing a Smithsonian Institution regent and other housekeep steps that all presidents do without mentioning tasks performed.

178) January 16, 2018-U.S. and China see risks of confrontation

China this month imposed stricter requirements on billions of dollars of American soybeans that threatens to curb the exports and punish a good size of the U.S. heartland. With this happening, President Donald Trump could follow through with his promise to get tough with China in trades. If Trump tries to levy trade sanctions, China is not going to take things lying down, and there will be some bad suffering for U.S. exporters. The Trump administration is getting ready to announce many actions including possible tariffs based on investigations into Chinese distorting trade and affecting U.S. firms and workers.

179) January 17, 2018-Trump administration appeals ruling on young immigrants under DACA
The Trump administration appealed a judge's ruling temporarily blocking its decision to end protections for hundreds of thousands of young immigrants. Attorneys for the U.S. Department of Justice said that they were appealing the January 9 ruling by a federal judge preventing President Donald Trump from ending the Deferred Action for Childhood Arrivals program (DACA). Attorney Jeff Sessions said in a statement that it defied **"law and common sense"** for a single federal judge to decide the DACA issue. DACA has protected about 800,000 people who were brought to the U.S. illegally as children or came with families who overstayed visas. The program includes hundreds of thousands of college-age students. The Trump administration is seeking the Supreme Court in hopes of reversing a federal judge's order allowing young, undocumented immigrants to remain in the United States.

180) January 18, 2018- Mr. President, get your facts straight
It was said for Trump to do what real journalist are supposed to do. Get your facts straight. A morning tweet **"Unemployment for Black Americans is the lowest ever recorded. Trump approval ratings with Black Americans has doubled. Thank you, and it will get even (much) better! @Fox News."** The first part of the tweet was deceptive, and the second part is totally wrong. Black

unemployment did fall to 6.8 percent in December, the lowest rate since the Bureau of Labor Statistics began tracking the data in 1972. The decline is black unemployment was started under President Barack Obama. Black unemployment began a steady decline in August 2011 which it went from 164 percent to 7.87 percent in January 2017. Trump's approval rating among blacks went down over the past year, not up.

181) January 21, 2018-Trump made 2,140 false or misleading claims

According to The Washington Post Fact Checker database that analyzes categories and tracks every suspect statement spoke by the president, showed that President Donald Trump has made 2,140 false or misleading claims one year after taking oath of office. From the earliest days as president, Trump repeatedly took credit for events or business decisions that happened before he took the oath of office. Sixty-two times he said that he secured business investments that had been previously announced and could easily be found on the internet. Trump has repeatedly asserted (61 times) that the Affordable Care Act was failing or on the edge of disaster. But the Congressional Budget Office said the Obamacare exchanges, despite well documented issues, is not imploding and is expected to remain stable for the foreseeable future. It seems like the only way you make things **"Great Again"** is to make them look bad to your followers and then talk as if you brought them back to fruition through your own genius way.

182) January 23, 2018- Trump ends shutdown, signs bill

The three-day shutdown of the government ended with President Donald Trump signing. The House and Senate approved a compromise to extend government spending until February 8, allowing the government offices to reopen. The deal was agreed to by 30 or so Senators calling themselves the Commonsense Caucus. Democrats need to keep the group together to put together an immigration deal that will protect "Dreamers". Democrats agreed to support the bill after winning a commitment from Senate Majority Leader Mitch McConnell, to bring up an immigration bill on February 8 or before then if there's bipartisan consensus around a specific proposal. The Democrats did get a little leverage and the promise of Senate vote on legislation to protect "Dreamers". This may be difficult with President Trump being elected on a hardline platform of curbing immigrations.

183) January 25, 2018- Trump: I'm looking forward to testifying before Mueller

Trump said he would be willing to answer questions under oath in an interview, which special counsel Robert Mueller has been seeking. **"I'm looking forward to it, actually. I guess they're talking about two or three weeks, but I'd love to do it."** Trump has said repeatedly, that "there's no collusion whatsoever" and he added **"there's no obstruction whatsoever."**

184) January 29, 2018-Trump's offer for 'Dreamers' good if he gets his $25 billion to build his wall.

In order to allow 1.8 million young immigrants without documentation to remain in the United States, Trump is asking in return $25 billion for his wall to keep any more immigrants from crossing the border illegally. In addition, Trump wants to end the policies that allow U.S. citizens to petition for permanent legal residency "green cards" for parents and siblings.

185) January 30, 2018-Trump rides on economic momentum created by Obama Administration.

It is expected that President Donald Trump, when delivering his State of the Union address, will be looking for approval in the economy, which he will claim "because of my policies". Trump claims he inherited a "mess" and transformed it. In real life, Obama inherited the mess, an economy free fall, losing 700,000 jobs/month which he turned around during his presidency term. Trump inherited an economy on joying a record stretch of months with private sector job growth. Black unemployment fell under Obama. Trump created slightly fewer new jobs in his first year than Obama did in his last. Trump is riding the economic momentum created under Obama.

186) January 31, 2018-Whoever became president, the economy would have gotten better due to Obama.

President Donald Trump's speech as he laid out the groundwork for a bipartisan achievement that has eluded him, on immigration, and a major new infrastructure initiative. Trump spoke about the economy with the rising stock market and low unemployment. These trends began in President Obama's first term, after the Great Recession, and the pace of growth actually slowed in the final quarter of 2017. That did not stop Trump from arguing that the country would have hit the skids if he had not been elected. Democrats have denied Trump any credit for the economy, arguing that his predecessor is responsible for the trends Trump inherited and that subsequent gains are little different from those in Obama's final years. Trump stated, **"I will not repeat the mistakes of the past administration that got us into this dangerous position."** One thing that was lacking was a thank you for the past presidents' accomplishments.

187) February 1, 2018-FBI has 'grave concerns' over Trump release of GOP memo

The FBI warned that it has "grave concerns" about a disputed Republican memo on secret surveillance during the 2016 campaign that President Donald Trump has promised to release, and that Democrats say is filled with distortions. The FBI had "limited opportunity" to review the classified four pages prepared by aides to Devin Nunes, a close Trump ally who chairs the House intelligence committee. The FBI warning increases the growing Republican effort to discredit.

188) February 5, 2018-House lawmakers question Trump exoneration claim, memo doesn't clear Trump

President Donald Trump's claim of exoneration in the Russia investigation was undercut by lawmakers who helped draft a controversial memo the president has embraced, alleging the FBI abused its surveillance powers. Trump seized on the memo after he'd declassified it over Justice Department objections, as confirming his own repeated contention that the investigation led by special counsel Robert Mueller is a "witch hunt". In a tweet, the president declared that the memo "totally vindicates" him.

189) February 7, 2018- "I'd love to see a shutdown" if Democrats refuse his proposal

Neither party appears to want a repeat of last month's three-day shutdown, but President Donald Trump seemed to want to close the government again if Democrats didn't give in to his demands. **"I'd love to see a shutdown if we can't get this stuff taken care of."** Trump's brash comments drew instant rebuke from lawmakers.

190) February 13, 2018-Trump budget plan adds to deficit, cuts domestic programs

Trump's budget calls for big cuts to domestic programs that benefit the poor and middle class, such as food stamps, housing subsidies and student loans. Social Security's disability program would have to reenter the workforce. The Public Broadcasting, The National Endowment for the Arts and Humanities, and the Institute of Museum and Library Services would be eliminated. This budget continues too much of Washington's spending, it does not balance in 10 years, and it creates a deficit of over a trillion dollars next year. In good times, the budget policy should be working to get the deficits down because bad times are sure to come.

191) February 14, 2018-GOP opposes allowing young immigrants to sponsor parents for legal status.

The Senate considers protections for young immigrants on those who achieve legal status, as being able to sponsor loved ones to join them in the United States. President Donald Trump, with legislation crafted by the GOP leaders, wants to block future immigrants from being able to petitions for relatives beyond spouses and minor children. Trump rejects what he calls **"chain migration"**, a term other view as derisive, in favor of giving visas to immigrants with specific skills or other sought-after experience. Republicans want to prevent the nearly 700,000 beneficiaries of the Deferred Action for Childhood Arrivals (DACA) program from helping the parents who brought them to the U.S. illegally as children earn permanent legal status.

192) February 16, 2018-Senate kill Trump's four immigration bills.

The Senate killed four immigration bills, including a Republican measure blocked by President Trump which would have provided a pathway to citizenship for more than 2 million DREAMERS. It would have allocated $25 billion to strengthen security, including the wall, and limited family-based immigration and barred the parents of DREAMERS from becoming citizens. The Department of Homeland Security said the bill would end the immigration enforcement in America.

193) February 17, 2018-Russians charged with meddling of the 2016 U.S. election.

The Justice Department charged 13 individuals and three companies with a long running scheme to criminally interfere with the 2016 U.S. presidential election. The Internet Research Agency was named in the indictment as the hub to trick Americans online into following and promoting Russian-fed propaganda that pushed 2016 voters toward then-Republican candidate Hillary Clinton. The indictment charges that the Russian efforts began in 2014 when three of the Russian conspirators visited 10 states, gathering intelligence about U.S. politics.

194) February 17, 2018- President Vladimir Putin assured Trump it wasn't true

Mr. Trump said that Mr. Putin had told him that Russia did not meddle, and he was inclined to believe him**. "Every time he sees me, he says, I didn't do that, and I really believe that when he tells me that, he means it,"** Mr. Trump said. In news conferences, on Twitter and at rallies Trump has called the Russia investigation "fake news" and repeatedly predicted that Mr. Mueller's investigation will end without finding much.

195) February 19, 2018-Students focus anger at President Trump

Students who escaped the deadly school shooting of 17 people at Marjory Stoneman Douglas High School in South Florida contended that President Donald Trump's response to the attack has been needlessly divisive. David Hogg, a 17-year old student said "You're the President. You're supposed to bring this nation together, not divide us. How dare you" he added. Hogg was responding to Trump's tweet that Democrats hadn't passed any gun control during the brief time they controlled Congress with a super majority in the Senate.

196) February 21, 2018-Trump purges bump stock ban

President Donald Trump directed the Justice Department to move to ban devices like the rapid-fire bump stocks used in last year's Las Vegas massacre. <u>**"We must do more to protect our children,"**</u> Trump said in response to the shooting in Parkland that left 17 dead. Trump signed a memorandum directing the agency to complete the review as soon as possible, <u>**"banning all devices that turn legal weapons into machine guns."**</u>

197) February 22, 2018-President Donald Trump's promises in gun control

Trump promised to be <u>**"very strong on background checks"**</u> and supported allowing some teachers and other school employees to carry concealed weapons to be ready for intruders. Besides concealed weapons by trained employees, Trump said he planned to go <u>**"very strongly into age, age of purchase."**</u> These promises were made to invited guests from survivors of school violence and their parents. The purpose of Trump's meeting was to show his resolve against gun violence in the wake of last week's shootings at Marjory Stoneman High School in Parkland Florida, and in past years at schools in Connecticut and Colorado. These episodes have prompted a renewal and growing call for stronger gun control. Trump invited his guests to suggest solutions and solicited feedback. He did not fully endorse any specific policy solution but pledged to take action.

198) February 23, 2018-Trump: Armed teachers could stop shootings

Trump wants to allow concealed-carry permits to schools to allow teachers, coaches and other officials to be armed against potential killers. Trump repeatedly berated the practice of declaring campuses as <u>**"gun free zones,"**</u> calling that an invitation to armed attackers. <u>**"We have to harden our schools, not soften them,"**</u>

Trump said. **"A gun free zone to a killer or somebody who wants to be a killer, that's like going in for the ice cream. That's like here I am, take me."** Trump had turned into a hearty supporter of arming teachers. He advocated for guns in schools, and then tweets several ideas, including raising the minimum age for certain gun purchases, building up the process of checking backgrounds of potential buyers and banning bump stocks. Trump suggested without evidence that up to 40 percent of teachers could be armed. He then recommended that **"we give them a little bit of bonus"** for bearing arms. When Trump has talked about gun control in the past, he immediately drops his support once the NRA opposes it. Will this time be different?

199) February 25, 2018-Trump talks new gun measures

After 17 people were killed by a teenager at the Florida school, Trump said that assault rifles should be kept out of the hands of anyone under 21. He endorsed more stringent background checks for gun buyers and ordered his Justice Department to work toward banning rapid-fire "bump stock" devices. The NRA, which spent about $30 million in support of Trump's campaign, is firmly opposed to raising the legal age for the purchase of long guns from 18 to 21. Gun owners of America issued on alert urging its 1.5 million members to call the White House and "tell Trump to OPPOSE all gun control."

200) February 26, 2018-The real test of President Trump is not words and empathy, but action.

President Trump said, **"I think we are going to have a great bill put forward soon having to do with background checks, having to do with getting rid of certain things and keeping other things, and perhaps we'll do something on age."** This statement is not very definitive. Trump has the tendency to make a statement and later change his mind based on the response from his followers, specifically the NRA. Trump will be faced with the resistance from gun owners, but with the NRA's independent expenditure arm which gave Trump's 2016 campaign millions of dollars, you know what his decision will be; follow what the NRA and gun owners want and not listen to the concerns of millions of school children asking for help.

201) February 26, 2018-NRA rejects Trump's age-limit proposal

The National Rifle Association rejected President Donald Trump's call for federal ban on rifle sales to those under 21. The NRA believes the age for purchases should not be raised from 18. According to the NRA and the age requirement, was only the step Trump was thinking about, not a hard-and-fast commitment. "These are not thing's he's discussing right now," an NRA spokeswoman said. A few elected officials whose positions have long aligned with those of the NRA, including Trump and Florida Governor Rick Scott, have expressed support for raising the age limit for gun sales nationwide or at the state level.

202) February 28, 2018-Teenagers through the first stone

Teenagers from Marjory Stoneman Douglas High School are students that are smart enough to understand that the real impediment to sensible gun control laws is not the second amendment but lawmakers who take the industry money. Senator Marco Rubio was asked by a Parkland student, "So Senator Rubio, can you tell me right now that you will not accept a single donation from the NRA in the future?" Senator Marco Rubio, who has received $3,303,355 from the NRA over the course of his career, had no response except to change the subject.

203) March 1, 2018-Trump: Send him "one terrific bill" on gun safety

President Donald Trump told bipartisan lawmakers to send him **"one terrific bill"** on gun safety, including restrictions based on people's age and mental health, and stronger background checks, proposals long opposed by the gun lobby. The president was non-committal when lawmakers called for a ban on assault weapons such as the AR-15 semi-automatic rifle used in the Parkland Florida shootings. He alluded to his signature proposal to arm some teachers but said he would defer to lawmakers on the proposal, which has drawn much opposition. Trump said, **"I will sign it and I will call whoever you want me to if I like what you're doing"** he added that legislation must be **"very, very powerful on background checks"** and **"very strong on mentally ill."** Trump told lawmakers several times not to include in a bill a ban on **"bump stocks"**, instead, Trump said, Congress should let him do it through executive order. Trump also said several times that he wants to be the president who finally gets something done to prevent school shootings.

204) March 5, 2018-Trump determined on tariffs despite warnings

President Donald Trump is determined to impose punishing tariffs on imported steel and aluminum, brushing aside an outcry from foreign allies, U.S. manufactures, Republican lawmakers and other presidential advisors that he may ignite a damaging trade war. Trump said on Twitter: **"Our friends and enemies have taken advantage of the U.S. for many years. Our steel and aluminum industries are dead. Sorry, it's time for a change!"**

205) March 8, 2018-Trumps steel tariffs reversal

The White House said that Mexico, Canada and other countries may be spared from President Donald Trump's planned steel and aluminum tariffs that are under national scrutiny, a move which could reduce the threats of retaliation by trading partners, lawmakers and business groups. A letter was written by 107 House Republicans that said, "We urge you to reconsider the idea of broad tariffs to avoid unintended negative consequences to the U.S. economy and its workers."

206) March 9, 2018-Will try to end N. Koreas nuke program, U.S. and S. Korea say

President Donald Trump met with S. Korea officials and it was agreed thru S. Korea that Trump would meet with Kim Jung Un by May to negotiate an end to Pyongyang's nuclear weapons program. South Korea National Security Advisor said "He (Kim) expressed his eagerness to meet President Donald Trump as soon as possible." President Trump appreciated the briefing and said he would meet Kim Jung Un by May **"to achieve permanent denuclearization"** The invitation was verbally given to Trump by the South Korean National Security Director, Chung Eui-young, not by Kim Jung Un personally.

207) March 9, 2018-Trump signs off on tariffs, Canada and Mexico exempt for now

President Donald Trump signed proclamation imposing tariffs on steel and aluminum imports and said they are designed to protect American industries. Trump said his plan does exempt Canada and Mexico from the tariffs. **"We have to protect and build our steel and aluminum industries, while at the same time showing great flexibility and cooperation towards those that are really friends of ours,"** Trump said. Trumps claim that the tariffs serve the need of national defense and the move is **"vital to our national security".**

208) March 14, 2018-President Trump dumps Secretary of State Rex Tillerson

President Donald Trump ousted Secretary of State Rex Tillerson and plans to nominate CIA Director Mike Pompeo to replace him. This would be a major change to his National Security Team amongst all the things Trumps staff has to contend with including possible talks with North Korea. Trump told reporters that he decided to fire Tillerson because they disagreed over strategy in key areas of foreign policy. Tillerson's voice was quivering when he thanked career diplomats for their "honesty and integrity" and the American people for "acts of kindness," but did not thank Trump or praise his policies.

209) March 15, 2018- White House nixes DACA for wall idea

The White House said that it does not favor an immigration agreement with Congress that would involve extending protections for certain young immigrants for three years in exchange for three years of border wall funding. President Donald Trump has proposed a path to citizenship for about 1.8 million immigrants brought to this country illegally as children in exchange for $25 billion for a border wall and other security measures, along with curbing legal immigration. The Department of Homeland Security is under court order to maintain the DACA protections while supporters of the program challenge Trump's decision to end it.

210) March 19, 2018-Trump slams Mueller, McCabe on Twitter

President Donald Trump lashed out at Special Counsel Robert Mueller. Trump has also challenged the honesty of Andrew McCabe, the newly fired FBI Deputy Director, and James Comey, the bureaus former director whom Trump fired last year over the Russia probe. **"The Mueller probe should never have been started in that there was no collusion and there is no crime. It** was based on fraudulent activities and a Fake Dossier paid for by crooked Hillary and the DNC, and improperly used in FISA Court for the surveillance of my campaign. WITCH HUNT!" Trump tweeted.

211) March 21, 2018-Trump Congratulates Putin

President Donald Trump was warned by his National Security Advisors, "Do Not Congratulate" Vladimir Putin, which was contained in his briefing materials, but Trump chose not to heed talking points from aides instructing him to condemn Putin about the recent poisoning of a former Russian spy in the United Kingdom with a powerful nerve agent, a case that both the U.S. governments have blamed on Moscow.

212) March 23, 2018-Trump tariffs upset Wall Street, China

President Donald Trump set in motion tariffs on as much as $60 billion in Chinese imports to the U.S. and accused the Chines of high-tech thievery. China threatened retaliation, and Wall Street cringed, recording one of the biggest drops of Trump's presidency. Trump declared the U.S. would emerge "much stronger, much richer."

213) March 24, 2018-Trump issues order taking aim at transgender troops

President Donald Trump released an order banning most transgender troops from serving in the military under "limited circumstances." Trump push for the ban has been blocked by several legal challenges and three federal courts have ruled against the ban. The Pentagon responded by allowing those serving to stay in the military and began allowing transgender individuals to enlist beginning on January 1.

214) March 29, 2018-Trump's failure on the border wall

One of the major campaign promises by Trump that he repeated over and over, was that he was going to build a wall along the U.S. and Mexican border. Trump emphasized to his followers consistently that Mexico will pay for it **"We're going to have our wall; we're going to get our wall."** Trump stated, **"Now, the obstructionist Democrats would like us not to do it, but believe me, if we have to close down our government, were building that wall."** In the end, Trump signed the spending bill but only received $1.6 billion for border security which was nowhere near the $25 billion the president had requested.

Chapter 5

215) April 2, 2018-Trump tweets: "No deal on DACA"
President Donald Trump went on an anti-immigrant tirade on Easter morning saying that there would be no deal to legalize the status of immigrants known as "dreamers". Trump put the future of millions of immigrants who were brought illegally to the United States as children into peril by promising **"No more DACA deal"**. After conceding DACA, Trump said he would like to reach a deal with Congress to protect dreamers from deportation in exchange for funding to build his long-promised wall of the U.S. Mexican border.

216) April 4, 2018- Military will be sent to guard border
President Donald Trump said the military will be sent to guard the U.S. Mexican border but did not offer any details on how this will be implemented. Trump continuously going to Twitter using his remarks to warn of threats posed by immigration. Sending the military put a new twist on Trump's strategy which centered on threats pressuring Congress to send him funding for a border wall.

217) April 4, 2018-55,000 DACA applications Ok'd so far this year
Trump said in a Twitter storm **"DACA is dead"**. But the numbers released by the Justice Department shows that the Trump administration has approved tens of thousands of applications in recent months for the Deferred Action for Childhood Arrivals program

which provides temporary protection to undocumented immigrants brought to the United States as children. More than 55,000 DACA initial and renewal applications were approved in the first three months of 2018.

218) April 4, 2018-Trump frustrated, sends military along U.S. Mexico border

President Donald Trump said until his wall is built, he will deploy "the military" along the U.S. Mexican border. Trump is frustrated and has initiated this deployment of military primarily because Mexico and Congress resist paying for the wall. Trump requested $25 billion for the border all but only received $1.6 billion. With the allocations for money in the budget funding being unclear. Sending the military to the southern border until his wall is built, could be for a very long time.

219) April 11, 2018-Deployment of troops to Mexico border begins

The deployment of National Guard member to the U.S. Mexico border at President Donald Trump's request was underway with a gradual ramp-up of troops under orders to help curb illegal immigration. Trump has called a crisis of migrant crossings and crime is why the troops are needed.

220) April 14, 2018-Trump: Ex-FBI director an 'untruthful slime ball'

President Donald Trump laced into James Comey as an "untruthful slime ball" as the White House and the National Republican Party mounted a withering counterattack against the former FBI director and his stringing new memoir. Press Secretary Sarah Sanders stood at the White House podium and called Comey "a liar and a leaker" who loyalty is "only to himself," adding that Comey will "be-forever known as a disgraced partisan hack." Ironically, the press secretary sounds similar to the language that President Donald Trump would also use to describe Comey.

221) April 16, 2018-Trump calls Comey "slipper" labeled him "the worst FBI Director in history, by far"

Trump pushed back again against Comey's claims that Trump sought his loyalty, saying, **"I hardly even knew this guy. Just another of his many lies."** He questioned Comey's intelligence and place in history, writing, **"Slippery James Comey, a man who always ends up badly and out of whack (he is not smart), will go down as the worst FBI Director in history, by far."** Trump also suggested Comey should be imprisoned, saying **"how come he gave up classified information (jail), why did he lie to Congress (jail)"** There is no indication Comey is under investigation for doing either.

222) April 20, 2018-What did Comey's memo say?

Concerns of President Trump as discussed in memos:
- A) Trump had serious concerns about the judgement of his first National Security Advisor Michael Flynn.
- B) Trump told Comey that Russian President Vladimir Putin told him that Russia had "some of the most beautiful hookers in the world"
- C) Trump tower discussion about encounter between Trump and prostitutes in Moscow.
- D) A White House dinner which Comey says Trump asked him for his loyalty.
- E) A private Oval Office discussion where Comey says the president asked him to end an investigation on Flynn.

The memos with more information was turned over to Mueller.

223) April 20, 2018-Rudy Giuliani joins Trumps legal team for Russia probe

Trump, by hiring Giuliani, is looking to bring his involvement with Special Counsel Robert Mueller's investigation to a close and is considering whether to sit for questioning by Mueller's team. Giuliani will be focusing in the Mueller investigation. Trump said, **"Rudy is great, and that he wants to get this matter resolved for the good of the country."**

224) April 25, 2018-Judge rules against ending DACA program

A federal judge ruled against the Trump administration's decision to end a program protecting some young immigrants from deportation, calling the Department of Homeland Security's rationale against the program "arbitrary and capricious." The judge gave DHS 90 days to "better explain its view that DACA is unlawful." If the department cannot come up with a better explanation, he wrote, it "must accept and process new as well as renewal DACA applications."

225) May 1, 2018-Stormy Daniels sues Trump.

Stormy Daniels filed a lawsuit against President Donald Trump alleging that he defamed her in a tweet that mocked the porn actress for saying a man once physically threatened her on Trump's behalf. The man suggested she would be harmed if she went public with her story about having a one-night stand with Trump.

226) May 3, 2018-Giuliani: Trump paid hush money.

Rudy Giuliani said that Trump made series of payments reimbursing his lawyer, Michael Cohen for a $130,000 settlement with an adult film actress which appeared to contradict Trump's assertion that he was unaware of the payment.

227) May 4, 2018-President confirms payment.
President Donald Trump said that his long-time lawyer Michael
Cohen was reimbursed through a monthly retainer for a $130,000
payment made to porn actress Stormy Daniels in 2016 to stop what
Trump called "false and extortionist accusations."

228) May 4, 2018- Giuliani news puzzles legal experts.
President Donald Trump and his new legal point man Giuliani are
off to an explosive start together admitting what Trump had only
recently denied, that he reimbursed his personal lawyer for hush
money to be paid to a porn actress before the election. Some legal
experts say Giuliani may have made things worse, not only for the
president, but also for Michael Cohen, the lawyer who paid Stormy
Daniels $130,000 shortly before the 2016 election to stay quiet
about an alleged affair with Trump.

229) May 5, 2018- Trump disputes Giuliani account.
President Donald Trump further confused his legal strategy, disputing an account from his attorney, Giuliani, that Trump paid
$130,000 in hush money to porn star Stormy Daniels, just a day
after he'd confirmed the remarks.

**230) May 5, 2018- Trump salutes NRA, strong
backing by NRA**
Trump has long enjoyed strong backing from the NRA, which spent
about $30 million in support of his presidential campaign. One
of the Parkland student survivors David Hogg criticized Trumps
appearance for the NRA, "It's kind of hypothetical of him to go
there after saying so many politicians bow to the NRA and are
owned by them. It proves that his heart and his wallet are in the
same place."

231) May 6, 2018- Plans to arm school teacher's stall

In the two months after the Florida school shooting that left 17 dead, Republican law makers across the country introduced 25 measures to arm teachers and staff in schools. Trump and the NRA called in states to arm teachers as a front-line defense against school shooters. In a survey of 1000 members, the National Education Association, found that 82 percent of educators said they would not carry a gun in school, including a substantial majority who own a gun. The idea of arming teachers is ill-conceived, preposterous, and dangerous. Teachers should be teaching, not acting as armed security guards, or receiving training to become sharp shooters.

232) May 7, 2018- Giuliani: 'We don't have to comply.'

President Donald Trump's attorney, Rudy Giuliani, who has already roiled the White House's legal tussle with adult film star actress Stormy Daniels, asserted Sunday that the president would not "have to" respond to a subpoena in the special counsel's ranging Russia investigation."

233) May 8, 2018- Trump jabs Kerry ahead of Iran-deal decision

Trump criticized John Kerry after reports that the former Secretary of State has been promoting the Iran nuclear deal. Trump said on Twitter: "The United States does not need John Kerry's possibly illegal Shadow Diplomacy in the very badly negotiated Iran Deal. He was the one that created this MESS in the first place."

234) May 9, 2018- Trump pulls U.S. out of Iran nuclear deal

President Donald Trump is pulling the United States out of the Iran nuclear deal and will reinstate a punishing array of U.S. economic sanctions on Tehran that were lifted under the landmark 2015 accord. In an 11-minute address, Trump called the Iran deal "decaying and rotten." The decision was more severe that diplomats had expected and sent shock waves around the globe. It could isolate the United States among its largest European allies, all of which had pleaded with Trump to keep the historic pact in place.

235) May 17, 2018- Trump Jr. can't recall discussing Russia Probe with father.

Donald Trump Jr. said he didn't think there was anything wrong with meeting a Russian lawyer at Trump Tower ahead of the 2016 presidential election or that the get together might have been part of a Russian government effort to aid his father. The president's eldest son also deflected multiple questions from the Senate Judiciary Committee, responding to dozens of queries by saying he could not recall.

236) May 18, 2018-Trump "Bigger than Watergate" to expose FBI source.

Trump reacted on Twitter that there was a top-secret source providing intelligence to the FBI as it began its investigation into Russia's interference in the election process. "Wow, word seems to be coming out that the Obama FBI SPIED ON THE TRUMP CAMPAIGN WITH AN EMBEDDED INFORMANT," Trump tweeted. "If so, this is bigger than Watergate."

237) May 20, 2018- Trump may plead the fifth

President Donald Trump's attorney, Rudy Giuliani, said he hasn't ruled out the possibility Trump will invoke the Fifth Amendment during questioning. As special counsel Robert Mueller's investigation continues to produce indictments, seeming to reach ever closer to the Oval Office, the Fifth Amendment and its protections against self-incrimination have been making news.

238) May 22, 2018- Farmers will come out on top, Trump promises "Under our potential deal with China, they will

<u>purchase from our Great American Farmers practically as much as our Farmers can produce,"</u> Trump tweeted.

Treasury Secretary Mnuchin, has said to expect to see a big increase of 35 to 45 percent in U.S. farm sales to China. Farm sales are feared by many Trump supporters in rural states that say they fear a U.S. trade war with China would hurt their export business.

239) May 23, 2018- North Korea summit less certain

Trump offers mixed signals on planned meeting with Kim. <u>"It may not work out for a June 12th meeting,"</u> then further confused the question by adding. <u>"There's a good chance we'll have the meeting."</u> Trump vowed to attend only if U.S. conditions are met. North Korean denuclearization, President Trump said, <u>"must take place,"</u> but he stopped short of demanding that Kim end his nuclear program attendance.

240) June 1, 2018- President now says Comey not fired over Russia Probe

President Donald Trump declared that he did not fire FBI Director James Comey over the Russia investigation, despite previously citing that as a reason. The president has said at least twice that Comey's firing in May 2017 was related to the FBI's investigation into whether Trump's campaign associates coordinated with Russia in an effort to sway the 2016 election. Trump tweeted, <u>"Not that it really matters but I never fired James Comey, because of Russia. Mainstream media loves to keep pushing that narrative, but they know it is not true."</u>

241) June 1, 2018-Trump action raises tensions on trade

President Donald Trump's decision to slap tariff on steel and aluminum from Canada, Mexico, and the European Union sharply escalated global trade tensions and widened a rift with America's closest allies. Canadian leaders reacted particularly angrily to the tariffs of 25 percent on steel and 10 percent on aluminum. Trump had justified the impart levies on the grounds of national security, a line of reasoning that Canadian officials called absurd, illogical and illegal.

242) June 1, 2018-U.S. Tariffs trigger retaliation
President Donald Trump imposed tariffs on imported steel and aluminum from the European Union, Canada, and Mexico, triggering immediate retaliation from U.S. allies and protest from American business and farmers.

243) June 2, 2018- Trump order to aid coal, nuclear plants
President Donald Trump directed Energy Secretary Rick Perry to prepare "immediate steps" to bolster struggling coal fired and nuclear power plants to keep them operating. Trump believes that keeping America's energy grid secure "protects our national security, public safety, and economy from intentional attacks and natural disasters." The Trump administration considers a plan to order operators of the nation's power grid to buy electricity from coal and nuclear plants to keep them open. The plan would exempt power plants from obeying a host of environmental laws and spend billions to keep coal-fired plants open.

244) June 5, 2018-Trump: An 'absolute right' to pardon self
President Donald Trump asserted two new and widely disputed claims in his assault on the Russia investigation that he has "the absolute right" to pardon himself and that the appointment of the special counsel for that inquiry was unconstitutional.

245) June 14, 2018- Legal entry to U.S. under siege.
President Trump acted differently since moving into the White House. His administration has granted fewer VISAS, approved fewer refugees, ordered the removal of hundreds of thousands of

legal residents whose home countries have been hit by war and natural disasters, and pushed congress to pass laws to dramatically cut the entire immigration system. The White House has argued the moves are necessary to protect national security and American workers.

246) June 15, 2018- Trump readying China tariffs
President Donald Trump has approved a plan to impose punishing tariffs on tens of billions of dollars of Chinese goods, a move that could put his trade policies on a collision course with his push to rid the Korean peninsula of nuclear weapons.

247) June 16, 2018-China strikes back, hikes tariffs on U.S.
China fired back on U.S. in a spiraling trade dispute with President Donald Trump by raising import duties on a $34 billion list of American goods including soybeans, electric cars, and whiskey. Beijing will impose an additional 25 percent tariff on 545 products from the United States which included orange juice, salmon, cigars, soybeans, electric cars, and whiskey. Additional tariffs would be medical equipment and energy products.

248) June 17, 2018-President Donald Trump lawyers and Robert Mueller heading towards showdown.
Rudi Giuliani, the president's personal attorney, said that he planned to use the inspector general's conclusions to undermine Mueller, suggesting he may ask Attorney General Jeff Sessions to appoint a second special counsel to examine the current probe. "We want to see if we can have the investigation and special counsel declared illegal and unauthorized."

249) June 18, 2018-Congressman compares presidents fear tactics to Nazi Germany

U.S. Representatives Lois Gutierrez slammed President Donald Trump's immigration policy of separating children from their parents at the border and compared Trump's actions to those used in Nazi Germany. "That's the way you got fascism in Germany. That's the first thing the Nazi's did in Germany. They said, 'Get rid of all those foreigners, and let's make this a German nation,'" said Gutierrez.

250) June 19, 2018- President brushes aside criticism of separating families

President Donald Trump stood defiant against a growing backlash over his administrations "zero tolerance" immigration policy that since April has separated at least 2,000 children from their parents crossing the southern border, and he continued to falsely blame Democrats for the hardline actions. "The United States will not be a migrant camp and it will not be a refuge holding facility, not on my watch."

251) June 20, 2018-Babies and other young children forcibly separated.

Trump administration officials have been sending babies and other young children forcibly separated from their parents at the U.S.-Mexican border to at last three "tender age" shelters in South Texas. Lawyers and medical providers who have visited the Rio Grande Valley shelters described playrooms of crying preschool-aged children in crisis. The doctors and lawyers said the facilities were fine, clean, and safe, but the kids, who have no idea where their parents are, were hysterical, crying, and acting out.

252) June 21, 2018-Trump helps the kids, but where is immigration reform?

President Donald Trump did the right thing reversing course to address on immigration crisis. He issued an executive order to end his administration's inhumane practice of separating children from their parents at the southern border. Nearly 2000 children had been sent alone to shelters because of Attorney General Session's decision to prosecute all adults, including parents, who violate immigration laws. The aggressive enforcement action, being a policy choice, was cruel, victimizing children.

253) June 21, 2018-Amid outrage Trump acts on border family separation.

Bowing to pressure from anxious allies, President Donald Trump abruptly reversed himself and signed an executive order halting his administration's policy of separating children from their parents when they are detained illegally crossing the U.S. border.

254) June 25, 2018-Trump is leading country toward disaster.

Everyday Trump is president, the United States drifts away from its ideals, and our future. We are not only poisoning our social landscape today but burying caches of poison that will plague us for years to come.

255) June 25, 2018-Trump pushes to strip rights from migrants.

President Donald Trump explicitly advocated depriving undocumented immigrants of their due process rights arguing that people who cross the border into the United States illegally must immediately be deported without trial, 'with no Judges or Court Cases'. Trump, in a tweet, described immigrants as invaders and wrote that U.S. immigration laws are "a mockery" and must be changed to take away trial rights from undocumented migrants.

256) June 26, 2018- Zero tolerance policy halted.

The nation's top border enforcement official acknowledged that authorities have abandoned, for now, the Trump administration's "zero tolerance" policy toward immigrant families after the president ordered the end to the separation of parents and children who cross the southern border.

257) June 27, 2018-U.S. Supreme Court ruled in favor of President Donald Trump's travel ban.

By a 5-4 vote, the U.S. Supreme Court ruled in favor of President Donald Trump's travel ban aimed at mostly Muslim nations. Under the ban, people from those nations generally are not allowed to emigrate here, nor are they allowed to work, study or take vacations in the United States.

258) June 30, 2018-G.M. tells Trump tariff plan puts U.S. jobs at risk.

General Motors warned that if President Trump pushed ahead with another wave of tariffs, the move could backfire leading to "less investment, fewer jobs, and lower wages" for its employees. The automaker said that the president's threat to impose tariffs on import of cars and car parts-along with an earlier spate of penalties-could drive vehicle prices up by thousands of dollars.

259) July 4, 2018-Trump: Deporting illegal immigrants is like 'liberating a town' in combat.

President Donald Trump likened federal immigration enforcement to war claiming that the work of deporting illegal immigrants is like "liberating a town or an area" in combat. "But when these people come into our country and come in illegally, and then they are dispersed throughout the country, and then all of a sudden you see nests of MS-13, you know, it's like you're liberating towns."

260) July 5, 2018-Trade-war showdown looms.

President Donald Trump is threatening tariff hikes on up to $450 billion of Chinese goods. Despite the threat from President Donald Trump of tariff hikes on Chinese goods, Beijing shows no sign it will scale back plans it sees as a path to prosperity and global influence.

261) July 6, 2018-U.S. says 3000 children need to be reunited with parents.

The Trump administration official in charge of caring for undocumented minors separated from their parents at the border said that his agency must reunite 3,000 children with their parents. Department of Health and Human Services Secretary Alex Azar said the work has been further complicated by the nation's "disjointed" immigration laws.

262) July 11, 2018-ICE grabbing legal immigrants too.

Jose Luis Garcia was convicted of a misdemeanor in 2001. The nearly 20-year-old conviction came roaring back when immigration agents arrested the 62-year-old man as he drank coffee and watered his lawn of his home in Arleta, California. Jose has been a lawful permanent resident since 1988. Legal immigrants in the U.S. have never been completely protected from possible deportation. The Trump administration has lowered the bar for whom immigration agents can go after. Jose's daughter thought this was only happening to people like they said, criminals, the gang members. President Donald Trump has vowed to crack down on immigrants with criminal records, saying they should be deported to their home countries.

263) July 12, 2018-Trump berates allies at summit.

President Donald Trump upended the show of unity at NATO's annual summit as many allies had feared, claiming that Germany "is totally controlled by" and "captive to Russia" and inflating demands that they spend more on defense to an unrealistic level. Trump increased his previous demands for NATO allies' defense spending saying each of the 29 member nations should budget an amount equal to 4 percent of their economies as measured by their domestic product, up from 2 percent. Trump told allies to do so immediately.

264) July 14, 2018-12 Russian agents charged in drive to upset 16 votes.

The special counsel investigating Russia interference in the 2016 election issued an indictment of 12 Russian intelligence officers in the hacking of the Democratic National Committee and the Clinton presidential campaign. The 29-page indictment is the most detailed accusation by the American government to date of the Russian government interference in the 2016 election, and it includes a litany of brazen Russian subterfuge operations meant to foment chaos in the months before Election Day.

265) July 15, 2018-Trump persistence in pursuing friendly ties with Putin.

Trump speaks fondly of Putin and a desire for better relations with Moscow. Trump has denied any collusion with Russia and has repeatedly cited Putin's denials of any Russian interference in the campaign, suggesting there is little or nothing he can do to demand accountability.

266) July 16, 2018-Trump calls E.U. a foe, says media is "enemy of the people".

President Donald Trump named the European Union as a top adversary of the United States and denounced the news media as the "enemy of the people" before his summit with Russia's Vladimir Putin. Trump said, "I think the European Union is a foe, what they do to us in trade, you wouldn't think of the European Union, but they're a foe."

267) July 17, 2018-Trump takes Putin's word on 16 interference.

President Trump stood next to President Vladimir V. Putin of Russia and publicly challenged the conclusion of his own intelligence agencies that Moscow interfered in the 2016 presidential election. Mr. Trump even questioned the determination by his intelligence officials that Russia had meddled in the election. "I have asked President Putin; he said it's not Russia."

268) July 17, 2018-Republicans criticize president's behavior.

Senator John McCain called it "disgraceful" Senator Bob Corker said he was "saddened" and "disappointed." Mostly however, Republican members of Congress reacted to President Donald Trump's performance beside Vladimir with silence.

269) July 18, 2018-Trump backs off summit statements.

Blistered by bipartisan condemnation of his embrace of a long time U.S. enemy, President Donald Trump backed away from his public undermining of American intelligence agencies, saying he simply misspoke when he said he saw no reason to believe Russia had interfered in the 2016 election.

270) July 18, 2018-Tariffs threaten newspapers.

About a dozen members of congress warned that newspapers in their home states are in danger of reducing news coverage, laying off workers or going out of business if the United States maintains recently imposed tariffs on Canadian newsprint. Newsprint is generally the second-largest expense for local papers. The tariffs have generally increased newsprint prices by 25 to 30 percent.

The newsprint tariffs reflect President Donald Trump's tough new approach to U.S trade relations.

271) July 19, 2018-Trump again says Russia is no threat.

The president's flat "no" came in response to a reporter's question about Russian threats. "Is Russia still targeting the U.S.?" "No" Trump responded looking directly at the questioner. He went on to say, "We are doing very well, probably as well as anybody has ever done with Russia." The president's apparent denial of an ongoing threat from Russia contradicted his chief intelligence advisor, director of National Intelligence Don Coates, who compared warning signs of cyber-attacks by Russia.

272) July 23, 2018- 'It is all a big hoax'.

Copping a week of drama, back tracking, a double negative and blistering statements from his allies about his attitude toward Russian election interference, President Donald Trump was back to "a big hoax." Trump cast doubt once again in a tweet, diminishing at least the significance, if not the evidence, of the interference and the U.S. investigation into Russia's actions.

273) August 2, 2018 President to Sessions: End Russia probe 'now'

President Donald Trump called on Attorney General Jeff Sessions to "stop this rigged witch hunt right now," "this is a terrible situation and Attorney General Jeff Sessions should stop this rigged witch hunt right now, before it continues to stain our country any further. Bob Mueller is totally conflicted, and his 17 Angry Democrats that are doing his dirty work are a disgrace to USA!" Trump wrote.

274) August 3, 2018-Agencies move to freeze MPG standards.

The Trump administration announced plans to freeze fuel-efficiency requirements for the nation's cars and trucks through 2026, a massive regulatory rollback likely to spur a legal battle with California and other states as well as create potential upheaval in the nation's automotive market. The proposal represents a reversal of the findings that the government reached under President Barack Obama.

275) August 4, 2018-China returns tariff threat.
The Chinese government threatened to dramatically escalate its economic standoff with President Donald Trump, vowing to impose tariffs on $60 billion in U.S. goods if the White House does not halt pending penalties on Chinese Imports.

276) August 6, 2018-Trump defends sons meeting with Russians.
President Donald Trump denied reports that he's privately fretting about his son's legal jeopardy yet acknowledged that Donald Trump Jr. met Russian representatives in June 2016 at Trump Tower "to get information on an opponent."

277) August 15, 2018-Trump lashes out at ex-aide.
President Donald Trump's campaign has filed an arbitration action against Omarosa Manigault Newman, alleging that the former White House aide, who published a tell all book, has broken a 2016 confidentiality agreement. In an earlier tweet Trump said, "When you give a crazed crying lowlife a break, and give her a job at the White House, I guess it just didn't work out."

278) August 17, 2018-Ex-security leaders blast Trump.
Former U.S. security officials issued scathing rebukes to President Donald Trump, admonishing him for yanking a top former spy chief's security clearance in what they cast as an act of political vengeance. Trump said he had to do "something" about the "rigged" federal probe of Russian election interference. Former CIA

Director John Brennan said Trump's decision to deny him access to classified information was a desperate attempt to end Mueller's investigation. Brennan called Trump's claims that he did not collude with Russia "hogwash."

279) August 17, 2018-Nation's newspapers slam Trump's attack on media

Hundreds of newspapers nationwide pushed back against President Donald Trump's frequent attacks on the media and his assertion that the news media are "the enemy of the people." The newspapers release editorials calling on Trump to curb his rhetoric about the news media. Trump often repeats the same words to describe the media- "dishonest", "disgusting", "fake", and "opposition party".

280) August 17, 2018-Trump gears up to strip more clearances

President Donald Trump has told advisers that he is eager to strip more security clearances as part of an escalating attack against people who have criticized him or played a role in the investigation of alleged Russia interference in the 2016 presidential campaign. Over the past 19 months, Trump has fired or threatened to take action against nearly a dozen current and former officials associated with inquiry, which he has labeled a "rigged witch hunt", including former FBI Director James Comey and other top FBI officials Sally Yates and Andrew McCabe, all three were dismissed.

281) August 21, 2018-Trump plan breathes new life into old plants.

The Trump administration is to unveil a sweeping rewrite of emissions rules for power plants that would boost to the coal industry, laying the groundwork for a revival of the most polluting facilities and abandoning Obama era mandates for re-orienting the electricity sector toward clean energy.

282) August 22, 2018-Local spotlight turns on Trump.

President Donald Trump suffered back-to-back legal blows after a whiplash series of court dramas that left his former campaign chairman and his formal personal attorney (fixer) facing jail time. A federal jury in Virginia found his former campaign manager, Paul Manafort, guilty on eight felony charges and longtime Trump Attorney Michael Cohen acknowledged violating campaign finance laws and said he did so at Trump's direction.

283) August 24, 2018-Trump, Sessions take feud public GOP. Senators Suggest new Attorney General coming.

President Donald Trump and Attorney General Jeff Sessions engaged in a public war of words over the Justice Departments securing a guilty plea this week from Trump's former lawyer and a guilty verdict against his former campaign chairman. The spectacle of the commander in chief's feuding with the nation's top law enforcement officer marked the latest argument in the long-soured relationship between the two.

284) August 29, 2018-Trump picks fight with Google.

President Donald Trump accused Google and other U.S. tech companies of rigging search results about him "so that almost all stories and news is BAD." He offered no evidence of this, but a top advisor said the White House is "taking a look" at whether Google should face federal regulation. Google pushed back sharply, saying Trump's claim simply wasn't so. "We never rank search results to manipulate political sentiment."

285) September 1, 2018-Trump edges closer to $200 billion China tariffs.

Trump's plan to bring down his biggest hit yet on China comes as trade talks show little signs of progress. Discussions between U.S. and Chinese officials yielded few results. The imposition of the $200 billion tariff would be the biggest so far and would mark a major escalation in the trade war between the two largest economies. It is likely to further unnerve financial markets that have been concerned about the growing tensions. China has threatened to retaliate by slapping duties on $60 billion of U.S. goods.

286) September 6, 2018-Trump rages at anonymous OP-ED.
A senior Trump administration official wrote an opinion piece in The New York Times claiming to be part of a group of people "working diligently from within" to impede President Donald Trump's "worse inclinations" and ill-conceived parts of his agenda. Trump said it was a "gutless editorial" and "really a disgrace", and his press secretary called in the official to resign. Trump tweeted "TREASON" and demanded that if "the GUTLESS anonymous person does indeed exist, the Times must, for National Security purposes, turn him/her over to the government at once!"

287) September 7, 2018-Obstruction a "no-go" in Trump talks, Giuliani says.
President Donald Trump will not answer federal investigators questions, in writing or in person, about whether he tried to block the probe into Russian interference in the 2016 election. Trumps lawyer, Rudy Giuliani said questions about obstruction of justices were a "no-go". Mueller's office previously has sought to interview Trump about obstruction, including his firing of former FBI Director James Comey and his public attacks on Attorney General Jeff Sessions.

288) September 7, 2018- Trump officials deny writing The New York Times op-ed.
One after another, President Donald Trump's top lieutenants stepped forward to declare "Not me". By email, by tweet and on

camera, the denials paraded in from Cabinet level officials, and even Vice President Mike Pence.

289) September 8, 2018-Obama decries Trump, politics of fear.

Former President Barack Obama issued a scorching critique of his successor, blasting President Donald Trump's policies and his pattern of pressuring the Justice Department. Obama also reminded voters that the economic recovery, one of Trump's favorite talking points, began on his watch. Obama also jabbed Trump in the issue the current president frequently heralds as one of his greatest achievements: the strong economy. Obama reminded that the economic recovery began during his administration and defended his handling of the 2008 economic collapse. "When you hear how great the economy's doing right, let's just remember when this recovery started."

290) September 9, 2018-Trump drama echo's Nixon's.

For months, the Trump administration and its scandals have carried whiffs of Watergate and drawn comparisons to the characters and crimes of the Nixon era. Nearly every element in President Donald Trump's trouble has a Watergate parallel. Special prosecution Robert Mueller is leading an independent investigation sparked by a break in at the Democratic National Committee, the same target that opened the Watergate can of worms, through the time the burglary was digital and linked to Moscow, not the Oval Office. "Everybody's trying to get me," Trump told an aide. Trump's list of those he considers enemies is obvious on his Twitter feed. It includes former political opponents, his own attorney general, his predecessor and former National Security officials, whose security clearance he has threatened.

291) September 11, 2018-President's own tweets indict him.
The president continues to strengthen the case that he is obstructing justice. The latest evidence: A tweet in which Trump condemned his own Justice Department and Attorney General Jeff Sessions for pursuing criminal charges against two Republican Congressmen running for re-election. "Two easy wins now in doubt," he lamented, "Good job Jeff." The definition of obstruction according to Merriam-Webster's "The crime or act of willfully interfering with the process of justice and law especially by influencing, threatening, harming, or impeding a witness, potential witness, juror or judicial or legal officer." The attorney general is clearly a "judicial or legal officer." He is clearly being influenced, threatened and impeded, by his boss, no less: the president, who can fire him at any time. And those threats are clearly being launched "willfully," since they are only the latest of many solves fired from the White House toward the Justice Department.

292) September 14, 2018-Trump disputes Puerto Rico toll.
President Donald Trump rejected the official conclusion that nearly 3,000 people died in Puerto Rico from last year's Hurricane Maria, arguing without evidence that the number was wrong and calling it a plot by Democrats to make him "look as bad as possible." Puerto Rico's governor last month raised Maria's death toll from 64 to 2,975 after the independent study found that the number of people who succumbed in the sweltering aftermath had been severely undercounted.

293) September 15, 2018-Manafort cooperating, Ex-Trump aide talks to Mueller.
President Donald Trump's former campaign chairman, Paul Manafort, agreed to provide testimony to special counsel Robert Mueller III as part of a plea deal. Flipping Manafort gives Mueller a cooperating witness who was at key events relevant to the Russia

investigation. Key events include Trump Tower meeting and a host of other behind-the-scenes discussions in 2016.

294) September 16, 2018-Mattis, Trump shows signs of discard.

When Defense Secretary Jim Mattis declared that he had "no plans" to cancel future joint military exercises with South Korean forces, it brought him a public rebuke from President Donald Trump. Trump fired back in a tweet, "there is no reason at this time to be spending large amount of money on joint U.S. South Korea war games." Associates say Mattis' frustration at Trump's often impetuous style and penchant for blindsiding the Pentagon with major policy announcements could prompt him eventually to quit.

295) September 20, 2018-Trump: "I don't have an attorney general".

Trump has long been publicly critical of Sessions' decision to recuse himself from the investigation into Russian interference in the 2016 election and said that he has regretted nominating him to lead the Justice Department. "I'm not happy at the border, I'm not happy with numerous things, not just this," referring to the Russian Investigation.

296) September 21, 2018- Trump slams GOP spending plan that lacks money for wall.

President Donald Trump complained that a spending plan pushed by congressional Republicans is "ridiculous" because it does not include funding for a border wall with Mexico. Trump tweeted that he wants to know "where is the money for Border Security and the WALL in this ridiculous spending bill." He added that "REPUBLICANS MUST FINALLY GET TOUGH" against Democrats he said are obstructing law enforcement and border security.

297) September 27, 2018-Trump: China threat to U.S. elections.

Taking center stage at the United Nations, President Donald Trump accused China of trying to interfere in the upcoming U.S. Congressional elections because it opposes his tough trade policies. "They do not want me or us to win because I am the first president ever to challenge China on trade." Asked what he had for evidence, Trump said there was "plenty" but didn't provide details, suggesting that some of the material was classified. "I don't like it when they attack our farmers, and I don't like it when they put out false messages. But be fare that we learned that they are trying to meddle in our election, and we are not going to let that happen, just like we're not going to let that happen with Russia."

298) October 2, 2018-Trump touts 'truly historic' trade deal.

President Donald Trump hailed the major revisions he was able to extract from Canada and Mexico to the 25-year-old North American trade agreement. Calling the deal "truly historic", Trump pledged "It will transform North America back into a manufacturing powerhouse." Trump was able to force Canada and Mexico to make major concessions from their initial position, but in the end the White House pulled back from some of its most stringent demands, including the possibility of terminating the North American Free Trade Agreement entirely.

299) October 3, 2018-President led push to silence porn star.

President Trump personally directed an effort to stop Stormy Daniels from publicly describing an alleged sexual encounter with him, people familiar with the events said. In a phone call, Mr. Trump instructed his then-lawyer Michael Cohen to seek a restraining order against the former adult film actress, whose real name is Stephanie Clifford, through a confidential arbitration proceeding, one of the people said. Mr. Trump told Mr. Cohen to coordinate the legal response with Eric Trump, one of the president's sons, and another outside lawyer who had represented Mr. Trump and the Trump Organization in other matters. Mr. Trump declined to answer questions about whether he had directed his son and Mr. Cohen to pay Mr. Clifford, saying: "I don't even know what you're talking about."

300) October 3, 2018-Trump took part in suspect schemes to evade tax bill.

President Trump participated in dubious tax schemes during the 1990's, including instances of outright fraud that greatly increased the fortune he received from his parents. Mr. Trump won the presidency proclaiming himself a self-made billionaire, and he has long insisted that his father, the legendary New York City builder Fred C. Trump, provided almost no financial help. Based on a vast trove of confidential tax returns and financial records, reveals that Mr. Trump received the equivalent today of at least $413 million from his father's real estate empire. He and his siblings set up a sham corporation to disguise millions of dollars in gifts from their parents, records and interviews show. Records indicate that Mr. Trump helped his father take improper tax deductions worth millions more. He also helped formulate a strategy to undervalue his parent's real estate holdings by hundreds of millions of dollars on tax returns, sharply reducing the tax bill when those properties were transferred to him and his sibling's.

301) October 9, 2018-Trump says he won't fire Rosenstein

President Donald Trump declared a reprieve for Rod Rosenstein, saying he has no plans to fire the deputy attorney general whose future has been the source of intense speculation. "I'm not making any changes," Trump told reporters as he returned to the White House after traveling with Rosenstein. "We just had a very nice talk. We actually get along."

302) October 12, 2018- Missing writer no reason to stop cash flow from Saudis, Trump says.

President Donald Trump defended continuing huge sales of U.S weapons to Saudi Arabia despite rising pressure from lawmakers to punish the kingdom over the disappearance of a Saudi journalist who lived in the United States and is now feared dead. As senators pushed for sanctions under a human rights law and also questioned U.S. support for the Saudi-led bombing campaign in Yemen, Trump appeared relevant to rock the boat in a relationship that has been very key to his strategy in the Middle East and which he described as "excellent." He said with holding sales would hurt the U.S. economy. <u>"I don't like stopping massive amounts of money that's pouring into our country. They are spending $10 billion on military equipment."</u> Trump maintained that the U.S. is being "very tough" as it looks into the case of Jamal Khashoggi, who has been missing since October 2.

303) October 14, 2018-Severe punishment vowed if U.S. find that Saudi's killed journalist.

President Donald Trump vowed "severe punishment" for Saudi Arabia if the United States determines that Saudi agents killed The Washington Post columnist Jamal Khashoggi, calling the journalist suspected murder "really terrible and disgusting." Trump said that the incident is being investigated, despite the mounting evidence that the Saudi regime was involved in the October 2 disappearance. "It's being investigated, it's being looked at very, very strongly. And we would be very upset and angry if that were the case. As of this moment, they deny it, and they deny it vehemently. Could it be them? Yes."

304) October 16, 2018-Trump floats idea of 'rogue killers".

Speaking to reporters, Trump said that he talked for about 20 minutes with the king and that the Saudi leader firmly denied the kingdoms involvement in Khashoggi's disappearance. <u>"I don't want to get into his mind, but it sounded to me like maybe these could have been rogue killers, who knows? We're going to try getting to the bottom of it very soon, but his was a flat denial."</u> Saudi Arabia so far has strenuously denied any knowledge of Khashoggi's whereabouts, saying that he walked out of the consulate soon after entering on October 2, without producing any evidence.

305) October 17, 2018-Trump warns against a rush to judgement.

The crown prince "told me that he has already started, and will rapidly expand, a full and complete investigation into this matter. Answers will be forthcoming shortly," Trump said in a tweet. The president later appeared to take a stronger stance in defense of Saudi Arabia, criticizing the global condemnation against the kingdom and comparing it to the allegations of sexual assault leveled against now-Supreme Court Justice Brett Kavanaugh during his confirmation hearing. <u>"Here we go again with your guilty until proven innocent,"</u> Trump told the Associated Press.

306) October 19, 2018-Trump: Military may be sent to border.

President Donald Trump threatened to summon the military to close the U.S.-Mexico border and up end a trade deal, expressing mounting frustration with a large caravan from Honduras, making its way toward the United States. Trump vowed to stop U.S. aid to Central American countries that do not disband the caravan and issued a fresh threat to the Mexican government, which said that it would treat those in the caravan no different than it does other migrants.

307) October 26, 2018-In reversal, Saudis suggest Khashoggi's killing planned.

Signaling a major pivot in its narrative, Saudi Arabia said evidence shows that the killing of journalist Jamal Khashoggi was premediated, an apparent effort to ease international outrage. A statement by Attorney General Saud Al Mojeb cited Turkish evidence that the slaying was planned, contradicting a Saudi assertion days ago that rogue officials from the kingdom killed him by mistake during a brawl inside their Istanbul consulate. The earlier assertion, in turn, backtracked from an initial statement that Saudi authorities knew nothing about what happened to the columnist for The Washington Post.

308) October 30, 2018-Troops on way to border as Trump decries invasion.

The Pentagon is sending 5,200 troops, some armed to the Southwest border in and extraordinary military operation to stop Central American migrants traveling north in two caravans that were still hundreds of mile from the U.S. President Donald Trump, eager to focus voters on immigration in the lead up to the elections, stepped up his warnings about the caravans, tweeting: <u>"This is an invasion of our country and our military is waiting for you!"</u>

309) October 30, 2018-Trump got struggling people to invest in scams.

A new lawsuit accuses President Trump, his company and three of his children of using the Trump name to entice vulnerable people to invest in sham business opportunities. The allegations take aim at the heart of Mr. Trump's personal narrative that he is a successful deal maker who built a durable business, charging he and his family lent their name to a series of scams. The 160-page complaint alleges that Mr. Trump and his family received secret payments from three business entities in exchange for promoting them as legitimate opportunities, when in reality they were get-rich quick schemes that harmed investors, many of whom were unsophisticated and struggling financially.

310) October 31, 2018-Trump: Citizens by birth to end.

President Donald Trump is vowing to sign an executive order that would seek to end the right to U.S. citizenship for children born in the United States to noncitizens, a move that most legal experts say would run afoul of the Constitution and that was dismissed by the House's top Republicans. Trump said he has discussed ending birth right citizenship with his legal counsel and believes it can be accomplished with executive action. "It was always told to me that you needed a constitutional amendment. Guess what? You don't," Mr. Trump said.

311) November 2, 2018- Canadians haven't forgiven, forgotten.

President Donald Trump disparaged Canadians as a bunch of trade cheaters and mercilessly mocked Minister Justin Trudeau as "very dishonest and weak" when the two countries were in the throes of difficult trade negotiations. But Trump's views and his tone seemed to change the minute the two sides struck a deal. The U.S. has "a great relationship with Canada, I think now it'll be better than ever," Trump boasted celebrating the new trade pact. Trudeau, he said, is a "good person who is doing a good job." For many Canadians, it's definitely not over. And it won't be for a long time, if ever. Canadians see Trump's attitude toward them as demeaning and his behavior as bully-ish, prompting calls to boycott American products.

312) November 2, 2018-Even tougher talk on border

President Donald Trump told the U.S. military mobilizing at the southwest border that if U.S. troops face rock throwing migrants, they should react as though the rocks were "rifles." <u>"This is an invasion,"</u> Trump declared. <u>"These illegal caravans will not be allowed into the United States and they should turn back now because they're wasting their time,"</u> Trump also tweeted a video alleging, without evidence, that Democrats were responsible for allowing a homicide immigrant into the U.S.

313) November 4, 2018-Some vets warn of politicizing forces.
After President Donald Trump ordered more than 5,000 U.S. troops to the southwest border days before the midterm election to intercept what he called an "invasion" of migrants, retired Marine Col. David Capan decided he could not stay silent. "The idea that a group of poor people from Central America, most of who are women and children, pose some kind of threat to the National Security of the United States is ridiculous." It's a misuse of active duty forces.

314) November 8, 2018-Mueller probe in peril?
Attorney General Jeff Sessions was pushed out after enduring more than a year of blistering and personal attacks from President Donald Trump, who inserted in his place a Republican Party loyalist with authority to oversee the remainder of the special counsel's Russia investigation. The move has potentially ominous implications for special counsel Robert Mueller's probe, given that the new acting attorney general, Matthew Whitaker, until now Sessions chief of staff has questioned the inquiry's scope and spoke publicly before joining the Justice Department about ways an attorney general could theoretically stymie the probe. Trump had repeatedly been talked out of firing Sessions until after the midterms, but he told confidants in recent weeks that he wanted Sessions out as soon as possible after the elections, according to a Republican close to the White House.

315) November 8, 2018-Trump scorns Republicans who lost for not embracing him.

President Donald Trump suggested House Republicans lost seats in the midterm elections because they didn't embrace his presidency, signaling some of them out by name. <u>"The candidates that I supported achieved tremendous success,"</u> Trump said.

316) November 8, 2018-A bipartisan nod and then back to the defiance.

President Trump threatened to adopt a "warlike posture" against Democrats if they use their newly wont control of the House to investigate his financial and political dealings, drawing a line at the start of a new era of divided government. The president began a post-election conference with an offer to work across party lines, but his conciliatory tone quickly turned contentious. And barely an hour later he announced the firing of Attorney General Jeff Sessions in defiance of Democrats who saw an effort to impede the Russia investigation.

317) November 9, 2018-Appeals court rules against Trump an ending to DACA.

A federal appeals court ruled that President Donald Trump cannot end an Obama administration program that protects undocumented immigrants brought to the USA as children. A panel of the U.S. court of appeals for the 9th circuit agreed with a federal judge's decision that Trump lacks the authority to eliminate the program.

318) November 10, 2018-Trump in acting AG: 'I don't know him'.

President Donald Trump denied even knowing the man he had named acting attorney general. Speaking to reporters Trump said, <u>"I don't know Matt Whitaker."</u> That contradicted Trump's remarks on Fox News, when he called Whitaker "a great guy" and said, "I mean, I know Matt Whitaker."

319) November 17, 2018-Trump says he answered questions from Mueller.

President Donald Trump said he had "very easily" answered written questions from special counsel Robert Mueller, though he speculated that the questions had been "tricked up" to try to catch him in a lie. "You have to always be careful when you answer questions with people that probably have bad intentions." Giuliani, president's attorney, has said repeatedly the president would not answer Mueller's questions on possible obstruction of justice. During months of back-and-forth negotiations with the special counsel office, Trump's lawyers have repeatedly counseled the president against sitting down for an in-person interview.

320) November 18, 2018- President tours area after blaze in North California killed 76.

Viewing the destruction of a wildfire that has killed more than 76 people, with 1,276 others still unaccounted for. Trump said he was stunned by the level of destruction. "Hopefully this will be the last of these, because it was a really, really, bad one." Trump was roundly criticized for erroneously blaming the fires on poor forest management and threatening to cut off funding to California. "There is no reason for these massive deadly and costly forest fires in California except that forest management is so poor. Billions of dollars are given each year, with so many lives lost, all because of gross management of the forests," Trump tweeted. "We've got to take care of the floors; you know the floors of the forest. It's very important," he said. He also alluded to Finland, saying that country focuses "on raking and cleaning, they don't have any problem." The reference to Finland puzzled some, because its ecosystem is so different than that of California.

321) November 19, 2018-Trump won't listen to tape. (Khashoggi's killing)

President Donald Trump acknowledged the existence of an audio recording of journalist Jamal Khashoggi's murder inside the Saudi Consulate in Istanbul but said he has not listed to what he called the "suffering tape" and dismissed a growing clamor among law-maker for Saudi Arabia to face more serious consequences for the killing. Based in part in the tape and other intercepted communications, the CIA has concluded that Saudi Crown Prince Mohammed Bin Salmon ordered last month's killing of Khashoggi, a prominent critic of Saudi leaders and a contributing columnist to The Washington Post. But Trump maintained in an interview on "Fox News" that the Crown Prince has told him "may be five different times" and "as recently as a few days ago" that he had nothing to do with the killing. Aides have said Trump has been looking for ways to avoid pinning the blame on Mohammed, a close ally who plays a central role in Trumps Middle East Policy. <u>"No reason for me to hear the tape, I know everything that went on in the tape without having to hear it, it was very violent, very vicious and terrible."</u>

322) November 19, 2018-Trump vows in action if AG kills probe.

President Donald Trump said he would not overrule his acting attorney general Matthew Whitaker, if he decides to curtail the special counsel probe being led by Robert Mueller III into Russian interference in the 2016 election campaign. "Look, it's going to be up to him, I would not get involved," Trump said. Trump also said he won't overrule man picked to replace Sessions on Mueller's investigation.

323) November 20, 2018-Trump criticism of retired admiral for not catching Bin Laden sooner draws fire.

President Donald Trump has ignited a firestorm of criticism and charges that he is politicizing the military by faulting a war hero for not capturing Al-Qaida leader Osama bin Laden sooner. Trump took shots at retired Adm. William McRaven in which he also asserted that the former Navy Seal, and former commander of U.S. Special Operations Command was a backer of Trump's 2016 rival, Hillary Clinton, and supporter of President Barack Obama. Lauren Panetta, who was CIA director during the bin Laden raid and later served as Secretary of Defense, said Trump owed an apology to McRaven and to all those in the military and intelligence agencies who played a role in tracking down Bin Laden and carrying out the risky raid into Pakistan. He called Trump's remark "patently ridiculous."

324) November 20, 2018- Ivanka Trump used private email for government business.

Ivanka Trump sent hundreds of emails last year to White House aides, cabinet officials and her assistants using a personal account, many of them in violation of federal records, according to people familiar with a White House examination of her correspondence. President Donald Trump made Hillary Clinton's use of personal email while she was secretary of state a focus of his 2016 presidential campaign, attacking his Democratic opponents as untrustworthy and dubbing her "Crooked Hillary."

325) November 21, 2018-Trump defends Saudi's in killing of Jamal Khashoggi.

President Donald Trump declared his strong support for Saudi Arabia, effectively ignoring the CIA's conclusion that Crown Prince Mohammed bin Salman ordered the brutal killing of journalist Jamal Khashoggi and asserting that it should not derail relations with a critical ally. Trump said U.S. intelligence would continue to "assess" information but that the United States "may never know all the facts surrounding the murder." But the president indicated that U.S. interests in Saudi oil production, weapons purchases and support for administration policies in the Middle East were more important than holding an ally to account, and he stressed the importance of staying in the kingdom's good graces.

326) November 21, 2018- Trump stands with Saudi's

President Donald Trump sought to extinguish questions about the future of U.S. relations with Saudi Arabia, pleading to remain a "steadfast partner" of the kingdom and dismissing U.S. intelligence conclusions that the Saudi Crown Prince had ordered the killing of a dissident journalist last month. In a White House statement that the president appeared to have penned himself. Mr. Trump suggested the U.S. wouldn't impose further punishment on Saudi Arabia over the killing and said it was unknowable whether Crown Prince Mohammed bin Salmon had ordered it.

327) November 21, 2018- Trump's view ignores CIA and stirs outrage on Capitol Hill.

President Donald Trump defied the nation's intelligence agencies and a growing body of evidence to declare his unswerving loyalty to Saudi Arabia, asserting that Crown Prince Mohammed bin Salman's culpability for the killing of Jamal Khashoggi might never be known. In a remarkable statement that appeared calculated to end the debate over the America response to the killing of Mr. Khashoggi, the president said, "It could very well be that the crown prince had knowledge of this tragic event, maybe he did and maybe he didn't." "We may never know all the facts surrounding the murder of Mr. Jamal Khashoggi, in any case, our relationship is with the Kingdom of Saudi Arabia."

328) November 22, 2018-President's embrace of Saudi Arabia causes rift among GOP.

President Donald Trump's embrace of Saudi Arabia has exposed a foreign policy rift in the Republican Party, as some of his GOP colleagues warn that not punishing the kingdom for its role in killing a U.S. based columnist will have dangerous consequences. Senator Bob Corker, the Republican Chairman of the Senate Foreign Relations Committee, said he was "astounded" by Trump's statement and likened it to a press release for Saudi Arabia. In his statement, Trump argued that punishing Saudi Arabia by "foolishly concealing" Saudi arms deals worth billions of dollars to the U.S. would benefit only Russia and China. Critics, including high-ranking officials in other countries, accused Trump of ignoring human rights and giving Saudi Arabia a pass for economic reasons.

329) November 22, 2018-Chief Justice Roberts rebukes Trump.

Chief Justice John Roberts directed a rare and pointed shot at President Donald Trump, defending the federal judiciary in the wake of Trump's criticism of an "Obama judge" who ruled against the administration's attempt to bar migrants who cross the border illegally from seeking asylum. "We do not have Obama judges or Trump judges, Bush judges or Clinton judges," Robert's said in a statement release by the court's public information office. "What we have is an extraordinary group of dedicated judges doing their level best to do equal right to those appearing before them." Trump had told reporters that he was "going to put in a major complaint" against the federal judge who temporarily blocked his administration from denying asylum to migrants who illegally cross the southern border.

330) November 23, 2018-Trump insists CIA wrong.
Trump in defiant remarks to reporters from his Mara Lago resort in Florida, defended his continued support for Mohammed in the face of CIA assessment that the crown prince had ordered the killing. "He denies it vehemently," Trump said of the crown prince. He reiterated that his own conclusion was that "maybe he did, maybe he didn't."

331) November 23, 2018-Trump threatens to close border.
Trump warned about the situation on the southern border pointing to the caravans of Central America migrants that have been making their way toward the U.S. and warning that, "If we find that it gets to a level where we lose control or people are going to start getting hurt, we're going to close entry into the country for a period of time until we get it under control."

332) November 24, 2018-Study contradicts Trump on global warming.
The federal government released a long-awaited report with an unmistakable message: The effects of climate change, including deadly wildfires, increasingly debilitating hurricanes and heat waves, are already battering the United States, and the danger of more such catastrophes is worsening. The report's sense of urgency and alarm stand in stark contrast to the lack of any apparent plan from President Donald Trump to tackle the problems, which, according to the government he runs, are increasingly cited.

333) November 25, 2018-Trump failed to give heartfelt thanks to our troops.
What Trump actually said to the troops amounted to naked political gasbagging. "That's why we're doing a strong border" he said in a phone call to a brigadier general in Afghanistan. "Large number of people, in many cases we have no idea who they are, and in many

cases, they are not good people. They are bad people." Trump, for his part, barely managed to squeeze in a thank you. He drifted instead from beating up on immigrants to beating up on judges. "There has been a lot of very bad court decisions, from the 9th circuit, which has become a big thorn in our side, always lose again and again, and you hopefully win at the Supreme Court." Once again, Trump showed himself incapable of empathy. Once again, it was all about himself.

334) November 26, 2018-Congress puts more heat on president.

Congressional Republicans continued to line up to criticize President Donald Trump over his defense of Saudi Crown Prince Mohammed bin Salmon, who the CIA believes ordered the killing of Saudi journalist Jamal Khashoggi. "I disagree with the president's assessment," Senator Mike Lee, R-Utah said "It's inconsistent with the intelligence I've seen. The intelligence I have seen suggest that this was ordered by the crown prince." Representative Maxine Waters of California tweeted, "Why does Trump have such an affinity for murderous autocrats? He defends Vladimir Putin of Russia, fell in love with Kim Jung Un of North Korea, admires Rodrigo Duterte of the Philippines and now refuses to accept CIA findings that the Saudi Crown Prince ordered Jamal Khashoggi's murder."

Chapter 6

335) November 27, 2018-Manafort's lies broke plea deal, more change possible.

Paul Manafort, President Trump's former campaign chairman, repeatedly lied to federal prosecutors in breach of a plea agreement he signed two months ago, the special counsel's office said in a court filing. Mr. Manafort's "crimes and lies" about "a variety of subject matters" relieve them of all promises they made to him in the plea agreement. But under the terms of the agreement, Mr. Manafort cannot withdraw his quality plea.

336) November 28, 2018-Trump slams Federal Reserve Chairman

President Donald Trump placed responsibility for recent stock market declines and this week's announcement of General Motors plant closures and layoffs on the Federal Reserve, shirking any personal blame for cracks in the economy and declaring that he is "not even a little bit happy with his hand-selected central bank chairman. Trump complained at length about Federal Reserve Chair Jerome "Jay" Powell, whom he nominated last year. When asked about declines on Wall Street and GM's announcement that it was laying off 15 percent of its workforce, Trump responded by criticizing higher interest rates and other fed policies, though he insisted that he is not worried about a recession.

337) November 29, 2018-Trump blasts Rosenstein over special counsel.

President Donald Trump sharply criticized Deputy Attorney General Rod Rosenstein hours after retweeting an image showing Rosenstein and several other current former officials locked in a prison cell. Trump has long vented about Rosenstein who appointed Robert Mueller to oversee the probe into Russian Interference in the 2016 campaign. The president has repeatedly sought to discredit the investigation as a "witch hunt." In an interview with the New York Post whey he believes Rosenstein belongs behind bars, Trump replied, "He should have never picked a special counsel." One of Trump's tweets, showed 10 current and former government officials behind bars and asked: "Now that Russia collusion is a proven lie, when do the trials for treason begin?"

338) November 29, 2018-GOP breaks with Trump on Saudis.

Defying President Donald Trump, Senators sent a strong signal that they went to punish Saudi Arabia for its signal that they went to punish Saudi Arabia for its role in the murder of journalist Jamal Khashoggi. By a 63-37 vote, the Senate opted to move forward with legislation calling for an end to U.S. involvement in the Saudi-led war in Yemen. Echoing Trump's public comments on the killing, Pompeo said that there was "no direct reporting" connecting the crown prince to the murder, and Mattis said there was "no smoking gun" making the connection. Trump has said it may never be known who was responsible for the killing, and in public comments he reinforced the United States long-standing alliance with the Saudis.

339) November 30, 2018-Cohen admits lying to Congress.

President Donald Trump's former lawyer, Michael Cohen, confessed in a surprise guilty plea that he lied to Congress about a Moscow real estate deal he pursued on Trump's behalf during the heat of the 2016 Republican campaign. He said he lied to be consistent with Trump's "political messaging." Cohen's plea arrangement made clear that prosecutors believe that Trump who insisted repeatedly throughout the campaign that he had no business dealings in Russia, was continuing to pursue the Trump Tower in Moscow project weeks after he had clinched the Republican nomination for president and well after he and his associates have publicly acknowledged. The negotiations about building the Moscow tower continued as late as June 2016, the same month Trumps oldest son met in Manhattan with a Kremlin-connected lawyer, even though Cohen told two congressional committees last year that the talks ended that January. Trump called Cohen a "weak person" who was lying to get a lighter sentence.

340) November 30, 2018-Cohen caves, boosting Mueller.

Justice Department Special Counsel Robert Mueller offered the most compelling case yet of President Donald Trump's ties with Russia and the efforts to conceal them when former Trump fixer Michael Cohen acknowledged that he lied to Congress about the president's interest in a Moscow development project. Mueller's team countered Trump's oft-repeated claims that he had no business interest in Russia.

341) December 3, 2018- CIA, says Crown Prince ordered journalists killing.

The CIA has evidence that Mohammad bin Salmon, the Saudi Crown Prince, communicated repeatedly with a key aide around the time that a team believed to have been under the aide's command assassinated Jamal Khashoggi, according to former officials familiar with the intelligence. The exchanges are a key piece of information that helped solidify the CIA's assessment that the crown prince ordered the killing of Mr. Khashoggi, a The Washington Post columnist and Virginia resident who had been critical of the Saudi government.

342) December 6, 2018-Mueller filings turn up heat on Trump and Company.

Democratic Rep. Jerrold Nadler of New York, the incoming chairman of the House Judiciary Committee, said in a statement: "The Special Counsel has now secured guilty pleas from President Trump's personal attorney, his campaign manager, his deputy campaign manager, a foreign policy advisor to his campaign, and his national security advisor.

343) December 9, 2018-Kelly to leave by end of month.

President Donald Trump announced that White House Chief of Staff John Kelly would exit his post by the end of the year, capping the retired Marine General's rocky tenure as the president's top aide and portending a major personnel shake-up as Trump prepares to navigate a divided congress and focuses on his reelection campaign.

344) December 10, 2018-House Dems raise prospect of impeachment, jail for Trump.

Top House Democrats raised the prospect of impeachment or almost certain prison time for President Donald Trump if it's proved that he directed illegal hush-money payments to women adding to the legal pressure on the president over the Russia investigation and other scandals. "There's a very real prospect that on the day Donald Trump leaves office, the Justice Department may indict him, that he may be the first prospect of jail time," said Rep. Adam Schiff, the incoming chairman of the House Intelligence Committee.

345) December 12, 2018- Trump threatens shutdown in public Oval Office dust up.

President Donald Trump, House Minority Leader Nancy Pelosi, and Senate Minority Leader Chuck Schumer clashed over funding for the border wall, and explosive Oval Office encounter that ended with Trump declaring he'd be proud to shut down the government to get what he wants. Trump also threatened that if Democrats don't provide enough votes to build the wall, "the military will build the remaining sections."

346) December 13, 2018-Cohen gets 3 years for hush money, lying.

A federal judge sentenced President Donald Trump's former attorney Michael Cohen to three years in prison for financial crimes and lying to Congress, as the disgraced "fixer" apologized but said he felt it was his duty to cover up the "dirty deeds" of his former boss, "My weakness could be characterized as a blind loyalty to Donald Trump."

347) December 14, 2018-Trump's defense: 'Advice of counsel'.

President Donald Trump offered a simple defense to accusations he broke campaign finance law by directing attorney Michael Cohen to orchestrate his hush money payments to conceal Trump's alleged affairs: He was following terrible advice from a bad lawyer. "I never directed Michael Cohen to break the law. He was a lawyer and he is supposed to know the law. It is called 'advice and consent,'" Trump wrote on Twitter.

348) December 14, 2018- Trump: Cohen broke law, not me.

President Donald Trump denied that he had directed his former personal attorney Michael Cohen to break the law during the 2016 campaign by buying the silence of women who claimed they once had affairs with the future president. In tweets, Trump did not dispute that he had directed Cohen to make the payments, as Cohen and federal prosecutors have alleged, actions that could imperil Trump. The president claimed that Cohen bore responsibility for any criminal violations of campaign finance law related to payments to former Playboy playmate Karen McDougal and adult-film star Stormy Daniels.

349) December 17, 2018-Report shows scale of Russia's efforts

A report prepared for the Senate that provides the most sweeping analysis yet of Russia's disinformation campaign around the 2016 election found the operation used every major social media platform to deliver words, images and videos tailored to voter's interest to help elect President Donald Trump, and worked even harder to support him while in office.

350) December 18, 2018- Russian trolls cast wide net.

Russia's sweeping political disinformation campaign on U.S. social media was more far-reaching than originally thought, with troll farms working to discourage black voters and "blur the lines between reality and fiction" to help elect Donald Trump in 2016, according to reports by the Senate intelligence committee. And the campaign didn't end with Trump's ascent to the White House. Troll farms are still working to stoke racial and political passions at a time of high political discord.

351) December 19, 2018-Flynn may go to prison after all.

A federal judge postponed the sentencing for Michael Flynn after he lambasted President Donald Trump's former National Security Advisor for trying to undermine the country and warned he might not spare Flynn for prison.

352) December 19, 2018-Trump Foundation to dissolve.
President Donald Trump's charitable foundation reached a deal to
go out of business, even as Trump continues to fight allegations,
he misused its assets to resolve business disputes and boost his run
for the White House. The foundation operated as "little more than
a checkbook to serve Mr. Trump's business and political interest"
says Attorney General Barbara Underwood.

**353) December 20, 2018-Trump orders U.S. forces
out of Syria.**
President Donald Trump called for a U.S. withdrawal from Syria
over the apparent objections of military advisors and a bipartisan
group of lawmakers. The withdrawal of the more than 2000 troops
is based on Trump's decision that the mission against ISIS is complete. Military leaders, including Defense Secretary Jim Mattis, in
recent weeks and months have spoken of the need for U.S. troops
to remain in the eastern part of the country to help stabilize it and
allow for negotiations to continue.

354) December 21, 2018-Government may hit the wall.
Showdown looms as Trump, Democrats face off over funding.
President Donald Trump said he would not sign a stop gap spending
bill unless it includes money to build a wall along the Mexico
border, sending large parts of the federal government lurching
toward shutdown. "I've made my position very clear. Any measure that funds the government must include border security." He
added, "walls work, whether we like it or not. They're better than
anything."

355) December 21, 2018- Defense Secretary quits in protest.
Secretary of Defense Jim Mattis told President Donald Trump that
he will resign February, handing the president a strongly worded
two-page letter that in effect rebuked the president for his military

policies and lack of respect for allies. The White House tried to persuade Trump to reconsider his plan to pull all U.S. troops out of Syria, a decision the secretary had strongly opposed before the president announced it on Twitter.

356) December 24, 2018-Mattis forced out early.

President Donald Trump, who aides said has been seething about news coverage of Defense Secretary Jim Mattis' pointed resignation letter, announced that he was removing Mattis' two months before his planned departure.

357) December 24, 2018-As stocks fall, Trump directs anger at Fed.

President Donald Trump has unabashedly hitched his political fortunes to a rising stock market. Now with stock prices in retreat, he has become increasingly fixated on the idea that one man is to blame for the recent rout: Jerome H. Powell, chairman of the Federal Reserve. Mr. Trump has said choosing Mr. Powell for the Fed job last year was the worst mistake of his presidency, and he asked aides whether he has the power to fire him.

358) December 24, 2018-Trump removes Mattis early.

President Donald Trump speeded up the departure of Defense Secretary Jim Mattis by two months while outlining a slower withdrawal from Syria, reshaping his evolving international policies and personnel amide torrent of largely negative reaction at home and abroad. Irked by the response to Mr. Mattis's resignation letter, which laid bare some of the core disagreements between the Pentagon Chief and the Republican president, Mr. Trump expedited the Defense Secretary's departure.

359) December 26, 2018-President says only wall funding ends shutdown.

President Trump promised to keep the federal government partially closed until Congress meets his demands for more than $5 billion for a U.S.-Mexican border barrier, saying thousands of federal employees were willing to work without pay if it meant securing funding for the wall.

360) December 26, 2018-Second migrant child dies in custody.

An 8-year old boy from Guatemala dies in government custody in New Mexico, U.S. immigration authorities said, marking the second death of an immigrant child in detention this month. The death came during an ongoing dispute over border security and with a partial government shutdown underway over President Donald Trump request for border wall funding.

361) December 27, 2018-Trump defends Syrian pullout on visit to Iraq.

President Donald Trump visited American military forces in Iraq, making his first trip to troops stationed in a combat zone only days after announcing his intention to withdraw the states from foreign wars in Syria and Afghanistan. Speaking to troops at Al Assad Air Base, Mr. Trump defended his move in Syria. "We're no longer the suckers, folks," the president said. "Our presence in Syria was not open-ended and was never intended to be permanent, eight years ago we went there for three months and we never left.

362) December 28, 2018-Trump's order to pull troops riles all sides.

President Donald Trump manages to do something remarkable with his abrupt order last week to withdraw all American troops from Syria and half from Afghanistan. Unite the left and the right against a plan to extract the United States from two, costly and increasingly futile conflicts. So chaotic was Mr. Trump's decision-making process; so transparent his appeal to his political base; and lacking in a cogent explanation to allies or the public that the presidents move short-circuited what many say is a much-needed national debate about the future of America's wars.

363) December 28, 2018-Trump goes to Iraq and lies to troops.

On his visit to Iraq, the president lied to the troops. How can you claim to honor people you are lying to? Lying signals contempt. "We are always going to protect you. And you just saw that, because you just got one of the biggest pay raises you've ever received. You haven't gotten one in more than 10 years. More than 10 years. And we got you a big one, I got you a big one." The military has received raises each year for the past 10 years. Trump wasn't finished, "They had plenty of people that came up, they said, you know we could make it smaller. We could make it 3 percent we could make it 2 percent, we could make it 4 percent," Trump told the troops about the latest pay raise. "I said no, make it 10 percent. Make it more than 10 percent."

364) December 29, 2018-Trump says he'll close border.

With the partial government shutdown headed toward its second week and no resolution in sight, President Donald Trump issued a string of tweets in which he once again vowed to close the entire U.S. border with Mexico and half aid to several Latin American countries unless Democrats agree to his demand for billions of dollars in wall funding.

365) December 31, 2018-Trump mulls slower Syria pullout.

President Donald Trump is re-evaluating a rapid pullout of U.S. troops from Syria but remains committed to pursuing the withdrawal he announced earlier. The president's decision earlier this month marked an abrupt shift in U.S. Middle East policy and helped prompt the resignation of Defense Secretary Jim Mattis amid broad concerns in Washington that a withdrawal could squander gains made by U.S. allied forces and allow Islamic state militants to regain a foot hold in the country.

366) December 31, 2018- Trump blames Democrats for deaths.

President Donald Trump said Democrats are to blame for the deaths of migrant children in U.S. custody at the Southern border, as he pressed lawmakers to approve funding for a border wall. In back-to-back tweets Mr. Trump said Democrats favor "pathetic immigration policies" that have given the false impression that people should attempt to enter the U.S. illegally. "If we had a wall, they wouldn't even try." Mr. Trump tweeted.

367) January 1, 2019- Trump reacting to pushback slows Syria troop withdrawal.

President Trump has agreed to give the military about four months to withdraw the 2000 United States troops in Syria, back tracking from his abrupt order two weeks ago that the military pull out within 30 days. "If anybody but Donald Trump did what I did in Syria, which was an ISIS loaded mess when I became President, they would be a national hero." Mr. Trump wrote. "ISIS is mostly gone."

368) January 2, 2019-President to nation: 'Enjoy the ride' in 19.

President Donald Trump got 2019 off to a whipsaw start using Twitter to insult a retired U.S. Commander in Afghanistan as a dumb loudmouth, sing the praises of an ultra-national formal aid and telling America to chill and "ENJOY THE RIDE". Trump's cheery tone in all caps tweet welcoming the New Year: "HAPPY NEW YEAR TO EVERYONE, INCLUDING THE HATERS AND

THE FAKE NEWS MEDIA! 2019 WILL BE A FANTASTIC YEAR FOR THOSE NOT SUFFERING FROM TRUMP DERANGEMENT SYNDROME, JUST CALM DOWN AND ENJOY THE RIDE, GREAT THINGS ARE HAPPENING FOR OUR COUNTRY!" Trump wrote.

369) January 3, 2019-Neitherside budges.

President Donald Trump rejected a plan from Democrats to reopen key parts of the federal government as a meeting of the country's top political leaders disbanded with no sign of progress toward ending the partial shutdown. The president is demanding more $5 billion to build a new wall along the U.S. Mexican border. Trump wants $5.6 billion for the construction of 200 miles of wall along the Mexican border. He also rejected the negotiating position of his own top advisors. Vice President Mike Pence approached Democrats with a compromise offer of $2.5 billion for border security and wall improvements. But Trump said he would never accept that deal. "Somebody said $2.5 billion for border security and wall improvements. But Trump said he would never accept that deal. "Somebody said $2.5 billion dollars." Trump said to reporters "No, Look, this is national security were talking about."

370) January 4, 2019-Trump, McConnell insist on bills with border wall funds.

The newly Democratic controlled House passed a package of bills that would reopen the federal government without paying for President Donald Trump's border wall, drawing a swift vote threat from the White House and leaving the partial shutdown no closer to being resolved. Senate Majority Leader Mitch McConnell, R-Ky., reiterated that the Senate will take up only government spending legislation that Trump supports.

371) January 5, 2019-Trump: "I can order wall built."

President Donald Trump offered his most robust public case for the border wall since the partial government shutdown began, expounding for an hour at the White House about the need for a barrier to keep out terrorist and dissuade migrants while asserting he has the legal authority to build it without congressional consent. In a forceful but meandering performance that included numerous false or questionable assertions. Trump announced he was considering declaring a "national emergency" to move forward on construction through executive power, argued his administration would use eminent domain to obtain private land along the U.S.-Mexico border, and suggested a steel wall could provide manufacturing jobs to U.S. companies.

372) January 5, 2019-Trump prepared to have impasse last for months.

President Trump threatened to keep the federal government partly closed for "months or even years" if he didn't get $5.6 billion for his wall at the southern border and he warned that he was considering declaring a national emergency to build it without congressional approval.

373) January 8, 2019-Impasse starting to leave a mark on the economy.

President Trump and congressional Democrats have made little progress in negotiations to end a shutdown that has affected about 800,000 federal workers, many of whom will miss their first paycheck this week, and who owe a combined $249 million in monthly mortgage payments. The effects of a prolonged shutdown have some Wall Street economists predicting a hit to the United States economy.

374) January 9, 2019- Trump makes case for wall.

President Trump, in a prime-time address, said a wall along the southern border is key to national security, as he called for lawmakers to fund it and end a partial government shutdown that is days away from becoming the longest in U.S. history. "A wall is absolutely critical for border security," Mr. Trump said, "It's also what professionals at the border want and need. This is just common sense." House speaker Nancy Pelosi and Senate Minority Leader Chuck Schumer issued an immediate televised response, rejecting the idea of a wall as unnecessary and accusing Mr. Trump of stoking fear to rally support for his cause.

375) January 9, 2019-President pleads for wall money.

In a somber televised plea, President Donald Trump urged congressional Democrats to fund his long-promised border wall, blaming illegal immigration for what he called a scourge of drugs and violence in the U.S. and framing the debate over partial government shutdown in stark terms. "This is a choice between right and wrong," he declared. Describing the situation at the border as a "growing humanitarian and security crisis," Trump urged Congress to give him the $5.7 billion he has repeatedly demanded for the wall.

376) January 9, 2019-Manafort accused of giving data to Russian

As a top official in President Donald Trump's campaign, Paul Manafort shared political polling data with a business associate tied to Russian intelligence according to a court filing. The document provided the clearest evidence to date that the Trump campaign may have tried to coordinate with Russians during the 2016 presidential race. The surprise disclosures about Mr. Manafort were the latest in two years of steady revelations about contacts between associates of Mr. Trump's and Russian officials or operatives. In another development the Russian lawyer who met with senior campaign officials at Trump Tower in June 2016 was charged with obstruction of justice in an unrelated case. The lawyer, Natalia V. Veselnitskaya, had pretended to a federal judge that she was purely a private defense lawyer when in fact she was working with the Russian government to thwart the civil prosecution of a Russian company.

377) January 11, 2019-Trump takes a step closer to taking emergency action.

President Donald Trump moved closer to declaring a national emergency to bypass Congress to secure funds for a border wall and resolve a government shutdown. "I have the absolute right to declare a national emergency," Trump said to reporters, "If this doesn't work," he said of getting Congress to include wall money in its final government funding bill, "probably I will do it. I would almost say definitely. This is a national emergency."

378) January 11, 2019-Cohen set to testify before Congress.

President Donald Trump's former lawyer, Michael Cohen, will testify publicly before a House Committee next month in a hearing that could serve as the opening salvo of a promised Democratic effort to scrutinize Trump, his conflicts of interest and his ties to Russia. Democrats say questioning will be limited to avoid interfering with open investigations, the hearing is still likely to pull back the curtain on key episodes involving Trumps personal life and business dealings, including hush money payments to women and a proposed Moscow real estate deal, that federal prosecutors have been dissecting for months.

379) January 12, 2019-Now working without a paycheck.

President Donald Trump cast fresh doubt on whether he would declare a national emergency to build a wall along the southern border, leaving lawmakers waiting for the president's next move as the government shutdown was poised to become the longest in history. The Democratic-led house voted on a measure to ensure that federal workers who are furloughed or working without pay are paid back once the government reopens. The bill, which passed the Senate, now goes to Trump for his signature. But it would do nothing to direct immediate help to the federal employees going unpaid, and the thousands of federal contractors who have been affected by the shutdown may never recoup their losses.

380) January 14, 2019-Trump faces 'nonstop' war for survival.

The president was asked over the weekend whether he is a Russian agent. And he refused to answer directly. The question which came from a friendly interviewer, not one of the "fake media' journalist he disparages, was "the most insulting thing I've ever been asked," he declared. But it is a question that has hung over his presidency now in two years. Mr. Trump faces the prospect of an all-out political war for survival that may make the still-unresolved partial government shutdown pale by comparison.

381) January 14, 2019-Trump didn't use note takers at Putin meeting.

President Trump didn't have official note takers present in his introductory meeting with Russian President Vladimir Putin and many top administration officials were never briefed on the discussion, according to several officials familiar with the matter. The president went to "extraordinary lengths" to keep his discussion with Mr. Putin from leaking, said one person familiar with the planning, including preventing any details from the meeting from circulating widely within the government. Mr. Trump said claims that he took extraordinary steps to keep his discussions with Mr. Putin secret were ridiculous.

382) January 15, 2019-As Russia works to weaken NATO, Trump talks of a U.S. withdrawal.

There are a few things that President Vladimir V. Putin of Russia desires more that the weakening of NATO, the military alliance among the United States, Europe, and Canada that has deterred Soviet and Russian aggression for 70 years. Last year President Trump suggested a move tantamount to destroying NATO: the withdrawal of the United States. Retired Admiral James G. Stavridis, the former Supreme Allied Commander of NATO, said an American withdrawal from the alliance would be "a geographical mistakes of epic proportion, even discussing the idea of leaving NATO, let alone actually doing so, would be the gift of the century for Putin," Admiral Stavridis said.

383) January 17, 2019-EPA nominee says climate change isn't 'greatest crises.

Andrew Wheeler, President Trump's nominee to lead the Environmental Protection Agency, found himself walking a tight road on the issue of climate change, he told Senators that climate change was not "the greatest crisis" facing our planet. Mr. Wheeler repeated the Trump administrations finding that its plan to revise the Clan Power Plan would still reduce planet warming emissions by 34 percent below 2005 levels by 2030. However, a Harvard University study disputed that finding that the Trump administrations plan would be worse for the planet than doing nothing at all. The study found that greenhouse gas emissions would "rebound" under the new policy by delaying the retirement of cool-fired power plants. Carbon emissions could rise in 18 states by as much as 8.7 percent by 2030, compared to having not carbon policy at all, the study found.

384) January 19, 2019-Mueller's office denies report that Trump told Cohen to lie.

Special Counsel Robert Mueller III's office denied an explosive report by Buzz Feed News that his investigators had gathered evidence showing President Donald Trump directed his former lawyer, Michael Cohen, to lie to Congress about a prospective business deal in Moscow. The story published by Buzz Feed attributed to two federal law enforcement officials an incendiary assertion: that Mueller had collected emails, texts, and testimony indicating Trump had directed Cohen to lie to Congress about the extent of discussions surrounding a proposed Trump Tower project in Moscow.

385) January 19, 2019-Probes ask if Trump had Cohen lie.

Lawmakers said they would investigate a report that President Trump directed his former lawyer Michael Cohen to lie to Congress about the president's involvement in a real-estate deal with Russia during the 2016 campaign. Rep. Jerrold Nadler, Chairman of the House Judiciary Committee, tweeted that the panels "job is to get to the bottom of it, and we will do that work." He added: "We know that the President has engaged in a long pattern of obstruction. Other Democratic members of the panel called for severe consequences if Mr. Trump is found to have directed his lawyer to lie to Congress.

386) January 20, 2019-Trump proposes DACA deal for wall funding.

In a bid to break the shutdown impasse and fund his long-promised border wall, President Donald Trump offered to extend temporary protections from deportation for young people brought to the U.S. illegally as children. The Democrats were quick to discuss it as a "non-starter." But Trump did not budge on his $5.7 billion demand for the wall. House Speaker Nancy Pelosi said that the proposal was "a compilation of several previously rejected initiatives, each which is unacceptable."

387) January 21, 2019-Giuliani: Trump did not tell Cohen to lie.

Rudy Giuliani vehemently denied that President Donald Trump asked his former attorney Michael Cohen to lie to Congress, he also said Buzz Feed be sued for reporting such allegations. Giuliani acknowledged that Trump might have spoken to Cohen about his testimony, but he shrugged it off, saying that would have been "perfectly normal." Giuliani reiterated that Trump was truthful in his repeated insistence that he wasn't doing business in Russia, saying the President was only minimally involved and the involvement only went as far as submitting a non-binding letter of intent, which he argues isn't the same as doing business. "All his concentration was 100 percent on running for president," Giuliani said.

388) January 21, 2019-Russia dealings said to continue till Trump win.

President Trump was involved in discussions to build a skyscraper in Moscow throughout the entire 2016 presidential campaign, his personal lawyer said, a longer and more significant role for Mr. Trump than he had previously acknowledged. The comments by his lawyer Rudolph W. Giuliani indicated that Mr. Trump's efforts to complete a business deal in Russia waned only after Americans cast ballots in the presidential election. The new timetable means that Mr. Trump was seeking a deal at the time he was calling for an end to economic sanctions against Russia imposed by the Obama administration.

389) January 23, 2019-Senate will hold competing votes to end shutdown.

The Senate will hold competing votes on President Trump's proposal to spend $5.7 billion on a border wall and a Democratic bill that would fund the government through February 8th without a wall. It will be the first time the Senate has stepped off the sidelines to try to end the month long government shutdown with most Republicans united behind Mr. Trump's insistence that any legislation to reopen the government include money for a border wall and most Democrats opposed to the linkage nether measure is expected to draw the 60 votes required to advance.

390) January 26, 2019-Trump accepts deal with no wall money.

After the longest government shutdown in history, Mr. Trump surrendered with nothing concrete (or steel) to show for the battle, taking essentially the same deal that was on the table in December that he originally rejected, touching off a 35-day impasse. For a president who believes in zero-sum politics and considers compromise a sign of weakness, it was a bruising setback, a retreat that underscored the limits of his ability to bull his way through the opposition in this new era of divided government. As it turned out, the art of the deal at this stage of Mr. Trump's presidency requires a different approach and the question is whether he can adjust.

391) January 26, 2019-Trump advisor Stone indicted.

Roger Stone, a long-time informal advisor to President Donald Trump, was arrested by the FBI on charges he lied and tried to tamper with a witness to hide the details of his efforts to learn about releases of Democrats' hacked emails during the 2016 campaign. Stone was charged with seven counts, including one count of obstruction of an official proceeding, five counts of false statements and one count of witness tampering.

392) January 27, 2019-Amid shutdown over wall, Trump club fired undocumented workers.

They had spent years on the staff of Donald Trump's golf club, winning employee of the month awards and receiving glowing letters of recommendation. But on January 18, about a dozen employees at Trump National Golf Club in Westchester County, New York, were summoned, one by one, to talk with a human resources executive from Trump headquarters. During the meetings, they were fired because they are undocumented immigrants. The fired workers are from Latin America. The firings show Trump's business was relying on undocumented workers even as the president demanded a border wall to keep out such immigrants.

393) January 28, 2019-Shutdown over.

The partial government shutdown ended when Trump backed off his demand that Congress commit $5.7 billion for a U.S.-Mexico border wall before federal agencies could resume work. The 800,000 federal workers who were affected will receive back pay, but contractors done have the same guarantee.

394) January 28, 2019-Trump ready to act on border 'with or without Congress'.

President Donald Trump will secure the U.S. border with Mexico "with or without Congress," acting White House Chief of Staff Mick Mulvaney said. "The president's commitment is to defend the nation, and he will do it either with or without Congress," Mulvaney said. The president is prepared to trigger 2nd shutdown over wall, aide says.

395) January 29, 2019-Cohen won't give in to Trumps intimidation.

Former Trump fixer/attorney Michael Cohen, who is set to appear before the House Oversight Committee next week, has just revamped his legal team in advance of his Capitol Hill testimony by adding powerhouse Chicago Attorney Michael Monico and his partner Barry Spevack. Monico told journalist that Cohen is preparing to tell the truth despite Trump's attempts to derail him.

396) January 30, 2019-U.S. Intelligence disputes Trump on global peril.

A new American intelligence assessment of global threats has concluded that North Korea is unlikely to give up is nuclear stockpile and that Iran is not, for now, taking steps necessary to make a bomb, directly contradicting the rationale of two of President Trump's foreign policy initiatives. The 42-page threat report found that American trade policies and "unilateralism," central themes of Mr. Trump's "America First" approach, have strained traditional alliances and prompted foreign partners to seek new relationships. Dan Coats, the National Intelligence Director, told lawmakers that the Islamic State would continue "to stoke violence" in Syria. He was backed up by the written review, which said there were thousands of fighters in Iraq and Syria and dozen Islamic state networks around the world. Just last month, Mr. Trump said "We have won against ISIS: We've beaten them, and we've beaten them badly," in announcing the withdrawal of American troops from Syria.

397) January 30, 2019-Trump political advisor Stone pleads not guilty.

Roger Stone entered a not guilty plea in federal court, after the longtime political advisor to President Donald Trump was arrested at his Florida home on charges from special counsel Robert Mueller of lying to Congress. Mr. Stone was charged in a seven-count indictment accusing him of misleading a House committee about efforts to obtain information about WikiLeaks plans to publish emails that Russian hackers stole from Democrats during the 2016 presidential election.

398) January 31, 2019-Trump rejects threat advice with 'Wrong!'

President Trump lashed out at the nation's intelligence agencies, accusing them of being "passive and naïve about the dangers posed by Iran, and defending his handling of Afghanistan, North Korea, and the Islamic State. A day after the agencies issued their annual assessment of global threats, warning of male factors like China and the Islamic State, Mr. Trump reignited a long-simmering feud with his own government, reacting as if the report was a threat to him personally. <u>"Perhaps Intelligence should go back to school"</u> he declared on Twitter in an indignant morning post.

399) February 2, 2019- U.S. to quit nuke pact with Russia.

The Trump administration announced that the United States will pull out of a nuclear arms control treaty with Russia, ending a cornerstone Cold War agreement and raising fears of a new nuclear arms race in Europe and Asia. President Donald Trump said Russia is violating the 1987 Intermediate Range Nuclear Forces, or INF, Treaty, a charge Moscow denies, leaving the United States at a disadvantage because of its own compliance at a time when global threats have changed considerably in the more than 30 years since the pact was signed. <u>"We cannot be the only country in the world unilaterally bound by this treaty, or any other,"</u> Trump said. <u>"We will move forward with developing our own military response options and will work with NATO and our other allies and partners to deny Russia any military advantage from its unlawful conduct."</u>

400) February 3, 2019-Bank rejected Trump for loan during 2016 race.

Donald J. Trump burning through cash. It was early 2016, and he was lending tens of millions of dollars to his presidential campaign and had been spending large sums to expand the Trump Organizations roster of high -end properties. To finance his business growth, Mr. Trump turned to a long-time ally, Deutsche Bank. Mr. Trump's loan request, which has not been previously reported, set off a fight that reached the top of the German bank, according to three people familiar with the request. In the end, Deutsche Bank did something unexpected. It said no.

401) February 6, 2019-Trump seeks to reset wall debate.
President Trump in his state of the Union renewed his call for a wall on the southern U.S. border, but without repeating his recent threats to declare an emergency and act unilaterally. Mr. Trump called for both parties to "work together, compromise and reach a deal" to pass a spending bill including funding for the project, but suggested some flexibility, on how extensive the wall would be and what it will take. "This is a smart, strategic, see through steel barrier, not just a simple concrete wall," Mr. Trump said. "It will be deployed in the areas identified by border agents as having the greatest need." If Congress fails to act, "I'll get it built," the president said.

402) February 8, 2019- Battle flares up over Trump's taxes.
With Democrats controlling the House and holding the legal key to seeking President Donald Trump's tax returns, Republican lawmakers are invoking privacy in defending his flank. At an oversight hearing, lawmakers examined proposals to compel president and presidential candidates to make years of their tax returns public. Getting Trump's returns has been high in the Democrats' list of priorities since they won control of the House in November's midterm elections but asking for them will probably set off a huge legal battle with his administration. Rep. John Lewis, D-GA., chairman of the oversight subcommittee, said the American public is intensely interested in the subject. "We ask the question: Does the public have a need to know that a person seeking or holding the highest office in our country obeys the tax laws?"
kept funding for physical barriers along the border far below

President Trump's request.

403) February 15, 2019-Trump to declare emergency to get funding for wall.

President Trump will declare a national emergency to bypass Congress and build his long-promised wall along the southwestern border even as he agreed to sign a spending package that does not finance it. But if he declares a national emergency to access billions of dollars for his wall, Mr. Trump could instigate a constitutional clash over the controls the federal purse and test the bounds of presidential authority in a time of divided government.

404) February 16, 2019-Trump calls emergency, defying Congress.

President Trump declared a national emergency on the border with Mexico in order to access billions of dollars that Congress refused to give him to build a wall there, transforming a highly charged policy dispute into a confrontation over the separation of powers outlined in the constitution. "We're going to confront the national security crisis on our southern border, and we're going to do it one way or another," "it's an invasion", he added. "We have an invasion of drugs and criminals coming into our country, I didn't need to do this, but I'd rather do it much faster, I just want to get it done faster, that's all."

405) February 17, 2019-Declaration draws suits, protests.

A day after President Donald Trump declared a national emergency in an attempt to circumvent congress and redirect taxpayer money to fund 230 miles of barriers along the U.S.-Mexican border. The designation has been beset with political and legal challenges. Democrats painted Trumps declaration as evidence of a Roque president who has finally gone too far, and they vowed to stop him.

Even in his declaration, Trump said he expected to be sued and anticipated the Supreme Court would ultimately decide the case.

406) February 19, 2019-States file suit against Trump.

A coalition of 16 states, including Illinois, filed a federal lawsuit to block President Donald Trump's plan to build a border wall without permission from Congress, arguing that the president's decision to declare a national emergency is unconstitutional. The complaint, filed by the attorney generals of nearly a third of the states and representing tens of millions of Americans, immediately became the heavy weight among a rapid outpouring of opposition to the president's emergency declaration.

407) February 20, 2019-Trump confident he'll prevail in border emergency lawsuit.

Presidential Donald Trump expressed confidence that he would prevail in a lawsuit filed by 16 states seeking to overturn his declaration of a national emergency at the U.S-Mexico border, saying the states are led "mostly by Open Border Democrats and the Radical left." Trump insisted that he had an "absolute right" to declare an emergency and said that it is on "open and closed case" that he can use the declaration to circumvent Congress to fund long sought barriers at the border.

408) February 23, 2019-House will vote to undo emergency declaration.

Speaker Nancy Pelosi began her push to overturn President Trump's emergency declaration, scheduling a House vote on legislation that would end the declaration, a timeline meant to force congressional Republicans to choose quickly between their president and the prerogatives of their branch of government.

409) February 23, 2019-Trump pivots once again, agreeing to leave 400 troops in Syria.

First, President Trump was going to pull as 2,000 troops out of Syria immediately. Then he was going to slow down the withdrawal. Then he was going to leave troops in neighboring Iraq. Now, in the latest about face, Mr. Trump has agreed to leave about 400 troops in Syria, 200 in a multinational force in the northeastern part of the country and another 200 at a small outpost in the southeast, where they will seek to counter Iran's influence throughout the country.

410) February 25, 2019-Democrats plan fight to release Mueller's report.

The chairman of the House Intelligence Committee said that House Democrats were prepared to go to court to force the release of the final report from the special counsel Robert S. Mueller III, and subpoena Mr. Mueller to testify if it was not made public. "We will take it to court if necessary," Mr. Schiff, Democrat of California said. "And in the end, I think the department understands they're going to have to make this public.

411) February 26, 2019-Emergency order draws new criticism.

Nearly 60 prominent former national security officials released a statement challenging President Trump's decision to invoke a national emergency to build a wall along the U.S.-Mexico border, arguing the move isn't justified and that the claim of an emergency lacks a factual basis. The statement is the latest rebuke of Mr. Trump by former national security officials. It is intended to bolster lawsuits challenging the emergency declaration.

412) February 26, 2019-Trump heads to Vietnam, Kim Summit.

Redefining success, President Donald Trump headed to his second meeting with North Korea's Kim Jong Un, determined to tamp down expectations that he'll achieve big strides toward denuclearization. "We want denuclearization and I think he'll have a country that will set a lot of records for speed in terms of an economy."

413) February 27, 2019-House rebukes Trump's emergency declaration.

The House passed a resolution to overturn President Donald Trump's declaration of a national emergency on the southern border as majority Democrats painted an apocalyptic portrait of a lawless chief executive who is out to gut the constitution. 13 Republicans defected to side with the Democrats on a vote that effectively become a test of GOP loyalty to Trump. Democrats argued that Trump's claim of a crisis at the border was baseless, and that he was embarking on the road to dictatorship by unilaterally declaring an emergency to try to get money from U.S. taxpayers to fulfill an unpopular campaign promise.

414) February 27, 2019-Cohen to testify Trump broke law in office.

Michael Cohen, Donald Trump's former lawyer, plans for the first time to publicly accuse the president of engaging, while in office, in criminal conduct related to a hush-money payment to a porn star. Appearing before the House Oversight Committee, Mr. Cohen also plans to make public some of Mr. Trump's private financial statements and allege that Mr. Trump at times inflated or deflated his net worth for business and personal purposes, including avoiding paying property taxes.

415) February 28, 2019-Cohen says Trump guided cover-up.
President Trump and his company's chief financial officer coordinated with Michael Cohen to pay for the silence of a porn star and conceal Mr. Trump's role in the deal, using sham invoices to cover it up, Mr. Cohen alleged in testimony to the House Oversight Committee.

416) February 28, 2019-Cohen accuses Trump of lies and cover-ups.
President Trump's long-time lawyer and fixer accused him of an expansive pattern of lies and criminality, offering a damming portrayal of life inside the presidents' orbit where he said advisors sacrificed integrity for proximity for power. He charged that Mr. Trump lied to the public about business interest in Russia, lied to reporters about stolen Democratic emails and told Mr. Cohen to lie about hush payments to cover up sexual misconduct. "He is a racist. He is a con man. And he is a cheat," Mr. Cohen said of the president.

417) March 1, 2019-Trump's talks with Kim break down.
U.S., North Korea point fingers over reason for summit. North Korea is disputing President Donald Trump's account of why the summit between Trump and Kim Jung Un collapsed, insisting the North demanded any partial sanctions relief in exchange for shutting down because North Korea's leader insisted that all the punishing sanction the U.S. has imposed on Pyongyang be lifted without the North committing to eliminate its nuclear arsenal.

418) March 1, 2019-Collapse of Hanoi talks, a setback for president.
President Donald Trump flew for 20 hours to this bustling Vietnamese capital determined to earn a place in history as the American statesman whose personal charm overcame decades of

intransigence and erased the North Korean threats. But the self-pro-
claimed master deal maker left Hanoi empty handed by his failure
to coax an erratic and reclusive dictator into giving up his arsenal.
Trump was so certain that he could broker an accord with Kim Jung
Un, even if an incremental one, that the White House announced it
had scheduled a joint signing ceremony at which the two leaders
would triumphantly conclude their two day nuclear summit. But
that event along with a working luncheon, was abruptly cancelled
amid a standoff over Kim's demand that the United States remove
all economic sanctions against North Korea without Pyongyang
completely ending its nuclear program.

**419) March 1, 2019-Senate Foes of Trump border emergency
close to a win.**
Senate opponents of President Donald Trump's declaration of a
national emergency at the Mexican border moved within a hair of
having enough votes to prevail, and one Republican suggested he
could face rejection by the GOP led chamber if he doesn't change
course. Trump's move would "turn a border crisis into a constitutional crisis," veteran Senator Lamar Alexander said on Senate floor.

**420) March 1, 2019- Democrats plan to follow up
Cohen leads.**
House Democrats said they would seek testimony from the chief
financial officer and other employees of the Trump organization,
potentially including members of President Donald Trump's family,
to follow up on accusations of wrongdoing Michael Cohen made
under oath before the House Oversight Committee.

421) March 1, 2019-GOP Senators warn on wall funds.
Senate Republicans are warning President Donald Trump against
moving forward with his national emergency declaration to build a
southern wall and pressuring him to restrict the project funding to

less controversial sources. Republicans are on the brink of attaining enough support for a resolution to disapprove of the declaration, potentially forcing Mr. Trump to use his veto power for the first time. Mr. Trump has already said he will veto the measure should Congress send it to his desk.

422) March 4, 2019-Panel eyes dozens of Trump associates.

The House Judiciary Committee plans to request documents from more than 60 associates of President Trump, including from his sons and from his longtime chief financial officer, as part of a House investigation into obstruction of justice corruption and abuse of power. "It's very clear that the president obstructed justice, 1,100 times he referred to the Mueller investigation as a witch hunt, he tried to protect former aide Mike Flynn from being investigated by the FBI. He fired former FBI directors James Comey in order to stop the Russian thing, as he told NBC News. He dangled pardons; he's intimidated witnesses."

423) March 5, 2019-Senate to rebuff Trump on Wall.

Senate Majority Leader Mitch McConnell said a resolution seeking to block President Trump from declaring a national emergency would pass the GOP-controlled senate, likely forcing the president to issue his first veto in a bid to secure the funding he wants for a border wall. Many Republicans said they were uncomfortable with Mr. Trump's circumventing congress to obtain more money to help fund a border wall after bipartisan legislation passed in February allocated $1.38 billion.

424) March 5, 2019-Trump says golf course 'furthers' U.K. relations.

President Trump has implied that a golf course owned by the Trump organization in Scotland helps cement the United States relationship with Britain, just a few days after a Scottish court ruled that the company had to pay expenses in a failed lawsuit. "Very proud of perhaps the greatest golf course anywhere in the world," Mr. Trump wrote on Twitter adding, "Also, furthers U.K. relationship." Mr. Lundmark, a professor of law at the University of Hull, in Northern England said in a telephone interview that the tweet "made me curious, I don't know what he's talking about does it further a relationship for him? For the United States? For us? How?"

425) March 6, 2019-President and his allies attack House investigation.

President Trump and close congressional allies denounced the investigations by House Democrats into possible obstruction of justice, abuse of power and corruption which Mr. Trump labeled a "big, fat, finishing expedition." The House Judiciary Committee requested records from more than 80 organizations and Trump associates among them former White House staff; executives from the president's real-estate business, including Mr. Trump's sons are officials who worked for the transition and inaugural committees. At the White House, Mr. Trump called the investigations a "disgrace to our country" and accused Democrats of wanting to "focus on nonsense."

426) March 6, 2019-Democrats target Trump's taxes.

Congressional Democrats are likely to request 10 years of President Donald Trump's tax returns in coming weeks, tailoring their inquiry in a way they hope will survive a court battle according to lawmakers and others involved in the discussions. Democrats are relying on a 1924 law that gives chairman of the House and Senate tax-writing committee's broad powers to demand the tax returns of White House officials.

427) March 6, 2019-How Trump's school hid his transcript.
In 2011, days after Donald Trump challenged President Barrack
Obama to "show his records" to prove that he hadn't been a "terrible student," the headmaster at New York Military Academy got
an order from his boss. Find Trump's academic records and help
bury them. The superintendent of the private school "came to me in
a panic because he had been accosted by prominent, wealthy alumni
of the school who were Mr. Trump's friends" and who wanted to
keep his records secret, recalled Evan Jones, the headmaster at the
time. He said, "You need to go grab that record and deliver it to
me because I need to deliver it to them." Cohen said that he sent
threatening letters to Trump's schools, warning that "we will hold
your institution liable" if any of his records are released. In his letter
to the President of Fordham University, where Trump spent his
first two years of college studying business administration, Cohen
demanded that the records be "permanently sealed" and said any
release was "criminality," which "will lead to jail time."

428) March 6, 2019-U.S. trade tariffs hit consumers hardest.
The Trump administrations trade initiatives have targeted China
and other foreign powers, but U.S. consumers have taken the hit,
according to two new studies. American consumers have been saddled with $69 billion in additional costs because of tariffs the U.S.
imposed last year, including on $250 billion on Chinese imports
as well as levies on steel and aluminum, according to a study by
economists working on a National Science Foundation grant. The
studies dispute President Donald Trump's off-repeated claim that
the costs of tariffs are born by foreign countries. U.S. manufactures
and producers, such as steel mills and washing-machine makers,
boosted income by $23 billion because tariffs on foreign com-
petition let them charge more for their products. The Center for
Economic Research concluded that tariffs gave U.S. producers the
ability to raise their prices when the tariffs were imposed on foreign

competition. Those foreign companies raised their prices too. Both studies share a conclusion: Although tariffs are formally assessed on U.S. importers when they bring in goods from foreign countries, the costs are passed on to the consumers.

429) March 7, 2019-Trade deficit defies Trump's efforts and promises.

The U.S. trade deficit reach edits highest sum ever last year, defying President Donald Trump's efforts and promises to shrink it through his economic policies. The irony is that those polices likely contributed to the deficit. Trump entered office insisting that decades of trade groups had crushed the U.S. economy and that he would forge new agreements that would diminish the deficits. It hasn't happened. The government said that the U.S. trade gap in goods and services reached $621 billion last year, its highest total since 2008. And the U.S. deficits in goods with China and Mexico surged to record highs. What's more, the tariffs Trump imposed on steel, aluminum and hundreds of billions worth of Chinese goods likely contributed to the trend. During 2018, American companies that import goods from China appeared to accelerate their spending on them to avoid Trump's future import taxes. "We've been losing, an average, $375 billion a year with China," the president said in February, referring to the 2017 deficit in goods between the United States and China. That imbalance surged to $419.2 billion in 2018 under Trump's watch.

430) March 8, 2019-Manafort sentenced to 47 months.

A federal judge sentenced Paul Manafort, who served as Donald Trump's 2016 campaign to 47 months in prison for dodging taxes and committing bank fraud much less than he could have faced. U.S. District Judge T.S. Ellis ordered the sentence saying guidelines calling for Mr. Manafort to spend between 19 and 24 years in prison were "out of whack." The judge said the roughly 4-year sentence was a suitable punishment for the crimes he said Mr. Manafort had committed.

431) Mach 8, 2019-Cohen sues Trump firm over nearly $2 million in legal fees.

Michael Cohen, President Donald Trump's former personal lawyer, is suing the Trump Organization for failing to reimburse him millions of dollars for his legal fees, fines and other cost. Cohen who testified before Congress at a contentious House Judiciary Committee hearing, said in a lawsuit filed in New York that the Trump Organization had breached a July 2017 agreement under which it agreed to cover the costs Cohen incurred while participating in ongoing investigations into his work for the company. Cohen is seeking more than $1.9 million that he has been ordered to pay as part of his sentence for crimes he committed while working for Trump.

432) March 9, 2019-U.S.-China trade talks hit a bump.

A U.S.-China trade accord is facing a new roadblock, as Chinese officials balk at committing to a presidential summit until the two countries have a firm deal in hand. A week ago, the sides appeared to be closing in on a draft accord. But Chinese leaders were taken aback by President Trump's failed meeting in Vietnam with North Korea leader Kim Jung Un. Mr. Trump's decision to break off talks and walk away sparked concern that China's President Xi Jinping could be pressured with take-it-or-leave-it demands at a potential summit at Mr. Trump's Mara-Lago estate.

433) March 10, 2019-Trump plan calls for allies to pick up U.S. military tab and pay a fee, too.

In private discussions with his aides, President Donald Trump has devised an eye-popping formula to address one of his long-standing complaints that allies hosting U.S. forces don't pay Washington enough money. Under the formula, countries would pay the full cost of stationing American troops on their territory, plus 50 percent more, said U.S. and foreign officials familiar with the idea, which could have allies contributing five times what they provide.

434) March 11, 2019- Trump again seeks funding for wall.
President Donald Trump will be making a significant request for border wall funds and seeking money to stand up Space Force as a new branch of military in the White House budget. For the first time, Trump plans to stick with strict spending caps-imposed years ago, even though lawmakers have largely avoided them with new budget deals. The president's plan promises to balance the budget in 15 years.

435) March 11, 2019-Trump ask for $8.6 billion for wall.
President Donald Trump is reviving his border wall fight, preparing a new budget that will seek $8.6 billion for the U.S.-Mexico barrier while imposing steep spending cuts to other domestic programs and setting the stage for another fiscal battle. Leading Democrats immediately rejected the proposal.

436) March 13, 2019-Senate to vote on ending aid to Saudi's for war in Yemen.
The Senate will vote on whether to cut off American military assistance for Saudi Arabia's war in Yemen preparing again to rebuke President Trump for his continued defense of the kingdom after the killing of the dissident journalist Jamal Khashoggi. Passage of the measures would prompt the first vetoes of Mr. Trump's presidency.

437) March 13, 2019-President's budget plan makes deep cuts to programs he brags about.
The Trump administrations annual budget proposal envisioned a series of cuts that contracted with the president's own words of

support for both programs and people, including some groups that make up his political base. To help make way for more military and border spending it would slash programs large and small, from Medicaid and Medicare, which President Trump as a candidate promised to protect, to safety nets for farmers.

438) March 14, 2019-Manafort hit with more prison time.

Paul Manafort was sentenced to federal prison for the second time in seven days, giving him a total sentence of 7 ½ years. Alexandria Virginia, where he was being held, prosecutors in New York announced a 16-count grand jury indictment charging the former Trump campaign chairman with mortgage fraud, falsifying business records and conspiracy. Trump would not be able to pardon Manafort, 69, on the state charges, which separate them from federal cases for which Manafort was just sentenced.

439) March 14, 2019-Senate votes to end aid to Saudi war in Yemen defying Trump.

The Senate again rebuked President Trump for his continued defense of Saudi Arabia after the killing of the dissident journalist Jamal Khashoggi, voting for a second time to end American military assistance for the kingdoms war in Yemen and to curtail presidential war powers.

437) March 14, 2019-Senate to rebuke Trump on wall, but veto expected.

The Senate is set to pass a resolution rejecting President Trump's emergency declaration to build more of the border wall. The Senate move would set the stage for Mr. Trump's first veto. Republicans have expressed concern over his action, saying it improperly bypassed Congress, and warned of the precedent it could set.

438) March 15, 2019-Senate rejects Trump's emergency declaration.

The Senate passed a resolution to overturn President Donald Trump's declaration of a national emergency at the U.S.-Mexico border, with 12 Republicans joining all the Democrats to deliver a rare bipartisan rebuke of the president. A short time later he added "I look forward to VETOING the just passed Democrat inspired Resolution which would OPEN BORDERS increasing crime, drugs, and trafficking in our country. I thank all the Republicans who voted to support Border Security and our desperately needed WALL." But for many GOP lawmakers, it was about what they saw as a bigger issue: the constitution itself, which grants Congress, not the president, control over government spending.

439) March 15, 2019-Defamation case against Trump to move forward.

President Donald Trump must face a defamation lawsuit brought by a former reality show contestant, a New York appellate court ruled, striking down his argument that a sitting president should be shielded from such claims. In overruling a request by Mr. Trump to halt or throw out the two-year case, the court found that "the president is still a person, and he is not above the law."

Chapter 7

440) March 16, 2019-Trump vetoes Border Resolution.
President Trump vetoed a congressional resolution disapproving of this national emergency declaration, asserting his authority to tap funding for barriers on the southern border even though the money hadn't been appropriated by lawmakers. <u>"Congress and I have the duty to pass this resolution, and I have the duty to veto it,"</u> Mr. Trump said, <u>"and I am very proud to veto it."</u> The Senate voted 59-44 to pass a resolution terminating Mr. Trump's declaration, with 12 Republicans joining Democrats in challenging Mr. Trump on his signature policy issue.

441) March 16, 2019- N. Korea threatens to halt nuclear talks with U.S. and resume tests.
North Korea threatened to suspend negotiations with the Trump administration over the North's nuclear arms program and said its leader, Kim Jung Un, would soon decide whether to resume nuclear and missile tests. After the Hanoi meeting ended without a deal, the North Korean leader had serious doubts about the merits of continuing negotiations with Mr. Trump.

442) March 18, 2019-Border battle goes to courts.
Congress can't stop President Trump's emergency declaration at the Mexican border, but the courts will have the final word. After the president's veto of a congressional resolution rescinding

his action, three little-known federal district judges have the best chance to block the emergency declaration. They will test Trump's theory that the judiciary is prejudiced against him. "They will sue us in the 9th circuit," Trump predicted when discussing his emergency declaration last month. "We will possibly get a bad ruling, and then we'll get another bad ruling, and then we'll end up in the Supreme Court."

443) March 18, 2019-Trump again takes aim at late Senators.
President Donald Trump is again training his fire on the late Senator John McCain, nearly seven months after the Arizona Republican's death from brain cancer. Trump piled on in his Saturday night tweet, criticizing McCain, as he has repeatedly done on the campaign trail and in interviews, for his vote against repealing the Affordable Care Act, aka Obamacare, in 2017.

444) March 18, 2019-Unfair to link mosque shorter Trump.
The man accused of the deadly shootings at mosques in Christchurch, New Zealand, left behind a lengthy document stating he was a white nationalist who hates immigrants and was set off by attacks in Europe that were perpetrated by Muslims. "Were/are you a supporter of Donald Trump?" was one of the questions he posed to himself in the document. His answer: "As a symbol of renewed white identity and common purpose? Sure. As a policymaker and leader? Dear god no."

445) March 19, 2019-President attacks GM and union over shutdown of Ohio plant.
President Trump entered office berating Detroit automakers for closing plants and sending jobs abroad. With another election on the horizon he has renewed the attack. Mr. Trump took to Twitter to demand that General Motors reopen a car plant in Ohio, a state that could play a pivotal role in his 2020 re-election campaign.

The president also criticized the United Auto Workers union and touted investments in the United States by Toyota and other foreign car companies. GM said in November that it would idle its factory in Lordstown, Ohio, as part of broader cutbacks that would eliminate a total of 14,000 jobs, and it stopped production there two weeks ago.

446) March 20, 2019-Trump advisors concede his tax cut fall short.

The Trump administration pushed a $1.5 trillion tax cut through Congress in 2017 on the premise that it would spark sustained economic growth. While the tax cuts have goosed the economy in the short term, officials now conceded there will be enough to deliver the 3 percent annual growth the president promised over the long term. To produce that average growth rate for the next decade, White House forecasters say, the American economy would need additional rollbacks in labor regulations, a $1 trillion infrastructure plan and another round of tax cuts.

447) March 20, 2019-Trump ramps up animosity against late Senator John McCain.

Carrying a bitter personal feud beyond the grave, President Donald Trump escalated his attacks on the late Senator John McCain, declaring he will "never" be a fan of the Vietnam War hero and longtime Republican lawmaker who died last year of brain cancer. "I was never a fan of John McCain, and I never will be," Trump told reporters in the Oval Office.

448) March 21, 2019-McCain death hasn't silenced a Trump feud.

John McCain has been dead for seven months, but President Trump's feud with him is very much alive, and in front of a military audience at a tank plant here in Lima, Ohio, he took it to a new level. He said he gave Mr. McCain "the funeral he wanted, and I didn't get 'thank you'," exaggerating the role he played in honoring the senator's death four days before his 82nd birthday. I have to be honest: I've never liked him much," Mr. Trump said.

449) March 21, 2019-Companies tune out Trump's ire.
This week, General Motors become the latest recipient of a barrage of tweets from Mr. Trump, who is angry about the company's closing of a plant in Lordstown, Ohio. The president told the company to reopen the plant or sell it "fast" to someone who would. He suggested that GM shutter a factory in China or Mexico instead. "Get that plant opened or sell it to somebody and they'll open it."

450) March 21, 2019-Trump: Let Mueller's findings be released.
President Donald Trump said that he believes special counsel Robert Mueller's report should be released to the public, even as he disparaged its very existence as "ridiculous." "Let it come out, let people see it, let's see whether or not it's legit."

451) March 22, 2019- My hope for the Mueller report (by James Comey).
The country is eagerly awaiting the special counsel Robert Mueller's report. May people who know what they want it to say, what they feel it simply must say, namely that Donald Trump is a criminal who should be removed from office. Or that he is completely innocent of all wrongdoing. Even though I feel Mr. Trump is morally unfit to be president of the United States, I'm not rooting for anything at all, except that the special counsel be permitted to finish his work, charge whatever cases warrant charging and report on his findings. I care only that the work be done well and completely. If it is, justice will have prevailed and core American values will have been protected at a time when so much of our national

leadership has abandoned its commitment to truth and the rule of law. I just hope we are up to it.

452) March 22, 2019-Hopes shift in Mueller probe.

It's a witch hunt, a vendetta, the worst presidential harassment in history. That's what President Donald Trump has shouted for two years about the special counsels Russia probe. With Robert Mueller's probe winding down, the president has grown increasingly confident the report will produce what he insisted all along, no clear evidence of a conspiracy between Russia and his 2016 campaign. No one knows what Mueller will say, but Trump, his allies and members are trying to map out the post-probe political dynamics.

453) March 23, 2019-Mueller probe ends with report.

Special counsel Robert Mueller presented his long-awaited report to the Justice Department, ending his nearly two-year investigation that has loomed over the Trump presidency and likely setting up a political battle over what he has found. In a letter to the majority and minority leaders of the House and Judiciary Committees, Attorney General William Barr said Mr. Mueller had concluded his investigation of Russian interference in the 2016 election and related matters, and said he would be able to alert Congress to Mr. Mueller's "principal conclusions" as soon as this weekend. Those conclusions are expected to be made public. The special counsel isn't recommending any further indictments, according to a senior Justice Department official.

454) March 23, 2019-Trump blocks planned North Korea sanctions.

President Trump said he wouldn't move forward with ah round of large-scale sanctions against North Korea, catching senior officials in his own administration by surprise and spurring confusion about his diplomatic surprise and spurring confusion about his diplomatic strategy to induce Pyongyang to give up its nuclear arsenal and programs. In a Twitter message Mr. Trump wrote: "I have today ordered the withdrawal of those additional sanctions!" "Once again, President Trump is making critical national security decisions on the fly, with tweets that directly conflict with the advice of his cabinet and experts," said Rep. Eliot Engel (D.N.Y.), chairman of the House Foreign Affairs Committee.

455) March 24, 2019-With Mueller's report in, interest turns to New York.

Evan as the special counsel, Robert S. Mueller III, submitted his confidential report to the Justice Department, Federal and State prosecutors are pursuing about a dozen other investigations that largely grew out of his work, all but ensuring that a legal threat will continue to loom over the Trump presidency.

456) March 24, 2019-Optimistic Trump allies await report.

The political showdown over the Russia investigation that could reshape the remainder of President Donald Trump's term began in earnest even before the special counsel's conclusion were known to the public, as Trump allies claimed vindication while Democrats demanded transparency and vowed to intensify their own probes. Trump and his attorneys and aides were clouded by uncertainty because they did not yet know the contents of Robert Mueller's report, which Attorney General William Barn and a small coterie at Justice Department official spent privately reviewing.

457) March 24, 2019-Mueller finds no Trump-Russia conspiracy.

President claims 'Exonerations,' but inquiry stops short of ruling out obstruction. The investigation led by Robert S. Mueller III found no evidence that President Trump or any of his aides coordinated with the Russia government's 2016 election interference. Mr. Mueller's team drew no conclusions about whether Mr. Trump illegally obstructed justice, Mr. Barr said, so he made his own decision. The attorney general and his deputy, Rod J. Rosenstein, determine that the special counsel's investigators had insufficient evidence to establish that the president committed that offense. He cautioned, however, that Mr. Mueller's report states that <u>"While this report does not conclude that the president committed a crime, it also does not exonerate him on the obstruction of justice issues."</u>

458) March 25, 2019-AG: No Russia Conspiracy.

Attorney General Barr says report neither accuses nor clears Trump of obstructing justice. On whether the president might have sought to obstruct the high-profile investigation, Mueller's team did not offer a definite answer. <u>"The special counsel did not draw a conclusion, one way or the other as to whether the examined conduct constituted obstruction,"</u> Barr's letter said<u>. "The special counsel states that 'while this report does not conclude that the President committed a crime, it also does not exonerate him,"</u> the letter said. Trump responded on Twitter, writing <u>"No Collusion, No Obstruction, Complete and Total EXONERATION. KEEP AMERICA GREAT!"</u>

459) March 26, 2019-Trump, citing 'Evil Deeds,' turns wrath on his critics.

President Trump and his Republican allies went on the offensive vowing to pursue and even punish those responsible for the Russia investigation now that the special counsel has wrapped up without finding a criminal conspiracy to influence the 2016 election. Mr. Trump, grim faced and simmering with anger, denounced adversaries who have pounded him for two years over Russian election interference, calling them <u>"treasons"</u> people who are guilty of <u>"evil</u>

deeds" and should be investigated themselves. "Those people will certainly be looked at," he said.

460) March 26, 2019-Democrats want full report; GOP says move on.

House Democrats pressed the Justice Department to provide the full report from special counsel Robert Mueller even as Republicans called for them to "move on" from the Russian investigation. President Donald Trump accused responsible for launching Mueller's probe of "treason things against our country" and said they certainly will be looked at.

461) March 27, 2019-Move to nullify health care act roils Democrats.

The Trump administration's decision to ask a federal appeals court to invalidate the Affordable Care Act has given House Democrats a new opening to pursue what they see as a winning political strategy: moving past talk of impeachment to put kitchen table issues like health care front and center.

462) March 27, 2019-President pivots to old foe: The ACA

Now that the pressure of special counsel Robert Mueller's investigation has been lifted, President Donald Trump is resuming an old battle: repealing Obamacare. Reversing an earlier position, Trump's Justice Department notified a federal appeals court in New Orleans that it would ask judges to toss out the entire Affordable Care Act, casting uncertainty over the future of a federal law that has extended health insurance to millions of Americans.

463) March 28, 2019-Fiery meeting swayed Trump in health fight.

The Trump administration's surprise decision to press for a court-ordered demolition of the Affordable Care Act came after a heated meeting in the Oval Office, where the president's acting chief of staff and others convinced him that he could do through the courts what he could not do through Congress: repeal his predecessor's signature achievement. Mick Mulvaney, the acting White House Chief of Staff had spent years in the House saying that the health laws should be repealed, and his handpicked head of the Domestic Policy Council Joe Grogan, supported the idea of joining a Republican attorney general lawsuit to invalidate the entire Affordable Care Act.

464) March 29, 2019-Data challenges Trump optimism on the economy.

President Trump is getting exactly what he wants on the economy, but it may not last. The Federal Reserve has abruptly stopped its march toward higher interest rates, as Trump demanded. But while Mr. Trump points with pride to last year's economic growth and promises even faster growth to come, there are signs that his most dependable talking point is eroding. The Commerce Department issued a downward revision of it's estimated for economic growth in the fourth quarter, pushing one measure of the full year's growth down as well.

465) March 29, 2019-Partisan fight over Barr memo escalates.

House Speaker Nancy Pelosi criticized Attorney General William Barr over his handling of the special counsel's report pressing the case for the full release of the documents as President Trump and Republicans continued to claim vindication in the Russian probe. Mrs. Pelosi said that the summary Mr. Barr provided to lawmakers was well short of what Mr. Barr provided to lawmakers was well short of what Congress required. "Show us the report and we can draw our own conclusions," Mrs. Pelosi said. "We don't need you interpreting for us. It was condescending, it was arrogant, and it wasn't the right thing to do."

466) March 29, 2019-Mexico wins U.S.-China trade war.

Companies shift production to duck stiff import taxes. The Trump Administrations trade war with China has turned out to be a windfall for another country the President frequently berates Mexico. Fuling Global Inc., a Chines Maker of plastic utensils that developed lucrative business making paper cups and straws for U.S. restaurants. But President Donald Trump opened all that with tariffs on $250 billion worth of Chinese imports, including paper products. So, the company found an alternative, opening a $4 million dollar factory in Monterey, Mexico, that will soon begin shipping millions of paper straws across the border. "We had to look for other ways to do business," said Fuling Chio F. Financial Officer Gilbert Lee. The move means the China based company will avoid the tariffs and make up for pricier Mexican labor with lower shipping cost.

467) March 29, 2019-More than 300 pages summed up in four.

Democrats intensified their demands for the Robert Mueller's full report after learning the special counsel's finding from his Trump-Russia investigation run to more than 300 pages, while President Donald Trump boasted of total exoneration based on a four-page summary by his attorney general. Democrats say they may subpoena the report if it's not forthcoming by their Tuesday deadline, which Barr has said will not be met.

468) March 30, 2019-Trump threatens to close border.

President Donald Trump declared that he is likely to shut down America's southern border unless Mexican authorities immediately halt all illegal immigration. Such a move could hit the economies of both countries, but the president emphasized: "I am not kidding around." "It could mean all trade" Trump said. "We will close it for a long time." The U.S. and Mexico trade about $1.7 billion in goods daily, according to the U.S. Chamber of Commerce, which said closing the border would be "and unmitigated economic debacle" that would threaten 5 million American jobs.

469) March 31, 2019- How Trump inflated his wealth, hid his debts.

When Donald Trump wanted to make a good impression on a lender, a business partner or a journalist, he sometimes sent them official looking documents called "Statements of Financial Condition." These documents sometimes ran up to 20 pats. They were full of numbers, laying out Trump's properties, debts and multimillion-dollar net worth. The documents were deeply flawed. Some simply omitted properties that carried big debts. Some assets were overvalued. And some key numbers were wrong. Trump's financial statements for 2011 said he had 55 home lots to sell at his golf course in Southern California. Those lots would sell for #4 million or more, the statement said. But Trump only had 31 lots zoned and ready for sale at the course, according to city records. He claimed credit for 24 lots and at least $72 million in future revenue he didn't have. He also claimed his Virginia vineyard had 2,000 acres, when it really has about 1200. He said Trump Tower has 68 stories, it only has 58. Since the 1980's Trump has defined himself by his wealth, but he has often avoided providing proof to back up his boasts or provided documents that inflated the real values. As President Trump has declined to release his tax returns, unlike every other president since Jimmy Carter.

470) March 31, 2019-GOP grapples with new ACA battle.

Republican unsure how to proceed after Trump vows reset ahead of the 2020 election. President Donald Trump's decision to revive the fight over the Affordable Care Act has stirred a political and policy debate among Republicans on how to approach the divisive issue heading into the 2020 election. Failing to repeal and replace the ACA is one of the biggest shortcomings of the president's first term in meeting its goals.

471) March 31, 2019-Trump seeks to cut aid to 3 Central American Nations.

Taking drastic action over illegal immigration, President Donald Trump moved to cut direct aid to El Salvador, Guatemala, and Honduras, whose citizens are fleeing north and overwhelming U.S. resources at the southern border. <u>"It would be easy to fix our weak and very stupid Democrat inspired immigration laws, in less than one hour, and then a vote, the problem would be solved. But the Dems don't care about the crime, they don't want any victory for Trump and the Republicans, even if good for USA!"</u>

472) April 1, 2019-White House redoubles border threat.

The White House doubled down on President Donald Trump' threat to close the U.S. border with Mexico, despite warnings that the move would inflict immediate economic damage on American consumers and businesses while doing little to stem a tied of migrants clamoring to enter the United States.

473) April 1, 2019-Trump aides: Health care plan in works.

White House counselor Kelly Anne Conway maintained that Republicans are "working in a plan" for replacing the Affordable Care Act after President Donald Trump surprised members on both sides of the aisle when he declared that the Republican Party <u>"will soon be known as the party of health care."</u> "There is a plan," she said. "We've been working on a plan for a long time. And we hope that Congress would come along."

474) April 1, 2019-Aide defends Trump plans to close border.

Mick Mulvaney, the acting White House Chief of Staff, defended President Trump's threat to end assistance to three Central

American countries and to close parts of the United States border with Mexico, saying that it would take "something dramatic" to prevent Mr. Trump from carrying out his plan.

475) April 2, 2019-House panel issues subpoena threat for report.

House Democrats threatened to issue subpoenas demanding a complete version of special counsel Robert Mueller's report on Russia interference in the 2016 election and alleged obstruction of justice by the president, escalating a political fight with the Trump administration over a document President Trump says exonerates him.

476) April 2, 2019-New questions on clearances in White House.

A whistleblower working inside the White House has told a House Committee that senior Trump administration officials granted security clearances to at least 25 individuals who applications had been denied by career employees for "disqualifying issues" that could put national security at risk. The memo does not identify any of the 25 people. But one of the senior White House officials appears to be Jared Kushner, the president's son-in-law and senior advisor.

477) April 2, 2019-As Russia barges in, Trump faces a redline moment in Venezuela.

Several Trump administration officials have warned Russia to not interfere in Venezuela, but President Trump has said little. For the past week, the Trump administration has escalated its warnings about Russia intervention in the Country, claiming that Moscow is helping to prop up President Nicolás Maduro of Venezuela and undermining the hopes of American officials that the Army War College in Carlisle, Pa, Secretary of State Mike Pompeo said flatly, "Russia's got to leave Venezuela."

478) April 3, 2019-Trump vows to close border, even if that means hurting the economy.

President Trump acknowledged that closing the southern border with Mexico could damage the United States economy but said protecting America's security was more important than trade. <u>"Sure, it's going to have a negative impact on the economy, but security is most important."</u> The president told reporters that if Mexico cannot restrict the flow of asylum seekers trying to cross into the United States, and if congress cannot agree to several immigration restrictions that Mr. Trump has long pushed for, <u>"the border is going to be closed."</u>

479) April 3, 2019-McConnell spurs Trump's retreat over health care.

President Trump backed off plans to introduce a Republican replacement for the Affordable Care Act after Senator Mitch McConnell privately warned him that the Senate would not revisit health care in comprehensive way before the November 2020 elections. Reversing himself in the face of Republican consternation, Mr. Trump said his party would not produce a health care plan of its own as he had promised, until after the elections, meaning he will not fulfill his first-term promise to repeal and replace his predecessor's signature program only if he wins a second term.

480) April 3, 2019-GOP puts off health care plan to after 2020.

Republicans said they plan to put off any new health care overhaul until after the 2020 election. President Trump flagged the shift in a series of tweets in which he continued to attack the Affordable Care Act but said any changes to it would have to wait for a GOP majority in both chambers in Congress.

481) April 3, 2019-Trump eases threat to close all of the U.S. Mexico border.

President Donald Trump eased up on his threats to shut the southern border as officials explored half-measures that might satisfy the president's urge for action like stopping only foot traffic at certain crossings. Facing a surge of Central American migrants trying to enter the country, Trump threatened last week to seal the border if Mexico did not immediately halt all illegal immigration into the U.S., a move would have enormous consequences on both side of the border. "Let's see if they keep it done, now, if they don't or if we don't make a deal with Congress, the borders going to be closed, 100%" Trump also said the he might only close "large sections of the border and not all of it."

482) April 4, 2019-House expands Trump inaugural probe.

The House Intelligence Committee is seeking an interview with and documents from a top organizer on Trump's inaugural committee, according to people familiar with the request, signaling that Congress is expanding its probe of how the fund raised and spent more than $100 million. A spokesman for the inaugural committee, raised a record amount more than twice what President Obama raised for his committee in 2009, declined to comment.

483) April 4, 2019- House panel seeks Trump tax returns.

The chairman of the House tax writing committee formerly requested President Trump's tax returns, kicking off what could be a bruising legal fight between Congress and the Trump administration. MR. Trump breaking with four decades of tradition from presidents and major party presidential candidates, hasn't released any tax returns voluntarily, despite saying repeatedly during the presidential campaign that he would do so. "We're under audit despite what people say, and we're working that out, I've been under audit for many years because the numbers are big, and I guess when you have a name you're audited. But until such time as I'm not under audit I would not be inclined to release the returns.

484) April 4, 2019-House panel ok's subpoenas for full Mueller report.

A House panel voted to authorize subpoenas to obtain Special Counsel Robert Mueller's full report on Russian interference in 2016 presidential election, laying down a marker in a constitutional power struggle that could end up in the courts.

485) April 5, 2019-Mueller team voices frustration.

Members of special counsel Robert Mueller's team have told associates they are frustrated with the limited information Attorney General William Barr has provided about their nearly two-year investigation into Russian interference in the 2016 election and whether President Donald Trump sought to obstruct justice.

486) April 5, 2019-Trump says he won't close south border.

Facing widespread opposition, President Donald Trump backed down from his threat to close the southern borders. Instead giving Mexico a "one-year warning" while leaving the administration with no clear path to deal with a record surge of migrant families. Trump had issued an ultimatum on Twitter late last week that he would move to seal the border to trade and travel if Mexico authorities do not halt illegal immigration.

487) April 6, 2019- "Our country is full" Trump says migrants straining system.

Declaring "our country is full", President Donald Trump insisted the U.S. immigration system was overburdened and illegal crossings must be stopped as he inspected a refurbished section of fencing at the Mexican border. "There is indeed an emergency on our southern border, it's a colossal surge, and it's overwhelming our immigration system, we can't take you anymore. Our country is full."

488) April 9, 2019-President ratchets up push to stem illegal immigration.

President Trump is shaking up the top ranks of the Department of Homeland Security and has instructed White House advisors to take a more direct role implementing immigration policy in an effort to slow the rise in families illegally crossing the southern border. Mr. Trump also told aides he wants to reinstate his family separation policy, which provoked a political outcry when it was implemented last spring in order to deter would be migrants. Mr. Trump recently told Stephen Miller, one of his most hardline advisors: "You're in charge" of the administration's immigration policy.

489) April 9, 2019-Policy of returning asylum seekers to Mexico blocked.

A federal judge blocked a Trump administration policy of returning asylum-seeking Central Americans to Mexico while their requests for admission to the U.S. are adjudicated. U.S. District Judge Richard Seeborg in San Francisco ruled the administration lacked a legal basis under current law for adopting the policy. He also found the policy ran afoul of the U. S's legal obligations not to remove people to a country where their lives or freedom are threatened.

490) April 10, 2019-Mueller report to come soon, Barr says.

Attorney General William Barr said he would deliver the special counsel's still secret report to Congress within a week and vowed to explain his reasons for blocking out parts of the roughly 400-page document. "I am relying on my own discretion to make as much of it public as I can, adding that he will color code the redactions and provide notes explaining the reason for each.

491) April 11, 2019-Barr, asserting 'spying' in 2016 cites questions but not evidence.

Attorney General William P. Barr said that he would scrutinize the FBI's investigation of the Trump campaign's ties to Russia, including whether "spying" conducted by American intelligence agencies on the campaign's associates has been properly carried out. "I think spying on a political campaign is a big deal," Mr. Barr said during testimony before the Senate Appropriations subcommittee, adding he wanted to look into both "the genesis and the conduct" of the FBI inquiry.

492) April 11, 2019-Treasury seeks delay on release of Trump's returns.

The Treasury Department said that it would not immediately comply with a congressional request to hand over President Trump's tax returns, setting up a protracted legal battle between two branches of the government. "The committee's request raises serious issues concerning the constitutional investigative authority, the legitimacy of the asserted legislative purpose and the constitutional rights of American citizens," Mr. Mnuchin wrote.

493) April 12, 2019-Trump changes tune on Wiki Leaks.

President distances himself from Assange's hacking organization after founder's arrest. President Donald Trump declared "I know nothing about Wiki Leaks" after its disheveled founder Julian Assange was hauled out of the Ecuadorian Embassy in London to face charges, a stark contrast how candidate Trump showered praise on Assange's hacking organization night after night during the final weeks of the 2016 presidential campaign.

494) April 12, 2019-White House asked ICE to let detainees go in sanctuary cities.

White House officials have tried to pressure U.S. immigration authorities to release detainees onto the streets of "sanctuary cities" to retaliate against President Donald Trump's political adversaries according to Department of Homeland Security officials and email messages reviewed by The Washington Post. Trump administration officials have proposed transporting detained immigrants to sanctuary cities at least twice in the past six months, once in November, as a migrant caravan approached the U.S. southern border, and again in February, amid a standoff with Democrats over funding for Trump's border wall.

495) April 13, 2019-Trump urged commissioner to shut border.

President Donald Trump last week privately urged Kevin McAleenan, the border enforcement official he was about to name as acting secretary of homeland security, to close the south western border to migrants despite having said publicly that he was delaying a decision in the step for a year. It was not clear what Mr. Trump meant by his request or his additional comment to Mr. McAleenan, that he would pardon him if he encountered any legal problems a result of taking the action. It was another instance of the president trying to undo a decision and to stretch the boundaries of his power, even when told there were legal issues at stake.

496) April 13, 2019-Trump revives idea on sanctuary cities.

President Trump revived and idea of relocating detained immigrants to so-called sanctuary cities, signaling he is couriering previously discarded options amid his growing frustration over the flow of Central American families seeking asylum at the southern U.S. border.

497) April 14, 2019-IRS given deadline to handover Trump's tax returns.

A top House Democrat ratcheted up his demand for access to President Donald Trump's tax returns, telling the IRS that the law clearly gives Congress a right to them. The government's failure to respond by April 23 deadline could send the dispute into federal court. Trump's treasury chief, who oversees the IRS, cited "complicated legal issues" and bemoaned "an arbitrary deadline" set by Congress, while saying he would answer in that time frame.

498) April 15, 2016-House Democrats want to question White House immigration advisor.

House Democrats are sharpening their focus on White House immigration advisor Stephen Miller, with key lawmakers saying he should be brought before congressional committees to testify about his role in recent policy controversies. The Washington Post reported that he played a key role in a plan first discussed last year to release undocumented immigrants into "sanctuary cities" represented by President Donald Trump's Democratic critics. While the plan never came to fruition because of objections from agency officials, Trump has since embraced the idea.

499) April 15, 2019-Buoyed by Attorney General, Trump is unfazed at Mueller report.

The case was closed for President Donald Trump on March 24, the day Attorney General William P. Barr delivered to Congress his four-page summary of the special counsel's 300-plus page report. "No Collusion, No Obstruction, Complete and Total EXONERATION," Mr. Trump wrote on Twitter that day. And in the weeks that followed, the president's message of vindication and revenge on his political antagonists has only intensified, as he has expressed no interest in reading the full report and leveled charges of treason against Democratic lawmakers.

500) April 15, 2019-Shifting Migrants remains possible.

White House Press Secretary Sarah Sanders said that President Donald Trump has asked his administration to take another look at a plan that would send migrant detainees to "sanctuary cities," in retaliation against Trump's political opponents. She said the proposal is not an "ideal solution," but that if the Democrats refuse to negotiate with Trump on border security, the White House is prepared to "put some of those people into their communities" and see how the Democrats react.

501) April 16, 2019-Mueller report set for release.

The Justice Department expects to release a redacted version of special counsel Robert Mueller's report on Donald Trump, his associates and Russia's interference in the 2016 election, setting the stage for further battles in Congress over the politically explosive inquiry. In a four-page letter to Congress, Barr said in March that Mueller <u>"did not find that the Trump campaign or anyone associated with it conspired or coordinated with Russia in its efforts to influence the 2016 U.S. presidential election."</u> Barr's letter also said the special counsel withheld judgement on whether Trump tried to obstruct justice during the investigation.

502) April 17, 2019-Trump vetoes Yemen measure.

President Trump issued the second veto of his presidency, refusing to sign a congressional resolution that would have ended America's role in the Saudi-led war in Yemen. The House and Senate had passed the resolution in a move to admonish the Trump administration over is support for Saudi Arabia. Its passage was a sign of the frustration on Capitol Hill with the Trump administration's support for the kingdom after the death of journalist Jamal Khashoggi at the hands of Saudi agents last year.

503) April 17, 2019-Attorney General Barr withholds bail to migrants seeking asylum.

The Trump administration took another drastic step to discourage migrants from seeking asylum, issuing an order that could keep thousands of them in jail indefinitely while they wait for a resolution of their asylum requests. In an effort to deliver on President Trump's promise to end "catch and release" at the border, Attorney General William P. Barr's order directed immigration judges to no longer allow some migrants who have sought asylum from posting bail. The order will not go into effect for 90 days and is all but certain to be challenged in federal court. But immigrant rights lawyers said it could hugely undermine the basic rights of people seeking safety in the United States.

504) April 18, 2019-Timing of today's release of Mueller report draws fire.

After nearly two years of waiting, America will get some answers straight from Robert Mueller, but not before President Donald Trump's attorney general has his say. The Justice Department is expected to release a redacted version of the special counsel's report on Russian election interference and Trump's campaign, opening up months, if not years, of fights over what the document means in a deeply divided country. Barr formulated the report's roll out and briefed the White House on his plans, according to a White House official who was not authorized to discuss the matter publicly. The White House declined to comment on an ABC News report that it had been briefed in the contents of Mueller's report beyond what Barr has made public.

505) April 19, 2019-Question of obstruction.

The long-awaited report from special counsel Robert Mueller details abundant evidence against President Donald Trump, finding 10 episodes of suspicious behavior, but ultimately concludes it was not Mueller's role to determine whether the commander in chief broke the law. "The evidence we obtained about the president's actions and intent presents difficult issues that would need to be resolved if we were making a traditional prosecutorial judgement," Mueller's team stated in the report. Mueller wrote that he would have exonerated Trump if he could, but he wasn't able to do that given evidence he uncovered. "At the same time, if we had confidence after a thorough investigation of the facts that the President clearly did not commit obstruction of justice, we would so state.

506) April 19, 2019-Mueller report adds to portrait of a man who shouldn't be president.

If President Donald Trump did not obstruct justice, it was not for lack of trying. But this should surprise nobody. The Mueller report, which by no means clears Trump of egregious misconduct. He's a man of low character doing a miserable job. The biggest take-away from the redacted version of special counsel Robert Mueller's report is that Trump repeatedly tried to kill an investigation into his presidential campaign's possible collusion with Russia, but his own people did not follow his orders. For more than two years, Trump has railed against Justice Department investigation, calling for various people to resign or be fired. He so openly attempted to obstruct justice that it no longer felt like obstruction of justice. It felt like Trump being Trump.

507) April 19, 2019-Barr's stance puts him in cross hairs.

President Trump has often said he wanted an attorney general who would protect him. Critics say William Barr, two months into his job as attorney general, is becoming that man. In public remarks before the Mueller report was issued, Mr. Barr several times underlined that the nearly two years old probe found no evidence that anyone affiliated with the Trump campaign coordinated with Russia in election interference in 2016. Without a determination from Mr. Mueller's team about whether Mr. Trump obstructed justice, Mr. Barr along with Deputy Attorney General Rod Rosenstein, made the decision to clear the president of a crime within two days of receiving the report on March 22.

508) April 20, 2019-Trump shifts tone on Mueller.
President Trump declared parts of special counsel Robert Mueller's report "total bullshit" as House Democrats demanded an unreduced version of a document whose findings reverberated through the capital. Mr. Trump in recent weeks had hailed the report as having exonerated him, after Attorney General William Barr in a letter to Congress said the special counsel hadn't established collusion with Russians or decided to charge the president with obstruction of justice. Mr. Trump questioned the authenticity of administration aides' notes that informed their accounts of the president's efforts to interfere in the investigation calling parts of the report "fabricated and totally untrue."

509) April 20, 2019-Mueller report offers no closure.
House Democrats vowed on Friday to pursue the revelations in the special counsel's report on President Trump but drew little Republican support in a nation still deeply polarized over the investigation that has dogged the White House for two years. While Mr. Trump had initially greeted the report as an exoneration, he spent at least part of the day in Florida stewing about disloyal aides who talked with investigators and sounded more defensive than celebratory. He expressed particular unhappiness over the report's inclusion of granular accounts of his efforts to derail the investigation based on FBI interviews and notes of his own advisors. "Statements are made about me by certain people in the Crazy Mueller Report, in itself written by 18 Angry Democrat Trump Haters, which are fabricated and totally untrue." He went on to vow to go after his pursuers, whom he called "some very sick and dangerous people

who have committed very serious crimes, perhaps even spying or treason."

510) April 22, 2019-Trump tariff on washers created jobs at high prices.

President Trump's decision to impose tariffs on imported washing machines has had an odd effect: It raised prices on washing machines, as expected, but also drove up the cost of clothes dryers, which rose by $92 last year. Calculations have been made that the tariffs brought in $82 million to the United States Treasury, while raising consumer prices by $1.5 billion. And while the tariffs did encourage foreign companies to shift more at the manufacturing to the United States and created about 1800 new jobs, the researchers conclude that those come at a step cost, about $817,000 per job.

511) April 22, 2019-Trump fails us as commander in chief.

The President of the United States, like all elected officials and public servants, swears to uphold and defend the Constitution against all enemies. But there is one responsibility the president must bear alone, and that is to act as the commander in chief, the guardian of our national security and defender of our nation from malevolent foreign powers. The Mueller report makes clear that Donald Trump has failed miserable in this sacred obligation. As a candidate and citizen, Trump had a responsibility to put a stop to this unethical and dangerous behavior in his organization. He had an obligation to report it to the FBI and to work with the government to thwart the Russian efforts. Instead he knowingly allowed his campaign and people close to him to continue their contacts with the Russians. Then he spent months lying, encouraging others to cover for him, and gas lighting an entire nation with talk of witch hunts and hoaxes.

512) April 23, 2019-Democrats issue subpoena for McGahn.

The Democratic chairman of the House Judiciary Committee issued a subpoena ordering former White House counsel Donald McGahn to testify before the panel and hand over documents and records pertaining to federal investigations of President Donald Trump, his finances, his campaign, and charges that he sought to obstruct justice. "The special counsel's report even in redacted form, outlines evidence that President Trump engaged in obstruction and other abuses," Judiciary panel Chairman Rep. Jerald Nader said in a statement calling McGahn "a critical witness to many of the allege instances of obstruction of justice and other misconduct described in the Mueller report."

513) April 23, 2019-Trump sues in bid to block subpoena of financial records.

President Donald Trump sued his own accounting firm and the Democratic Chairman of the House Oversight Committee at the same time, trying to con unusual tactic to stop the firm from giving the committee details about Trump's past financial dealings. The move amounts to Trump, the leader of the executive branch of government, asking the judicial branch to stop the legislative branch from investigating his past. A spokeswoman for Mazars (Trump's accounting firm" confirmed that the company had received the lawsuit. "As a firm we will respect this process and will comply with all legal obligations."

514) April 23, 2019-Trump and allies ramp up attacks on McGahn.

Mr. Trump and his surrogates began attacking Mr. McGahn shortly after the report by the special counsel, Robert S. Mueller III, revealed he was the chief witness to the president's attempts to undermine the inquiry. Mr. Trump denied that he ordered Mr. Mueller fired, say he had instead wanted Mr. McGahn to alert the

Justice Department to what the president contended were several conflicts of interest of Mueller. But Mr. McGahn reminded the president that he had indeed told him to fire the special counsel. Mr. McGahn said that he had no choice to reveal to investigators the president's attempt to have Mr. Mueller fired because he was not protected by attorney-client privilege in his role as White House counsel.

515) April 23, 2019-Dems clash with Trump officials.

The struggle between House Democrats and the Trump administration over investigations intensified as a former White House official defied a subpoena and the Treasury Department ignored a deadline for providing President Donald Trump's tax returns. "It appears that the President believes that the constitution does not apply to his White House, that he may order officials at will to violate their legal obligations, and that he may obstruct attempts by Congress to conduct oversight," House Oversight and Reform Committee Chairman Elijah Cummings said in a statement.

516) April 24, 2019-Mnuchin says he'll decide on Trump tax returns by May 6.

Treasury Secretary Steven Mnuchin told a key lawmaker he would make a final decision to whether he will furnish President Donald Trump's tax returns by May 6, committing for the first time to a specific deal in what has become a major Washington power struggle. Mnuchin's resistance is part of a broader Trump administration effort to block myriad congressional investigations into the White House and Trump's business background.

517) April 24, 2019-Are Trump's acts impeachable?

President Trump has been consulting the Constitution. He recited part of Article II, Section 4, and the provision that allows Congress to remove federal officials who commit "treason, bribery, or other high crimes and misdemeanors." Mr. Trump wrote that he had done none of these things: "There were no crimes by me (No Collusion, No Obstruction), so you can't impeach." The president's analysis had two shortcomings. It misstated the conclusion of the report issued by the special counsel, which made no definitive judgement and whether Mr. Trump had violated criminal laws concerning obstruction of justice. And it failed to take account of what the framers meant by "other high crimes and misdemeanors."

518) April 25, 2019-Trump is setting course to battle House Oversight.

The Trump administration escalated its defiance of Congress, as the Justice Department refused to let an official testify on Capitol Hill and President Trump vowed to fight what he called a "ridiculous" subpoena ordering a former top aide to appear before lawmakers. "We're fighting all the subpoenas, these aren't like, important people. The Democrats are trying to win 2020." Mr. Trump's flurry of moves to block multiple congressional investigations signaled a new phase of constitutional friction that could redefine long murky boundaries of Congress power to conduct oversight of the executive branch and the power of presidents to keep government affairs secret from lawmakers.

519) April 26, 2019-Trump disputes Mueller claim.

President Trump said in a tweet that he never asked then-White House Counsel Robert Mueller directly contradicting a detailed account in Mr. Mueller's report. "As has been reported incorrectly by the Fake News Media, I never told then White House Counsel Dan McGahn to fire Robert Mueller, even though I had the legal right to do so," Mr. Trump wrote on Twitter. "If I wanted to fire Mueller, I didn't need McGahn to do it, I could have done it myself."

520) April 27, 2019-President says U.S. didn't pay for release of Warmbier.

President Trump said the U.S. didn't pay a $2 million hospital bill presented by North Korea or make any other payment to Pyongyang when it secured the release of American college student Otto Warmbier in 2017. The Washington Post reported that Mr. Trump authorized a government official to sign off on a $2 million invoice issued by the North Koreans as a condition of Mr. Warmbier's release.

521) April 28, 2019-Trump cheers economy, mocks candidates at rally.

President Donald Trump cheered the thriving U.S. economy and criticized his Democratic presidential opponents. Trump warned his supporters that Democrats would take away their guns, promised anew to build a wall along the U.S. border with Mexico and pledged to come up with a plan for healthcare after the next election. Trump has long derided the news media as "fake news" and "the enemy of the people."

522) April 29, 2019-Ending family separation has led to disaster at border, Trump says.

President Donald Trump said that ending the practice of separating children from their families at border crossings has been "a disaster" that has resulted in a surge of people coming into the country illegally, though he overstated the increase as measured by the government. Trump said the practice had served as an effective "disincentive" for people who wish to enter the country illegally.

523) April 30, 2019-Trump's anti-abortion incitement.

Donald Trump's false and misleading claims hit a milestone, topping 10,000. His untruths, which lately average almost two dozen a day, have long since stopped being news, becoming instead irritating background noise. He told a particularly lurid lie about infanticide at a political rally in Wisconsin. Trump described a hideous scenario that he insists Democrats approve of. "The baby is born," said Trump. "The mother meets with the doctor, they take care of the baby, and they wrap the baby beautifully," at this time, he seemed to mime rocking an infant, "and then the doctor and the mother determine whether or not they will execute the baby." He made a chopping motion with his hand.

524) April 30, 2019-Battle intensifies on subpoena requests.

With President Trump vowing to "fight all the subpoenas," Democrats have aggressively issued subpoenas since taking over the House, including calling for an unreacted version of special counsel Robert Mueller's report on Russian interference in the 2016 election and any obstruction of justice by Mr. Trump. The White House and Justice Department have ordered several and former administration officials not to testify. Moreover, lawyers representing Mr. Trump's real estate business are suing to stop his accounting firm from giving his financial records to Congress.

525) May 1, 2019-Mueller at odds with Barr's view of investigation.

Robert S. Mueller III, the special counsel, wrote a letter in late March to Attorney General William P. Barr objecting to his early description of the Russia investigation's conclusions that appeared to clear President Trump on possible obstruction of justice. The letter adds to the growing evidence of a rift between them and is another sign of the anger among the special counsel's investigators about Mr. Barr's characterization of their findings, which allowed Mr. Trump to wrongly claim he had been vindicated.

526) May 2, 2019-Attorney General, Democrat clash over Mueller report.

Attorney General William Barr criticized Robert Mueller's decision not to reach a conclusion about whether President Trump obstructed justice during a contentious hearing that laid bare a rift between him and the special counsel over the politically charged investigation. When Mr. Mueller, driven largely by Justice Department policy against indicting a sitting president, declined in his report to make a recommendation about whether Mr. Trump obstructed justice during the investigation. Mr. Barr determined the special counsel's evidence was insufficient to establish Mr. Trump committed a crime.

527) May 3, 2019-Pelosi says Barr lied to Congress.

Speaker accuses the attorney general of a crime. House Speaker Nancy Pelosi accused Attorney General William Barr of misleading Congress in appearances on Capitol Hill. "He lied to Congress, if anybody else did that, it would be considered a crime. Nobody is above the law." At issue is Mr. Barr's testimony April 9 before the House in which he professed ignorance about reported complaints from the special counsel's team over Mr. Barr's handling of the public roll out of the report. It is now known that Mr. Mueller himself raised concerns in March 25 and March 27 letters to Mr. Barr about the attorney general's characterization of Mr. Mueller's report in a four-page summary that Mr. Barr sent to Congress. The second letter was followed by a phone call between the two.

528) May 4, 2019- 'Russian Hoax' is joke shared in call to Putin.

President Donald Trump telephoned President Vladimir V. Putin of Russia for what both men described as a lengthy conversation, in which they dismissed two years of investigations into Russia's interference in the 2016 presidential campaign as a "Russian Hoax" and a mountain that <u>"ended up being a mouse."</u> Mr. Trump's dismissal of Russian election interference runs counter to the assessments of the nation's intelligence agencies as well as Mr. Mueller's report, while his characterization of Mr. Putin's role in Venezuela contradicts the views of his own top advisors. They accuse Russia of propping up the Venezuelan president, Nicholas Maduro, in defiance of an American led pressure campaign to force him from his power.

529) May 5, 2019- 'Own the Center-Left' Pelosi tells Democrats or risk a disputed win.

Speaker Nancy Pelosi does not believe President Donald Trump can be removed through impeachment, the only way to do it, she said this past week is to defeat him in 2020 by a margin so "big" he cannot challenge the legitimacy of a Democratic victory. <u>"We have to inoculate against that, we have to be prepared for that,"</u> as she discussed her concern that Mr. Trump would not give up power voluntarily if he lost re-election by a slim margin next year. "Our passions were for health care, bigger paychecks, cleaner government.

530) May 5, 2019- 'Investigate the investigators in new Trump rallying cry.

For President Donald Trump's re-election effort, "Investigate the investigators." Is becoming the new "Lock her up." Trump has long sought to paint his political opponents as criminally suspect, spending much of 2016 leading "lock her up!" chants that targeted his Democratic rival, Hillary Clinton. After Trump's own conduct became the subject of Mueller's criminal investigation, which did not establish that his campaign conspired with Russia's election interference but indicated that he may have obstructed justice, the president is aiming to change the narrative by highlighting the allegations of improper spying by the FBI.

531) May 5, 2019-Low key aide's notes aided Mueller.

The notes scribbled rapidly on a legal pad, captured the fear inside the White House when President Donald Trump raged over the Russia investigation and decreed, he was firing the FBI director who led it. "Is this the beginning of the end?" The public airing of the notes, which document the-White House counsel Donald McGahn' s contemporaneous account of events and his fear that the president was engaged in legally risky conduct, has infuriated from a news report in February 2018 that McGahn kept a written record of their encounters, according to Mueller's report. "Watch out for the people that take so-called 'notes' when the notes never existed until needed," Trump tweeted a day after the release of special counsel Robert Mueller's report.

532) May 6, 2019-Trump issues Tariff threat.

President warning to China takes Beijing by surprise and could imperil talks this week. President Trump threatened to drastically ramp up U.S. tariffs on Chinese imports, a surprise twist that put an accord in doubt Beijing considered pulling out of talks scheduled to begin this week in a pair of Twitter messages, Mr. Trump wrote he planned to raise levels on 200 billion in Chinese imports to 25% starting Friday, from 10% currently. He also wrote he would impose 25% tariffs "shortly" on $325 billion in Chines goods that haven't yet been taxed.

533) May 6, 2019-Trump opposes letting Mueller offer testimony.

President Trump reversed himself and said that the special counsel, Robert S. Mueller III, should not testify before Congress, setting up a potentially explosive confrontation with Democrats over presidential authority and the separation of powers. The president argued on Twitter that Mr. Mueller's report on Russian interference in the 2016 election, which found no conspiracy between Moscow and Mr. Trump's campaign but did not exonerate the president on obstruction of justice, was conclusive and that Congress and the American people did not need to hear from Mr. Mueller. "Bob Mueller should not testify," he said, "No redo for the Dems."

534) May 7, 2019-Tax returns and Barr subpoena fuel latest clash on Capitol Hill.

The Trump administration ruled out turning over President Trump's tax returns to the White House and girded for a contempt of Congress resolution against Attorney General William P. Barr. Mr. Trump and his administration resisted the Democrats' oversight efforts on multiple fronts. Treasury Secretary Steven Mnuchin told the chairman of the House Ways and Means Committee, Richard E. Neal of Massachusetts, that he would not grant access to six years of personal and business tax returns. He said the demand "lacks a legitimate legislative purpose," a view that Democrats are almost certain to contest in court. The Democrats were already moving against Mr. Barr.

535) May 8, 2019-Ex-White House lawyer defies House subpoena.

Former White House counsel Dan McGahn defied a House Judiciary panel subpoena for materials he provided special counsel Robert Mueller, raising the specter of a legal fight as President Donald Trump pushes back against Democratic-led investigations. McGahn's refusal to provide the documents came at the instruction of the White House which suggested they could be subject to executive privilege. Such a claim con shield some presidential material from disclosure.

536) May 9, 2019-Senate calls son of president to testify.

The Senate Intelligence Committee has subpoenaed Donald Trump Jr., the president's oldest son, who met with Russians in June 2016 after being promised political dirt about Hillary Clinton. The move by the Republican-led committee is a sign that some members of the president's party are not aligned with his desire for a swift end to all of the Russia inquiries.

537) May 9, 2019-Panel urges contempt for Barr as president asserts privilege.
The House Judiciary Committee voted to hold Attorney General William Barr in contempt as the Democratic led chamber and President Trump continued along a collision course over special counsel Robert Mueller's report. The conflict is now expected to lead to federal court and a legal battle with few precedents.

538) May 11, 2019-China Trade talks end without deal.
Beijing plans to retaliate on tariffs. Chinese trade negotiations failed to break on impasse following two days of globally watched trade talks, as both sides tried to prevent sentiment from detreating further. President Trump said newly imposed 25% U.S. tariffs on $200 billion in Chinese imports would remain in place pending future negotiations.

539) May 12, 2019-Trump's defiance testing Congress over-sight role.
President Donald Trump and his allies are working to block more than 20 separate investigations by Democrats into his actions as president, his personal finances and his administration's policies. Trump's noncooperation strategy has shifted from partial resistance to all-out war as he faces mounting inquiries from the Democratic controlled House, a strategy that many legal and congressional experts fear could undermine the institutional power of Congress. All told, House Democrats say the Trump administration has failed to respond to or comply with at least 79 requests for documents or other information. The president is blocking aides from testifying,

refusing entire document request from some committees, filing lawsuits against corporations to bar them from responding to subpoenas and asserting executive privilege to keep information about the special counsel's Russia investigation from public view.

540) May 12, 2019- House Dem subpoenas Trump's tax returns.

A top House Democrat issued subpoenas for six years of President Donald Trump's tax returns. Ways and Means Committee Chairman Richard Neal, D. Mass., issued the subpoenas days after Mnuchin refused to comply with demands to turn over Trumps returns. Mnuchin told the panel he wouldn't provide Trump's tax records because the panel's request "lacks a legitimate legislative purpose," as Supreme Court precedent requires.

541) May 12, 2019- On global stage, a whole world of trouble.

"We've made a decisive break from the failed foreign policy establishment that sacrificed our sovereignty, surrendered our jobs and tied us down to endless foreign wars." "In everything we do, we are now putting America first."

Still Trump has plenty of unfinished business. Since taking office, he has specialized in publicly hectoring friendly partners, embracing foes and resisting too much advice. Critics have labeled him an unreliable force, while allies say he has followed through on a promise to disrupt foreign policy.

542) May 13, 2019-Tariffs on China will exact cost for both sides.

President Donald Trump' Chief Economic Advisor said that American consumers would bear some pain from the escalating trade war with China, Mr. Trump's claim that his tariffs are a multi-billion-dollar, mostly one-way payment by China to the American Treasury. "In fact, both sides will pay, both sides will suffer on this."

Mr. Kudlow's acknowledgment of economic pain, while widely shared by economists, contradicted the president's view that trade wars are easy to win and that the burden falls disproportionately on America's trading partners.

543) May 14, 2019-Beijing hits back with tariffs.

The United States and China traded blows in the latest escalation of their tariff war, unnerving Wall Street and threatening to draw American consumers into the fray for the first time. Both nations, which just days earlier had anticipated sealing a comprehensive commercial deal, instead took steps to raise new trade barriers. In Beijing, the Chinese government announced plans to impose tariffs on $60 billion in American products in retaliation for U.S. tariffs that President Donald Trump increased. Trump, meanwhile, began the process of expanding U.S. tariffs to cover all $540 billion in Chinese imports, a potentially seismic jolt to the global economy that is expected to raise prices for everyday products such as cellphones, sunglasses, cameras, and televisions. There will be price hikes at Target, Costco, Home Depot, and Walmart. The importers are going to pass on some or all of the tariff to the consumer, and that will become much more readily apparent and harder to mask.

544) May 15, 2019-Trump: Farmers bailout coming.

President Donald Trump rushed to placate furious farmers and Senate Republicans about his escalating trade war with China, with lawmakers now considering a package of fresh bailout funds to quell a rebellion in agricultural states. Trump suggested the standoff could last years and lead to structural charges in the global economy. Trump offered conflicting forecast, musing that a deal could come next month but also predicting a furious economic battle with Beijing.

545) May 15, 2019-Judge skeptical of Trump bid over financial files.

A federal judge in Washington expressed astonishment at arguments raised by President Donald Trump's lawyers seeking to block his accounting firm from turning over years of financial records to the Democratic-controlled House Oversight and Reform Committee and seemed to signal a swift ruling in favor of lawmakers.

546) May 16, 2019-Trump's plan upends rules on migration.

President Trump will unveil a plan to overhaul parts of the nation's immigration system that would impose new security measures at the border and significantly increase the educational and skills requirements for people allowed to migrate to the United States. The proposal would vastly scale back the system of family-based immigration that for decades has allowed immigrants to bring their spouses and children to live with them. In its place, it would provide new opportunities for immigrants who have specific skills or job offers to work in the United States, provided they can demonstrate proficiency and educational attainment, and pass a civics exam. The proposal calls for construction of some of the border wall that is a preoccupation of Mr. Trump's and vehemently opposed by Democrats and upends family-based migration in ways that Democrats and immigrant advocates have long opposed.

547) May 17, 2019-Trump pushes for 'merit' system.

Immigration plan favors point system over family policy. President Donald Trump said the he wanted to provide a sharp contrast with Democrats by aiming to upend decades of family-based immigration policy with a new approach that favors younger, "totally brilliant," high skilled workers he says won't compete for U.S. jobs. "We want immigrants coming in. We cherish the open door." Trump said his new system with points given for those with advanced degrees, job offers, and other attributes, will make it exactly clear what standards we ask you to achieve."

548) May 17, 2019-Mr. Trump's 'bold' immigration plan.

"This is the big, beautiful, bold plan, the most complete and effective security package ever assembled, sweeping modernization of our dysfunctional legal immigration process." Should Democrats somehow fail to embrace and enact his plan, the president had an answer. "We will get it approved immediately after the election, when we take back the House, keep the Senate, and of course, hold the presidency."

549) May 18, 2019-Trump removes tariffs on metal from two allies.

President Donald Trump agreed to lift tariffs on metal imports from Mexico and Canada, removing a major irritant for two important allies that in exchange agreed to stop punishing American farmers with their own takes on pork, cheese, and milk. At the same time Mr. Trump postpones a decision on whether to impose tariffs on automobiles imported from Europe, Japan, and other countries for six months, setting a tight deadline for the United States to reach trade deals that have so far proved elusive.

550) May 18, 2019-Trump says he should have been told about Flynn.

President Trump, who waited several weeks to oust then national security advisor Mike Flynn after learning that federal investigators were examining his activities, complained that he wasn't warned early enough, that Mr. Flynn was under investigation. It now seems that General Flynn was under investigation long before was common knowledge, "why was I not told so that I could make a change?" Mr. Trump received several warnings about Flynn soon after his election. On November 10, 2016, President Obama warned him against hiring Flynn as his national security advisor, citing Mr. Flynn checkered service as head of the Defense Intelligence Agency. A week later, Mr. Trump announced he had chosen Mr. Flynn for the National Security Advisor job.

551) May 19, 2019-Michigan GOP congressman: Trump's conduct 'impeachable'

Representative Justin Amash, R-Mich., a critic of President Donald Trump, became the first Republican congressman to say the president "engaged in impeachable conduct" based on the Mueller report. Amash wrote that after reading the 448-page report, he had concluded that not only did Mueller's team show Trump attempting to obstruct justice, but that Attorney General William Barr had "deliberately misrepresented" the findings. "Contrary to Barr's portrayal, Mueller's report reveals that Trump engaged in specific actions and a pattern of behavior that meet the threshold for impeachment," Amish wrote.

552) May 20, 2019-Trump activity raised red flag inside his bank.

Anti-money laundering specialist at Deutsche Bank recommended in 2016 and 2017 that multiple transactions involving legal entities controlled by Donald J. Trump and his son-in-law Jared Kushner, be reported to a federal financial watchdog. The transactions, some of which involved Mr. Trump's now defunct foundation, set off alerts in a computer system designed to detect illicit activity, according to five current and former back employees. Compliance staff members who then reviewed the transactions prepared so-called suspicious activity reports that they believed should be sent to a unit of the Treasury Department that polices financial crimes. But executives at Deutsche Bank, which has lent billions of dollars to the Trump and Kushner companies, rejected their employee's advice. The reports were never filed with the government. The nature of the transactions was not clear. At least some of them involved money flowing back and forth with overseas entities or individuals, which bank employees considered suspicious.

553) May 21, 2019-President bars McGahn testimony.
President Donald Trump directed former White House Counsel Don McGahn to rebuff a congressional subpoena to testify, escalating a standoff over a key witness to the president's efforts to curtail and shut down the special counsel's Russia investigation. The Trump administration has repeatedly blocked congressional Democrats' subpoenas and requests for documents and testimony since Democrats took control of the House in January. Mr. Trump has said he plans to fight "all the subpoenas."

554) May 21, 2019-Judge: Trump can't stop subpoena of his records.
A federal judge denied President Donald Trump's bid to quash a House subpoena for years of his financial records from his accounting firm and stayed his order seven days to give the president's lawyer's time to appeal. "So long as Congress investigates on a subject matter on which legislation could be had; Congress acts as contemplated by Article I of the Constitution, "District Judge Amit Mehta said in a 41-page opinion.

555) May 21, 2019-Secrecy battle builds as judge rebuffs Trump.
The fight over President Trump's systematic stonewalling of Congress escalated on two fronts, as a federal judge upheld a subpoena for his financial records even as the White House instructed its former top lawyer to defy a subpoena to testify before lawmakers. In the first court test of Mr. Trump's vow to resist "all" subpoenas by White House Democrats, a judge ruled that his accounting firm, Mazars USA, must turn over his financial records to Congress,

rejecting his lawyers argument that lawmakers had no legitimate power to demand files.

556) May 22, 2019-Calls swell for Trump impeachment probe.
More Democrats are calling for impeachment proceedings against President Donald Trump after his latest defiance of Congress by blocking his former White House lawyer from testifying. "We are confronting what might be the largest broadest cover up in American history," House Majority Leader Steny Hoyer told reporters. If a House inquiry "leads to other avenues including impeachment, so be it." As Democrats weigh their options, Trump is almost taunting them by testing the bounds of executive power in ways few other administrations have. The White House contends that even former employees like McGahn do not have to abide by subpoenas from Congress.

557) May 23, 2019-President walks out on Pelosi, Schumer.
President Trump said he wouldn't work with Democrats while investigations of him continue and abruptly ended a meeting with the party's leaders, casting fresh doubt on a divided Washington's ability to complete big-ticket legislation in the next 18 months.

558) May 23, 2019- Trump records move 2 steps toward light.
For three years, Donald J. Trump has treated the details of his personal and business finances as a closely guarded secret. A federal judge in Manhattan ruled against a request from President Trump to block his longtime lender, Deutsche Bank, firm complying with congressional subpoenas seeking his detailed financial records. In Albany, New York lawmakers approved a bill that would allow Congress to obtain Mr. Trumps state tax returns.

559) May 23, 2019- Trump: Drop inquiries or no deals.

President Donald Trump informed Democratic leaders that he wouldn't work with them on shared priorities such as infrastructure and bringing down the cost of prescription drugs unless they abandoned investigations into his presidency. Trump said he told House Speaker Nancy Pelosi and Senate Minority Leader Charles Schumer at a White House meeting that it would be impossible to go forward on discussions while "phony" congressional investigations hang over his administration.

560) May 24, 2019-Farmers stung by trade strife, get $16 billion.

President Trump unveiled a $16 billion bailout for famers hurt by his trade war with Beijing. Mr. Trump, flanked by farmers in cowboy hats said, China had "taken advantage" of the United Sates for far too long and vowed to protect an industry that has been "used as a vehicle" by Beijing to hurt American economy. "Farmers have been attacked by China" Mr. Trump said, adding that if the United States is in a trade war, "We're winning it big."

561) May 24, 2019-Trump slams Rex Tillerson as 'dumb as a rock'.

President Donald Trump lashed out at former Secretary of State Rex Tillerson, calling him 'dumb as a rock' and claiming the former diplomat lied when he claimed that Russian President Vladimir Putin was more prepared than Trump for a meeting in Germany. "Rex Tillerson, a man who is 'dumb as a rock' and totally ill prepared and ill equipped to be Secretary of State, made up a story (he got fired) that I was out prepared by Vladimir Putin at a meeting in Hamburg Germany," Trump wrote on Twitter. "I don't think Putin would agree, look how the U.S. is doing.

562) May 24, 2019-U.S. plans more troops for Middle East.
The Trump administration is planning to send several thousand additional troops to the Middle East and is moving toward a decision to rush billions of dollars in weapons to allies in the region. Meanwhile, the Trump administration expected to declare an emergency under U.S. arms-control laws amid the increased tensions with Iran, a step that would allow it to sidestep normal congressional review and rush billions of dollars in weapons to key Middle East allies. The declaration is expected to come by week's end, allowing the U.S. to move ahead with weapons sales to Saudi Arabia and the United Arab Emirates.

563) May 24, 2019-Barr gets power to declassify probe Intel.
President Donald Trump empowered the U.S. attorney general to declassify information about the origins of the investigations into Russia's election meddling, escalating a probe that the president has said would show crimes committed by his political opponents. "Today's action will help ensure that all Americans learn the truth about the events that occurred, and the actions that were taken, during the last presidential election and will restore confidence in our public institutions, the White House said in a statement.

564) May 25, 2019-Order to review secrets pits CIA vs. Justice Department.
President Trump's order allowing Attorney General William P. Barr to declassify any intelligence that led to the Russia investigation sets up a potential confrontation with the CIA. It effectively strips the agency of its most critical power: choosing which secrets it shares and which ones remain hidden. Mr. Trump said that he wanted Mr. Barr to "get to the bottom" of what the intelligence agencies knew about the investigation into his campaign. He promised, "We're exposing everything."

565) May 25, 2019-Trump allows weapons sales to Gulf allies.
President Trump circumvented Congress by declaring an emergency war over Iran and moving forward with arms sales to Saudi Arabia, the United Arab Emirates and Jordan that had been blocked by Congress since last year. Mr. Trump also announced that he would order about 1,500 additional troops to the Middle East to increase protection of those American forces already there. The weapons sales decision immediately drew criticism from lawmakers, who are also furious over the civilian death toll from the Saudi led air campaign in Yemen.

566) May 25, 2019-Critics fear Trump freed AG to blur probes origin.
Intelligence professionals warned that President Donald Trump's decision to give his loyal Attorney General Carte Blanch to disclose still secret material from the Russian investigation will let William Barr cherry pick intelligence to paint a misleading picture about what started the probe. The president claims his campaign was spied upon, through Trump administration officials have said they have no specific evidence that anything illegal was done when the campaign came under FBI surveillance approved by a court. Trump gave Barr full authority to publicly disclose information about the origins of the investigation that the president reportedly has dismissed as a "hoax."

567) May 26, 2019-Trump vows to appeal ruling blocking key sections.
A federal judge has blocked President Donald Trump from building key sections of his border wall with money secured under his declaration of a national emergency, delivering what may prove a temporary setback on one of his highest priorities. U.S. District Judge Hayward Gillian Jr.'s order, prevents work from beginning on two of the highest priority, Pentagon-funded wall projects, and one

spanning 46 miles in New Mexico and another covering 5 miles in Yuma, Arizona. Trump pledged to file an expedited appeal on the ruling.

568) May 27, 2019-Dems, Republicans criticize presidents 'confidence.'

Members of both parties criticized President Donald Trump's handling of North Korea after the president tweeted that he has "confidence" in Kim Jong Un. "North Korea fired off some small weapons, which disturbed some of my people, and others, but not me. I have confidence that Chairman Kim will keep his promise to me."

569) May 28, 2019-In climate fight Trump will put science on trial.

President Trump has rolled back environmental regulations, pulled the United States out of the Paris climate accord, brushed aside dire predictions about the effect of climate change, and turned the term "global warming" into a punch line rather than a prognosis. In the next few months, the White House will complete the rollback of the most significant effort to curb greenhouse-gas emissions, initiated during the Obama administration. And, in what could be Mr. Trump's most consequential action yet, his administration will seek to undermine the very science on which climate change policy rests.

570) May 29, 2019-Trump diverges from key advisor on Iran and Kim.

President Trump was grousing about John R. Bolton, his National Security Advisor. Guest heard the president complaining about the advice he was getting and wondering if Mr. Bolton was taking him down a path he did not want to go. Mr. Trump and his national security advisor has spilled over into public, sowing confusion around the world about America's foreign policy, particularly on matters of war and peace. The president declared that, unlike his national security advisor, he was not seeking regime change in Iran and he asserted that, contrary to what Mr. Bolton had said, recent North Korean missile tests did not violate United Nations resolutions.

571) May 30, 2019-Breaking silence, Mueller declines to absolve Trump.

Robert S. Mueller III, the special counsel, declined to clear President Trump of obstruction of justice in his first public characterization of his two-year investigation of Russia's interference in the 2016 presidential election. "If we had confidence that the president clearly did not commit a crime, we would have said so."

572) May 30, 2019-Mueller shifts burden to Congress.

Special Counsel Robert Mueller said if he had confidence President Trump didn't commit a crime, he "would have said so," suggesting in his first public remarks on the Russian investigation that it was Congress's job to formally accuse a sitting president of wrong doing.

573) May 31, 2019-Trump prepares Mexico tariffs.

President Trump said the U.S. would impose escalating tariffs on all Mexican imports beginning June 10, in an effort to push the country to deter the flow of asylum-seeking Central American families to the southern border. The president said the tariff on America's third largest trading partner would begin at 5% and grow steadily, hitting 25% by October 1 unless Mexico takes satisfactory action to halt migrants.

574) May 31, 2019-Trump accuses counsel of a personal vendetta.

President Trump lashed out angrily at Robert S. Mueller III accusing him of pursuing a personal vendetta as Mr. Trump sought to counter increasing calls among Democrats for his impeachment.

A day after Mr. Mueller, the special counsel, spoke out for the first time and refused to exonerate the president, Mr. Trump dismissed the Mueller investigation as hopelessly tarnished and expressed aggravation that he could have dogged him since the early days of his administration.

575) May 31, 2019-Trump erupts after Mueller says he's not exonerated.

President Donald Trump angrily assailed special counsel Robert Mueller's motives, a day after Mueller bluntly rebuffed Trump's repeated claims the Russia investigation had cleared him of obstructing justice. Trump tweeted he had "nothing to do with Russia helping me get elected." Mueller's report said Russia interfered in the election in hopes of getting Trump elected. Then on the White House South Lawn, Trump told reporters: "Russia did not help me get elected. You know who got me elected? You know who got me elected? I got me elected. Russia didn't help me at all."

576) June 1, 2019-Tariffs on Mexico will hit cars, heavy equipment hard.

Mexico is an integral part of the U.S. economy. It's the source of most of America's imported beer and tractors, to say nothing of the rest of the $346.5 billion in goods it sent the U.S last year. All those goods may soon be hit with a 5% tariff. President Donald Trump said the tariffs will begin at 5% on June 10th. They will rise on additional five percentage points each month until they hit 25% on Oct 1. Those tariffs will remain elevated "until Mexico substantially stops the illegal inflow of aliens coming through its territory," the White House said.

577) June 1, 2019-Trump's Mexico threat jolts GOP, law-makers and spooks the market.

President Trump's threat to punish Mexico with tariffs until it restrains the flow of migrant's rattled financial markets, and the Mexican government, American businesses and Republican law-makers pressed Mr. Trump to back down. Two of Mr. Trump's top economic advisors, including his trade representative, Robert Lighthizer, raised concerns about the tariffs.

578) June 1, 2019-President is betting the American economy on one tariff threat after another.

President is upending the United States economy and perhaps jeopardizing his re-election prospects with an abrupt escalation of protectionist trade policies. Mr. Trump announced that he would soon impose a 5% tariff on imports from Mexico, which could quickly grow to 25%, unless Mexican officials stop the flow of immigrants across America's southern border. The move capped a furious month of cross-border tariff threats that has rattled investors and raised economist concerns about a slowdown in global growth.

579) June 3, 2019-Trump's Mexico threat spooks companies.

The trade fight between the U.S. and China has pushed firms to shift manufacturing to Mexico to avoid tariffs and keep prices steady. Now the prospect of new U.S. tariffs over immigration threatens to disrupt that shift and drive up cost for American consumers. If the U.S. begins hitting Mexico with steep tariffs, as President Trump last week threatened to do unless the country stems cross-border migrant flows, companies will start running out of options for affordable products.

580) June 4, 2019-Mexico tries to alter rush towards tariffs.

Mexico launched a counter-offensive against the threat of U.S. tar-iffs, warning not only that it would hurt the economies of both countries but also could cause a quarter-million more Central Americans to migrate North, making the case against the threat by President Donald Trump of levying a 5% tariff on Mexico imports by June 10. Trump asserts Mexico has taken advantage of the United States for decades but that the abuse will end when he slaps tariffs on Mexico imports.

581) June 5, 2019-GOP senators warn against tariffs.
Defiant Republican senators warned Trump administration officials that they were prepared to block the president's effort to impose tariffs on Mexican imports, threatening to assemble a veto-proof majority to mount their m since he took office.

582) June 5, 2019-Pressured by president, Republican push back on Mexico tariff threat.
Republican senators sent the White House a sharp message warning that they were almost uniformly opposed to President Trump's plans to impose tariffs on Mexican imports, just hours after the president said lawmakers would be "foolish" to try to stop him.

583) June 6, 2019-President warns of fading chance for Mexico deal.
The United States barreled closer to imposing tariffs on all the Mexican imports as high stakes negotiations at the White House failed to immediately resolve President Trump's demand that Mexico prevent a surge of Central America migrants from flowing across the south western border. Mr. Trump declared on Twitter that "not nearly enough" progress had been made and warned that "if no agreement is reached tariffs of the 5% level will begin on Monday, with monthly increases as per schedule.

584) June 6, 2019-Programs for child migrants halted.

The Trump administration is canceling English classes, recreational programs, and legal aid for unaccompanied minors staying in federal migrant shelters nationwide, saying the immigration influx at the southern border has created budget pressures.

585) June 7, 2019-Trump signs $19.1 billion bill takes credit for aid to Puerto Rico.

President Donald Trump signed a $19.1 billion disaster relief bill and took credit for aid to Puerto Rico, assistance he had opposed for months that caused long delays in getting help to states. Trump tweeted photos of himself holding the signed bill and wrote, "Just signed disaster Aid Bill to help Americans who have been hit by recent catastrophic storms. So important for our GREAT America farmers and ranchers. Help for GA, FL, IA, NE, NC, and CA." "Puerto Rico should love President Donald Trump. Without me, they would have been shut out!"

Chapter 8

586) June 7, 2019-In lead up to D-Day tribute, Trump blasts Mueller and Pelosi.

President Donald Trump called former special counsel Robert Mueller "a fool" and derided House Speaker Nancy Pelosi as "a disaster" during a television interview conducted at the site of a solemn ceremony in France commemorating the 75th anniversary of the D-Day invasion. Trump said that Mueller, a former Marine who served in Vietnam, had made "such a fool out of himself" last week when he made a public statement regarding his investigation into Russian election interference. Trump also referred to Pelosi as "Nervous Nancy."

587) June 8, 2019-Deal might put bombs' secret in Saudi hands.

When the Trump administration declared an emergency last month and fast tracked the sale of more American arms to Saudi Arabia, it did more that anger members of Congress who opposed the sale on humanitarian grounds. It also raised concerns that the Saudi's could gain access to technology that would let them produce their own versions of American precision guided bombs, weapons they have used in strikes on civilians since they began fighting a war in Yemen four years ago.

588) June 8, 2019-Tariffs on Mexico averted.
President Donald Trump announced that a deal was in place that would avert threatened tariffs on Mexican imports in exchange for Mexico taking "strong measures" to curb the influx of Central American migrants at the U.S. southern border.

589) June 10, 2019-Threats are part of Trumps playbook.
President Trump's threat to impose tariffs on Mexico was met with alarm from business leaders and many in his own party who responded with corresponding relief when the threat was withdrawn. No one, however, should have been surprised. Using threats of punitive action against allies to force negotiation has become a staple of Mr. Trump's diplomatic playbook, from dangling the prospect of U.S. withdrawal from the North Atlantic Treaty Organization if Western nations didn't increase their contribution to, in this case, hitting one of the U.S.'s largest trading partners with tariffs if it didn't do more to stem migration across the southern U.S. border. As Mr. Trump views it, the threat creates leverage and leverage strengthens the U.S.'s hand. In his 1987 book "The Art of the Deal," he wrote: "The best thing you can do is deal from strength, and leverage is the biggest strength you can have."

590) June 10, 2019-Trump claims secret in deal with Mexico, defying news.
President Trump asserted that there were secret, undisclosed elements to his new immigration agreement with Mexico as he sought to deflect criticism that he achieved less than he had claimed with his threat to impose punitive tariffs.

591) June 11, 2019-Hailing tariffs as win, Trump ponders more.
President Trump has concluded his tariff threat worked and Mexico to stop the flow of migrants. He pivoted back his to his trade fight

with China and vowed to hit Beijing with more tariffs if it did not accede to America's trade demands. "The China deal's going to work out," Mr. Trump said in an interview on CNBC. "You know why? Because of tariffs. Because right now China is getting absolutely decimated by companies that are leaving China, going to other countries, including our own, because they don't want to pay the tariffs."

592) June 11, 2019-Trump: Federal Reserve is 'very destructive to us.'

President Donald Trump complained that President Xi Jinping enjoys a major advantage in the U.S.-China trade war in that he controls China's central bank while Trump must deal with a Federal Reserve that is "very destructive to us." Trump noted that China's president, by contrast, is essentially head of the Chinese central bank. "He can do whatever he wants," Trump said. "We have people on the Fed that really weren't, you know, they're not my people."

593) June 11, 2019-Mexico denies Trump's claim of secret concessions in deal.

Three days after U.S. President Donald Trump announced a deal with Mexico to stem the flow of migrants at the southern border; the two countries appear unable to agree exactly what's in it. Stung by criticism that the agreement mostly ramps up border protection efforts already underway, Trump hinted at other; secret agreements he says will soon be revealed.

594) June 11, 2019-President levels new tariff threat against China.

President Donald Trump threatened to impose large tariffs in $300 billion in imports if Chinese leader Xi Jinping didn't meet with him in Japan later this month, showing he plans to immediately pivot from his trade war with Mexico back to Beijing. "We do not want a trade war, but we are not afraid of fighting one. If the U.S. is ready to have equal consultations, our door is open. But if it insists on escalating trade frictions, we will respond to it with resolution and perseverance," said Geng Shuang, spokesman for China's Ministry of Foreign Affairs.

595) June 12, 2019-Trump insists he has secret deal but gives no details.

President Trump waved a piece of paper that he said was part of a "very long and very good" secret agreement with Mexico, refusing to describe it but vowing that it will go into effect whenever he wants it too. Mr. Ebrard, Mexico's foreign minister, insisted that such a deal has not been reached with the United States, saying only that the two sides have agreed to potentially revisit the issue in the future.

596) June 12, 2019-House votes to allow panel to take Barr, McGahn to court.

The House took its strongest step yet in the standoff with President Donald Trump over congressional oversight, voting to seek court enforcement of subpoenas for Attorney General William Barr and former White House counsel Donald McGahn. The House passed a resolution that would empower the House Judiciary Committee to go to court against Barr and McGahn over non-compliance with requests for documents and testimony.

597) June 13, 2019-Trump clamps lid on documents.

President Donald Trump asserted executive privilege to keep secret the documents related to adding a citizenship question to the census as a House panel voted to hold two cabinet members in contempt for defying subpoenas for the documents.

598) June 13, 2019-Trump said he'd listen to foreign in formants.

President Trump said that his campaign might be willing to accept information from foreign governments that was damaging to his 2020 rivals, adding that he might not divulge such information to the Federal Bureau of Investigation. "It's not an interference, they have information, and I think I'd take it, if I thought there was something wrong. I'd go maybe to the FBI, if I thought there was something wrong." But Mr. Trump maintained that he believed there wasn't anything wrong with listening. "If somebody called from a country, Norway (and said) 'we have information on your opponent', oh, I think I'd want to hear."

599) June 14, 2019-Pelosi rips Trump's view on foreign help.

House Speaker Nancy Pelosi said President Trump stated openness to accepting damaging information about his rivals from foreign governments showed he didn't know right from wrong. "We have a president ignoring the law, not honoring his oath of office. The president gave us once again evidence that he does not know right from wrong."

600) June 15, 2019-Under fire, Trump pivots and says he'd call FBI.

President Trump appeared to back track somewhat on accepting campaign help from Russia or other foreign governments without necessarily calling the FBI, saying that he would certainly inform law enforcement authorities if he were approached. Under fire for saying earlier in the week that "I'd take it" and scoffing at the nation that he should call authorities, Mr. Trump shifted by saying that, while he would still look at incriminating information pro-vided by a hostile foreign power about an election opponent, he would "absolutely" report such an encounter. "Of course, you give it to the FBI or report it to the attorney general or somebody like that," Mr. Trump said.

601) June 15, 2019-Trump's foggy truth meets fog of war.
For two and a half years in office, Mr. Trump has spun out so many misleading or untrue statements about himself, his enemies, his policies, his politics, his family, his personal story, his finances and his interactions with staff that even his own former communications director once said "he's a liar" and many Americans long ago concluded that he cannot be trusted. To President Trump the question of culpability in the explosions that crippled two oil tankers in the Gulf of Oman is not question at all. "It's probably got essentially Iran written all over it," Trump declared.

602) June 16, 2019-Trump: If I lose in '20, market will tank.
President Donald Trump, gearing up for the official start of his 2020 campaign, warned that the U.S. would face an epic stock market crash if he's not re-elected. "If anyone but me take over, there will be a market crash, the likes of which has not been seen before."

603) June 19, 2019-Trump says ICE ready to deport millions.
President Donald Trump has begun his re-election bid by reviving a campaign promise to deport "millions of illegal aliens" from the United States, saying his administration will get to work on the goal "next week" with raids across the country.

604) June 19, 2019-Trump trying to sell himself as 2020 rebel.
President launches re-election bid with familiar themes. Addressing a crowd of thousands in Orlando. Trump complained that he had been "under assault from the very first day" of his presidency by a "fake news media" and illegal witch hunt" that had tried to keep him and his supporters down. He painted a disturbing picture of what life would look like if he loses in 2020, accusing his critics

of "Un-American conduct" and telling the crowds that <u>"Democrats</u> <u>want to destroy you and they want to destroy our country as</u> <u>we know it."</u>

605) June 20, 2019-EPA establishes plan on climate change friendly to coal.

The Trump administration replaced former President Barack Obama's effort to reduce planet warming pollution from coal plants open longer and undercut progress on reducing carbon emissions. The rule represents the Trump administration's most direct effort to protect the coal industry, it is another significant step in dismantling measures aimed at combating global warming, including the roll-back of tailpipe emissions standards and the planned withdrawal from the Paris climate agreement.

606) June 20, 2019-With talk of 'treason,' Trump crosses a line.

First it was <u>"the failing The New York Times."</u> Then <u>"Fake News."</u> Then <u>"enemy of the people."</u> President Trumps escalating attacks on The New York Times have paralleled his broader barrage on American media. He's gone from misrepresenting our business, to assaulting our integrity, to demonizing our journalists with a phrase that's been used by generations of demagogues. Mr. Trump said the Times and committed <u>"a virtual act of treason."</u> Treason is the only crime explicitly defined in the U.S. constitution. Article III reads: "Treason against the United States, shall consist only in levying war against them, or in adhering to their enemies, given them aid and comfort," to ensure that it couldn't be abused by politicians for self-serving attacks on rivals or critics. The crime almost never prosecuted, but Mr. Trump has used the word dozens of times.

607) June 20, 2019-Trump power plan keeps coal stoked.

President Donald Trump is keeping a signature campaign promise to boost the coal industry, but environmentalist say the energy plan his administration rolled out would lead to premature deaths, increase the risk of lung disease and hasten climate change. The Affordable Clean Energy (ACE) rule, an amendment to the Clean Air Act, is likely to extend the lives of potentially scores of aging coal fired power plants across the country whose carbon emissions are blamed for contributing to global warming.

608) June 20, 2019-EPA defies climate warnings.

Despite scientist's increasingly urgent warnings, the Trump administration ordered a sweeping about-face on Obama-era efforts to fight climate change, easing restrictions on coal-fired power plants in a move it predicted would revitalize America's sagging coal industry. The EPA move follows pledges by candidate and then President Donald Trump to rescue the U.S. coal industry. It's the latest and one of the biggest of dozens of environmental regulatory roll backs by his administration.

609) June 21, 2019-Senate blocks Trump on arms deals, his use of special power.

The senate passed three measures to block President Donald Trump from using his emergency authority to complete several arms sales benefiting Saudi Arabia and the United Arab Emirates, but fell short of the support needed to overcome a pledged veto. Trump has cited rising tensions with Iran as justification for using his emergency powers to complete the deals. Democrats and Republicans have been troubled by Trump's embrace of Saudi Arabia, which has endured despite international condemnation of its leaders' reported role in the killing of Saudi journalist Jamal Khashoggi.

610) June 23, 2019-Trump pushes back ICE sweep.
President Donald Trump gives Democrats, GOP two weeks to work
out immigration solution. Trump delayed a nationwide immigration sweep to deport people living in the United States illegally,
including families, saying he would give lawmakers two weeks to
work out solutions for the southern border.

**611) June 24, 2019- In playing down killings of Khashoggi,
Trump cites buying power of Saudi's.**
President Trump shrugged off the brutal dismembering of Jamal
Khashoggi, a The Washington Post columnist, just days after a
United Nations report described how a team of Saudi assassins
called Mr. Khashoggi a "sacrificial animal" before his murder. The
U.N. urged an FBI investigation into the slaying. But in an interview with NBC's "Meet the Press, Mr. Trump said the episode had
already been thoroughly investigated. He said the Middle East is a
vicious, hostile place" and noted that Saudi Arabia is an important
trading partner with the United States.

**612) June 25, 2019-Trump again chides Fed for interest
rate increase.**
President Trump continued his assault on the Federal Reserve,
blaming the central bank for reining in a United States economy
that's on track to reach its longest expansion in history. Mr. Trump,
in a pair of tweets, said the economy and stock market would have
been even stranger had the Fed kept interest rates low rather than
raising rates four times in 2018. "Now they stick, like a stubborn
child, when we need rate cuts, and easing, to make up for what
other countries are doing against us. Blew it!" Mr. Trump tweeted.

613) June 26, 2019-Mueller to testify to Congress.
Former special counsel Robert Mueller will testify to Congress
in a public session next month about his investigation of Russia's

interference in the 2016 election and possible obstruction of Justice by President Donald Trump, a reluctant witness, long sought by House Democrats. Mueller has agreed to appear before both panels on July 17.

614) June 27, 2019-Trump says he made Fed chair, but now wants to trade him in.

President Donald Trump is keeping up his attacks on Federal Reserve Chairman Jerome Powell, saying he "made" Powell but now would like to trade him in for Mario Draghi, the head of the European Central Bank.

615) June 27, 2019-Dems emoluments lawsuit against Trump can proceed.

Rejecting a request from President Donald Trump, a federal judge in Washington D.C., cleared the way for nearly 200 Democrats in Congress to continue their lawsuit against him alleging that his private business violates an anti-corruption provision of the Constitution. U.S. District Judge Emmet Sullivan declined to put the case on hold and said lawmakers could begin this week seeking financial information, interviews and other records from Trump Organization.

616) June 28, 2019-Chief Justice sides with liberals in halting citizenship question on census for now.

A deeply divided Supreme Court halted the Trump administration plans to ask U.S. residents on the 2020 census whether they are citizens, in a ruling that voiced blunt concerns about the White House motivations. The court, in a strongly worded opinion by Chief Justice John Roberts, said commerce Secretary Wilbur Ross, who made the decision to add a citizenship question, hadn't explained his real reasons for doing so, leaving the legality of his actions in question. "If judicial review is to be more than an empty ritual, it must demand something better. Then the explanation offered for the action taken in this case," Chief Justice Robert's wrote.

617) June 28, 2019-Justices block citizenship query from census.

The Supreme Court temporarily blocked the Trump administration's plan to add a citizenship question to the 2020 census, giving opponents new hope of defeating it. The ruling by Chief Justice John Roberts questions the rationale for the administration's effort just as challenging states and immigrant rights groups have done. Robert's wrote, "The sole stated reason seems to have been controverted."

618) June 29, 2019-Trump's breakfast invitation helps rebuild a Crown Princes' standing.

No one is more important to Saudi efforts to rehabilitate their defacto ruler after the bone-saw killing and dismemberment of Jamal Khashoggi then President Donald Trump, who joked around with the Crown Prince. Mr. Trump's willingness to embrace Prince Mohammed as if nothing were wrong sent a powerful signal to the rest of the world and represented a cold-eyed calculation that America's relationship with Saudi Arabia is more important than the death of Mr. Khashoggi.

619) June 29, 2019-Supreme Court agrees to hear 'Dreamers case'.

At stake are protections for nearly 800,000 young immigrants. The Supreme Court agreed to resolve their fate. By agreeing to take the case, the Supreme Court also provided a window of opportunity during which the Republicans and Democrats could permanently resolve the status of the young immigrants, perhaps by giving them a chance to earn citizenship.

620) July 3, 2019-House panel sues for Trump tax returns.
The House tax-writing committee sued the Treasury Department and the Internal Revenue Service for access to President Donald Trump's tax returns, hoping federal judges will pry loose records that the administration has refused to hand over. Mr. Neal, House Ways and Means Committee Chairman is asking the courts to enforce a subpoena that Mr. Mnuchin and IRS Commissioner Charles Rettig have defied. The lawsuit seeks a court order that would immediately require the officials to produce six years' worth of Mr. Trump's tax returns and audit records.

621) July 3, 2019-Citizen question dropped from census.
The Trump administration dropped plans to add a citizenship question to the 2020 census from, a turnaround after days of defiant statements following last week's Supreme Court decision to halt the query. Mr. Trump said he was "looking...very strongly" at delaying the census, which federal law directs to start on April 11, 2020.

622) July 4, 2019-It's a 'far better' life in detention, Trump says.
President Trump said that migrants were "living far better" in Border Patrol detention centers that in their home countries, one day after his own administration reported that children in some facilities were denied hot meals or showers, and that cells were so crowded that migrants begged to be freed.

623) July 4, 2019-U.S. aims to put citizenship item back in census.
Citing Trump's orders, emergency meetings and Justice Department reversal follow a tweet. A day after pledging that the 2020 census would not ask respondents about their citizenship, Justice Department officials reversed course and said they were hunting for a way to restore the question on orders from President Trump.

624) July 5, 2019-Tomorrow's children cannot afford Trump's ignorance on climate change.

There is one sense in which Donald Trump truly is the greatest American president. Given his ignorant determination to move us backward rather than forward on the issue of climate change, he is a greater threat than any other president has been to the children of tomorrow. That threat was apparent when the leaders of the Group of 20 nations renewed their commitment to the Paris climate accord while Trump stood alone against the rest of the world and over-whelming scientific consensus.

625) July 5, 2019-Trump is losing his trade war.

Donald Trump's declaration that "trade wars are good and easy to win" will surely go down in the history books as a classic utter-ance-but not in a good way. Instead it will go alongside Dick Cheney's prediction, on the eve of the Iraq war that "we will, in fact, be welcomed as liberators." That is, it will be used to illus-trate the arrogance and ignorance that so often drives crucial policy decisions. For the reality is that Trump isn't winning his trade wars. True, his tariffs have hurt China and other foreign economies. But they've hurt America too: economist at the New York Fed estimate that the average household will end up paying more than $1,000 a year in higher prices.

626) July 6, 2019-As Biden looms, Trump is still running against Obama.

It took all of 1 minute, 9 seconds for Trump to go after Obama and engage in a debate that has consumed much of his own time in office over who was the best president. It was the former President Barack Obama who started the policy of separating children from their parents at the border, Mr. Trump claimed falsely, and it was Mr. Obama who had such a terrible relationship with North Korea that he was about to go to war. Mr. Obama had it easy on the economy, Mr. Trump added, but let America's allies walk all over him. "If you look at what we've straightened out, the –I call it the Obama-Biden mess." Mr. Trump has been determined to minimize or undo Mr. Obama's accomplishments, and lately has even suggested that his predecessor was behind a deep-state conspiracy with law enforcement and intelligence agencies to thwart his 2016 candidacy.

627) July 6, 2019-Justice Department reaffirms goal for the census.

Justice Department lawyers told a federal judge that they would press ahead in their efforts to add a citizenship question to the 2020 census but indicated they did not know yet what kind of rationale they would put forward. Just hours before President Trump told reporters on the South Lawn of the White House that he was considering four or five options, including an executive order, to restore the question.

628) July 6, 2019-Trump says he wasn't aware of undocumented workers at his club.

President Donald Trump said he did not know about the dozens of undocumented workers employed at his golf courses over many years because he no longer runs his business. But groundskeepers, maids, and kitchen staff interviewed by The Washington Post in recent months say they worked without legal documents at Trump's clubs long before he entered politics and made illegal immigration his core issue. When asked about his knowledge of undocumented workers, Trump said, "Well, that I don't know, because I don't run it, but I would say this, probably every club in the United States has that, because it seems to me, from what I understand, a way that people did business, we've ended whatever they did, the rules now are very strict." Trump Organization officials have said that these workers used fake documents to get their jobs and that the company fired them once they found out.

629) July 7, 2019-Deadline up, so are ICE raids imminent.

President Donald Trump said his administration will move forward "fairly soon" with a plan to arrest thousands of migrant families in surprise roundups across major U.S. cities. Trump's threats have left immigrants living in the United States illegally in a fog of dread, putting neighborhoods on edge and making residents fear venturing outside.

630) July 8, 2019-Trump dismisses reports of poor care of children.

President Trump and his top immigration officials contested reports that migrant children were being held in horrific conditions in federal detention facilities. Accounts of disease, hunger, overcrowding, have multiplied in recent days. Pressed on a report by The New York Times and the El Paso Times in which border patrol agents and others had visited a facility in Clint, Texas, described crying children, cases of chickenpox, scabies and shingles and inadequate medical care. Speaking to reporters, Mr. Trump called the report about the Clint facility a "hoax". "The Fake News Media, in particular the Failing @NYTimes is writing phony and exaggerated accounts of the Border Detention Centers" Trump tweeted.

631) July 8, 2019-Detention-Center policies defended.

U.S. officials defended the Trump administrations immigration policies on several fronts, pushing back forcefully against criticism of conditions at migrant detention facilities. Also speaking on ABC, Democratic Rep. Rashida Tlaib of Michigan said she saw people sleeping on floors who said they hadn't bathed in 15 days. "Literally every single woman confirmed what the one woman said which is, 'I asked for water and they said go drink it from the toilet,' Mr. Tlaib said.

632) July 10, 2019-House Panel to weigh subpoenas of several Trump officials.

In an escalation of the showdown between the Trump administration and Congress, a House panel will vote this week on whether to demand testimony from a dozen current and former administration officials and confidents of President Trump who were involved in some of his business and personal dealings-that would allow subpoenas for documents and testimony from the presidents son-in-law Jared Kushner, as well as former National Security Advisor Mike Flynn, former Attorney General Jeff Sessions, form Attorney General Rod Rosenstein and former White House Chief of Staff John Kelly-seeking testimony from the editors of the National Enquirer tabloid-also seeking to force testimony from a number of Trump confidants including former campaign manager Corey Lewandowski and former White House Staff Secretary Rob Porter.

633) July 11, 2019-Appeals court rules in favor of Trump in emoluments case.

A federal appeals court sided with President Donald Trump, dismissing a lawsuit claiming the president is illegally profiting from foreign and state government visitors at his luxury hotel in downtown Washington.

634) July 12, 2019-President tries new way to get citizenship data.

President Donald Trump abandoned his quest to place a question about citizenship on the 2020 census and instructed the government to compile citizenship data from existing federal records instead, ending a bitterly fought legal battle that turned the non-partisan census into and object of political warfare. Mr. Trump announced that he was giving up on modifying the census two weeks after the Supreme Court rebuked his administration over its effort to do so. Mr. Trump had insisted that his administration "must" pursue that goal.

635) July 12, 2019-Biden calls the president a threat to U.S. security.

Joseph R. Biden Jr. delivering a sweeping foreign policy address that denounced President Trump as incapable of global leadership-Mr. Biden offered a scathing assessment of Mr. Trump's leadership, saying, the president's judgement has tarnished the country's reputation and undermined its ability to achieve its foreign policy goals. "The threat that I believe President Trump poses to our national security and where we are as a country is extreme." He criticized the president's "chest thumping" and called him inept at global and domestic leadership.

636) July 13, 2019-ICE raids on migrants to start Sunday, Trump says.

President Donald Trump said that immigration authorities plan to begin carrying out mass arrests of migrants Sunday. "We are really specifically looking for bad players but were also looking for people who come into our country not through the process, they just walked over a line, and they have to leave." Trump's threats to arrest migrant families have left many fearful of going to work, school or even to the grocery store.

637) July 15, 2019-Trade war has companies aiming at Asia & Mexico.

The tariffs that President Donald Trump has slapped on Chinese imports haven't sparked the widespread return of manufacturers to the U.S. that Trump envisioned. About 41% of American companies are considering moving factories from China because of the trade war, or already done so, but fewer than 6% are heading to the U.S. companies are largely eyeing South East Asia and Mexico. Trump tweeted <u>"companies will relocate to U.S."</u> and <u>"if the tariffs went on at higher levels, they would come back, and fast."</u>

638) July 15, 2019-Dems call Trump's 'go back' tweets racist.
President Donald Trump's opponents accused him of xenophobia and racism after he posted tweets calling on an unspecified group of Democratic congress women to <u>"go back and help fix"</u> the countries he said they <u>"originally came"</u> from before trying to make legislative changes in the USA. <u>"Why don't they go back and help fix the totally broken and crime infested places from which they came. Then come back and show us how it is done. These places need your help badly, you can't leave fast enough!"</u>

639) July 16, 2019-Trump defends tweets.
(Congress women respond say president wants to pit us against one another)
President Donald Trump defended racist remarks about four minority lawmakers by alleging that they <u>"hate our country"</u> and should leave if they are unhappy. When asked whether he was bothered that many people viewed the remarks as racist and that white nationalists found common cause with them, Trump said<u>: "It doesn't concern me because many people agree with me. And all I'm saying: They want to leave, let them leave."</u>

640) July 16, 2019-Trump targets asylum request.
(Migrants would have to ask other countries first)
The Trump administration moved to prove at most, migrants from claiming political asylum in the USA, requiring them to make their claims in other countries first.

641) July 16, 2019-Trump puts new limits on asylum at border.

The Trump administration moved to dramatically limit Central American migrants' ability to seek asylum at the U.S. border with Mexico, on escalation of the presidents push to stem the flood of border crossers that is severely straining the U.S. immigration system. Migrants who pass through another country first must seek asylum there rather than at the U.S. border, where they will be in eligible to do so. Trump officials said the Immigration and Nationality Act gives the attorney general the authority to set new limitations on who can seek asylum.

642) July 16, 2019-President steps up attack on four Congresswomen.

President Trump, under fire for comments that even members of his own party called racist, amplified his attacks on four Democratic congress women of color saying that they hated America and that one of the first two Muslims elected to Congress sympathized with Al Qaeda. The House strongly condemns President Trump's racist comments that have legitimized increased fear and hatred of new Americans and people of color. It mentions both Mr. Trump "go back" tweet and his branding of immigrants and asylum seekers as "invaders."

643) July 17, 2019-Lawsuit targets new Trump asylum limits.

Facing legal challenges and armed with few details on how the Trump Administration planned to carry out its new asylum policy, U.S. immigration agents proceeded as usual on the border. Civil right and immigration groups filed a lawsuit challenging new administration rules that could dramatically limit asylum claims by Central American migrants seeking entry into the U.S.

644) July 17, 2019-House condemns Trump's tweets.

A divided House voted to condemn President Donald Trump's racist remarks telling four minority congresswomen to "go back" to their ancestral countries. Trump insisted in a string of tweets that he's not a racist- "I don't have a Racist bone in my body" he wrote. The Republican National Committee provided a list of comments to bolster Trumps contention, but in none did the four women say they hate America or wanted to leave as the president asserted.

645) July 18, 2019-House targets Saudi Arms sales.

The House sent President Donald Trump a trio of resolutions aimed at blocking arms sales to Saudi Arabia and the United Arab Emirates, joining the senate in disapproving of administration ties to the Gulf nations but setting up a likely presidential veto. Both chambers passed a resolution earlier this year that would end U.S. military assistance for the Saudi led coalition in Yemen, but President Trump vetoed the measure and the senate did not muster the votes needed to override it. Administration officials have hesitated to blame Crown Prince Mohammed bin Salmon for the death of Mr. Khashoggi, a columnist for The Washington Post and a U.S. resident through the Central Intelligence Agency concluded that Prince Mohammed likely ordered the killing.

646) July 18, 2019-House kills impeachment push, but lawmakers vote to hold Barr, Ross in contempt over census.

The House killed a maverick Democrats effort to impeach President Donald Trump for his recent racial insults against four lawmakers of color. The House voted to hold Attorney General William Barr and Commerce Secretary Wilbur Ross in criminal contempt.

647) July 19, 2019-President says he tried to stop NC rally chant.

President Donald Trump chided his supporters who chanted "send her back" when he questioned the loyalty of a Somali-born congresswoman. The crowds "send her back" shouts resounded for 13 seconds as Trump made no attempt to interrupt them. "I was not happy with it. I disagree with it" and "would certainly try" to stop any similar chant at a future rally."

648) July 21, 2019-Attaching Democrats to radical socialist.

President Trump has made branding Democrats as out of the mainstream economy-wrecking socialists one of the center piece of his re-election strategy. He has sought to do so partly by making four junior Democratic members of Congress-all women of color who are on the left side of the party's ideological views with the Democrats seeking their party's presidential nomination. Mr. Trump said: "A vote for any Democrat in 2020 is a vote for the rise of radical socialism and the destruction of the American dream." All Democrats are not socialists. Most Democrats are not socialist. Of the 24 candidates for president only Senator Bernie Sanders of Vermont identifies himself as a Democratic socialist.

649) July 21, 2019-Trump turns to old tactics: Using race for his gain

Over decades in business, entertainment and now politics, Mr. Trump has approached America's racial, ethnic and religious divisions opportunistically, not as the nation's wounds to be healed but as openings to achieve his goals, whether they be ratings, fame, money or power, without regard for adverse consequences. He was accused by government investigators in the 1970's of refusing to rent apartments to black tenants (he denied it but settled the case) and made a home for himself in the 1980's by championing the return of the death penalty when five black and Hispanic teenagers were charged with raping a jogger. They were later exonerated. He threatened to sell his Mar-a-Largo estate to the Unification Church in 1991 and unleash "thousands of Moonies" if city officials in Palm Beach, Florida did not allow him to carve up his property. His own campaign in 2016 was marked by slurs against Mexicans, a proposed Muslim ban and other factors.

650) July 21, 2019-House Dems to focus on obstruction with Mueller.

Democrats on the House Judiciary Committee who will question former special counsel Robert Mueller plan to focus on a narrow set of episodes laid out in his report, on effort to direct American's attention to what they see as the most egregious examples of President Donald Trump's conducts.

651) July 22, 2019-Trade war leads Chinese spending in U.S. to plunge.

Growing distrust between the United States and China has slowed the once steady flow of Chinese cash into America, with Chinese investment plummeting by nearly 90 percent since President Trump took office. The fallout, which is being felt broadly across the economy, stems from tougher regulatory scrutiny in the United States and a less hospitable climate toward Chinese investment, as well as Beijing's tightened limits on foreign spending. It is affecting a range of industries including Silicon Valley start-ups, the Manhattan real estate market and state governments that spent years wooing Chinese investment, underscoring how the world's two largest economics are beginning to decouple after years of increasing integration.

652) July 22, 2019-President keeps up attack on 'squad'.

President Trump continued to target four progressive lawmakers knows as the "squad" while his senior advisors pushed back against assertions from Democrats that he was a racist. Mr. Trump kicked off the fight a week ago by saying the four Democratic lawmakers, all of them minority women, should return to the "totally broken and crime infested places from which they came and fix them." The president tweeted that he doesn't think the U.S. House lawmakers are "capable of moving the country." That followed similar suggestions that the four lawmakers- "hate the U.S."

653) July 23, 2019-Trump expands fast-track deportation authority.

The Trump administration announced that it will vastly extend the authority of immigration officers to deport migrants without allowing them to appear before judges, its second major shift on immigration in eight days. Starting today, fast-track deportations can apply to anyone in the country illegally for less than two years. Previously, those deportations were largely limited to people arrested almost immediately after crossing the Mexican border.

654) July 24, 2019-Will Mueller shift U.S. impeachment mode.

Robert Mueller's testimony before the White House Judiciary and Intelligence committees is not about gathering new evidence. It is a Democratic sponsored public relations campaign, and it's long overdue. If people believe that the Russia investigation is a "witch hunt" as President Donald Trump has endlessly claimed, no amount of testimony detail will matter. The primary questioning should debunk Trump's false claims that Mueller found no obstruction or collusion.

655) July 24, 2019-President sues to keep state returns confidential.

President Trump sued New York state officials and the House Ways and Means Committee to try to block congressional Democrats from using a recently enacted New York law to obtain his state tax returns. Breaking from decades of tradition, Mr. Trump refused to release his tax returns during the 2016 presidential campaign, say that he was under audit but suggesting that someday he may make them public.

656) July 25, 2019-Mueller rejects Trump's claims.

Robert Mueller, the taciturn lawman at the center of a polarizing American drama, dismissed President Donald Trump's claims of "total exoneration" in the federal probe of Russia's 2016 election interference. Mueller warned that Moscow's actions represented-and still represent-a great threat to American democracy.

657) July 25, 2019-A priest says Mr. Trump should quit for hate talk.

Father D 'Silva, the diminutive priest, now 82, and officially retired, once again affirmed those basic principles and called leaders to account. In his sermon, he spoke of how the "current occupant of the White House spews hatred, bigotry and intolerance" and must resign.

658) July 25, 2019-Mueller sticks to his report, rejects 'witch hunt' rebuke.

Mr. Mueller, in his first appearance to answer lawmakers' questions about his nearly two-year investigation, stood by his refusal to exonerate Mr. Trump and he criticized the Republican president for his limited answers to investigators. He also rejected several of Mr. Trump's criticisms of his probe, say: "It is not a witch hunt" and "it was not a hoax." He also described Russian election interference as an ongoing threat. "The Russian government's effort to interfere in our election is among the most serious."

659) July 26, 2019-Tainted elections, Congress does little.

A report from the Senate Intelligence Committee concluded all 50 states were targeted in 2016 and that ahead of the 2018 election "top election vulnerabilities remained" But there is no help coming from Congress. Senate Majority leader Mitch McConnell blocked a House-passed bill that would authorize $775 million to beef up state election systems.

660) July 27, 2019-Ruling allows shift of funds to build wall.

The Supreme Court gave President Trump a victory in his fight for a wall along the Mexican border by allowing the administration to begin using $2.5 billion in Pentagon money for the construction. While the order was only one paragraph long and unsigned, the Supreme Court said the groups challenging the administration did not appear to have a legal right to do so.

661) July 27, 2019-White House give NTO 90 days to close loophole used by China.

The Trump administration escalated pressure on the World Trade Organization, giving the international group a 90-day ultimatum to alter a provision that the United States has long allowed China to game the global trading rules.

662) July 28, 2019- Trump attacks Rep. Elijah Cummings' district.

President Donald Trump denigrated a majority black district represented by a congressional nemesis as a "disgusting, rat and rodent infested mess," broadening a campaign against prominent critics of his administration that has exacerbated racial tensions. Trump lashed out in tweets against Rep. Elijah Cummings, the powerful House Oversight Committee chairman, claiming his Baltimore-are district is "considered the worst run and most dangerous anywhere in the United States."

663) July 29, 2019-Trump assails black lawmaker as 'racist'.
Facing growing accusations of racism over his incendiary tweets, President Donald Trump labeled a prominent black congressman as racist himself and accused Democrats of trying to "play the race card."

664) July 30, 2019-Trump ally sought Saudi funds for nuclear deal.
Tom Barrack, an equity investor and a close ally of President Donald Trump, sought Saudi government funding in a bid to buy U.S. nuclear-reactor builder Westinghouse, according to a House report that discloses new details of an effort to transfer sensitive nuclear technology to the kingdom. The new report based on 60,000 newly obtained documents, says that Mr. Barrack and the group of ex-military officers, whose company was known as IP3, solicited Saudi funds even as they lobbied for and obtained Trump administration support for their strategy.

665) July 30, 2019-U.S. China talks resume, but deal seems unlikely.
Mr. Trump and his advisors are playing down the likelihood of reaching an agreement in the short term, and the president suggested that China was trying to drag out the negotiations in the hope that someone else might occupy the Oval Office come January 2021.

666) July 30, 2019-Trump has no authority as critic, Baltimore says.
The last time Donald J. Trump blamed a black man for the condition of this undoubtedly troubled city, the year was 2015, the death of Freddy Gray in police custody had spawned a racial uprising, and the black man in question was President Barack Obama. "Our great African American president hasn't exactly had a positive impact on the thugs who are so happily and openly destroying Baltimore!" Mr.

Trump wrote then on Twitter. Now Mr. Trump is president himself, and he has written off this entire city as "disgusting, rat and rodent infested" place where "no human being would want to live" and blaming it's longtime and revered congressman, Representative Elijah E. Cummings for the city's problems.

667) July 30, 2019-Senate fails in effort to override veto of bill on Saudi arms sales.
President Trump again succeeded in turning back bipartisan congressional efforts to rebuke his lock-step support for Saudi Arabia after the Senate failed to override his veto on a series of measures that would have blocked billions of dollars of arms sales to the Persian Gulf region.

668) July 31, 2019-Over 900 migrant children separated.
Federal immigration authorities have separated more than 900 children from their parents in the past year. The ACLU said the average age of children was 9 years old and 185 of the children were younger than 5. The ACLU sued the Trump administration last year to stop the government from separating thousands of migrant children from their parents after crossing the border illegally, under a zero-tolerance policy that sought to prosecute nearly all adult illegal border crossers. President issued an executive order abandoning the policy in June 2018, amid broad outcry from immigration advocates and lawyers, Democratic lawmakers and some Republicans. A Federal Judge in San Diego that same month barred matter of policy. More than 2000 children were separated the roughly two months that the separation policy was in place, and an internal watchdog report concluded that thousands more were likely separated in the months before.

669) July 31, 2019-Trump: "I'm the least racist person" in the world.

"I think I'm helping myself," Trump told reporters while defending his recent attacks on African American and Hispanic lawmakers. He said he is pointing out "the tremendous corruption" in cities like Baltimore. <u>"I am the least racist person there is anywhere in the world."</u>

670) August 1, 2019-Trump's $16 billion farm bailout will make rich farmers richer.

The Trump administration last week revealed details of a $16 billion aid package for farmers hit in the U.S.-China trade war, with provisions meant to avoid large corporations scooping up big payouts at the expense of farmers. According to a report released by the non-profit Environmental Working Group (EWG), most of the $8.4 billion given out so far in last year's farm bail out went to wealthy farmers, exacerbating the economic disparity with smaller farmers.

671) August 2, 2019-Trump escalates fight over trade with Chinese.

A vow of more tariffs. Move by U.S. would virtually tax virtually all imports from Beijing. President Trump, frustrated by increasingly fruitless negotiations with China, said that the United States would impose a 10 percent tariff on an additional $300 billion worth of Chinese imports next month, a significant escalation in a trade war that has dragged on for more than a year. Mr. Trump had agreed in June not to impose more tariffs after meeting with Chinese president, Xi Jinping, and agreeing to restart trade talks. But Mr. Trump said he was moving ahead with the levies as of Sept. 1 as punishment for China's failure to live up to its commitments, including buying more American agriculture products and stemming the flow of fentanyl into the United States.

672) August 2, 2019-North Korea launches more missiles.
North Korea launched its third missile test in just over a week, in what President Donald Trump described as a test involving short-range missiles with which he had "no problem." At the White House, Mr. Trump appeared to shrug off the test that was launched early in Asia. "They are very standard," Mr. Trump told reporters, adding that he never made an agreement with the North Korean Leader, Kim Jong Un that forbade the testing of short-range missiles.

673) August 2, 2019-Trump plans new tariffs on China.
Markets fall as trade conflict escalates; levies would hit nearly all goods in the country. President Trump moved to extend tariffs to essentially all Chinese imports, escalating a trade conflict that is poised to hit U.S. consumers in the pocketbook and roiling financial markets. The new tariffs would take effect Sept 1 and cover $300 billion in Chinese goods-including smart phones, apparel, toys, and other consumer products.

674) August 3, 2019-Tariff fight knocks off China as top U.S. trading partner.
The standoff between Washington and Beijing has cost China its position as the top U.S.'s trading partner, a shift that could accelerate as President Donald Trump moves to ratchet up tariffs even more. Stocks swooned for a second day, as Beijing vowed to retaliate if Mr. Trump makes good on his threat from a day earlier to impose 10% tariffs Sept 1 on $300 billion in Chinese goods that are currently not subject to levies.

675) August 5, 2019-Trump's advisors opposed China tariffs.
At campaign rallies before last year's midterm elections, President Trump repeatedly warned that America was under attack by immigrants heading for the border. "You look at what is marching up, that is an invasion!" he declared at one rally. "That is an invasion!"

Nine months later, a 21-year-old white man is accused of opening fire in a Walmart in El Paso, killing 20 people and injuring dozens more after writing a manifesto railing against immigration and announcing that "this attack is a response to the Hispanic invasion of Texas." The suspect wrote that his views "predate Trump" as if anticipating the political debate that would follow the blood bath. But Mr. Trump did not originally inspire the gunman, he has brought into the mainstream polarizing ideas and people once consigned to the fringes of American society.

676) August 6, 2019-Trump condemns racism, focuses on mental illness.

President Donald Trump urged the nation to condemn bigotry and White supremacy after a pair of mass shootings and focused on combating mental illness over new gun-control measures in remarks delivered from the White House. "In our voice, our nation must condemn racism, bigotry, and White supremacy," Trump said. "Hatred warps the mind, ravages the heart and devours the soul." Trump condemned the "two evil attacks" and vowed to act "with urgent resolve." He outlined a number of possible steps, including "red flag laws" that focus on better identifying mental ill people who should not be allowed to purchase firearms. "Mental illness and hatred pull the triggers. Not the gun." Trump also called for cultural changes, including stopping the "glorifications of violence in our society" in video games and elsewhere.

677) August 7, 2019-Experts: Mental illness not main driver of mass shootings.

President Donald Trump's focus on "mentally ill monsters" oversimplifies the role of mental illness in public mass shootings and downplays the ease with which Americans can get firearms, experts say. "Mental illness and hatred pull the trigger, not the gun," Trump said. The president described the perpetrators as "a wicked man" and "another twisted monster." In response, mental health experts repeated what they have said after previous mass shootings: Most people with mental illness are not violent, they are far more likely to be victims of violent crime that perpetrators, and access to fire-arms is a big part of the problem. "If mental illness were the driving factor, we would expect the countries with highest suicide rates to have higher rates of public mass shootings. That's not what we see, said Adam Lankford, University of Alabama criminologist.

678) August 7, 2019-Trump's trade fight with China creates pain for all including Midwest farmers.

When he set out to extract concessions from China and other coun-tries, President Donald Trump assured Americans that "Trade wars are good, and easy to win." He regarded previous presidents as easy marks for devious foreign governments, and he thought his tough tactics would force rivals to back down. But after, two years of negotiations with Beijing, victory has proved elusive. What was mostly an exercise in posturing and demands is turning to produce mass casualties. Any business that depends on exports to China is at risk. Lamented American Farm Bureau Federation President Zippy Duvall, "We stand to lose all of what was a 9.1 billion market in 2016, which was down sharply from the 19.5 billion U.S. famers exported to China in 2017." Manufacturers like Boeing, Caterpillar and Deere also stand to forfeit sales.

679) August 7, 2019- 'Red flag' gun laws gain stream.

Despite frequent mass shootings, Congress has proven unable to pass substantial gun violence legislation, in large because of resis-tance from Republicans. But a bipartisan proposal by Senators Lindsey Graham, RSC and Richard Blumenthal, D. Conn, is gaining momentum after the weekend mass shootings in Texas and Ohio. The still emerging plan would create a federal grant program to encourage states to adopt "red flag" laws to take guns away from people believed to be a danger to themselves or others. A similar bill never came up for a vote in the GOP-controlled Senate last year, but both parties express hope that this year will be different. President Donald Trump has signaled support for the plan.

680) August 7, 2019-Trump campaign challenges California tax return law.

President Trump and the Republican National Committee filed a pair of lawsuits against officials in California challenging a new law requiring presidential candidate to release five years of tax returns in order to be placed on the state primary ballot in 2020.

681) August 7, 2019-President Trump's fruitless trade war.

President Trump told the American people that confronting China would be quick and painless and would result in clear gains for the American economy, a philosophy summarized most famously in his Twitter boast: <u>"Trade wars are good, and easy to win."</u> Today, two years after the Trump administration imposed its first punitive measures on China, the United States is mired instead in an escalating trade conflict with no clear strategy, no discernible goals and no end in sight.

682) August 8, 2019-McGahn is 'most important witness.'

The House Judiciary Committee asked a federal judge to couple Don McGahn, whom lawmakers consider their "most important" witness in any potential impeachment proceedings against President Donald Trump. "Given McGahn' s central role as witness to the president's wide-ranging potentially obstructive conduct, the Judiciary Committee cannot fulfil its constitutional investigative, oversight and legislative responsibilities-including its consideration of whether to recommend articles of impeachment-without hearing from him," the lawsuit says.

683) August 9, 2019-Shootings lead Trump to study fire-arms checks.

In the wake of two mass shootings, the divisive politics of gun control appeared to be in flux as President Trump explored whether to back extend background checks on gun purchases and Senate Majority Leader Mitch McConnell signaled that he would at least be open to considering the idea. It is not clear that either the president or Mr. McConnell will embrace such legislation, which both of them have opposed in the past and which would have to overcome opposition from the National Rifle Association and the powerful conservative constituencies.

684) August 10, 2019-Trump is optimistic on gun talks.

President says Senate GOP, NRA are open to background checks, neither has endorsed. President Trump expressed hopes that Republicans would join with Democrats to consider proposals expanding background checks following a pair of mass shootings last week, adding that he believes the National Rifle Association wouldn't stand in the way of the effort. "We have tremendous support for really commonsense, sensible, important background checks." "I think in the end, Wayne and the NRA will either be there or maybe will be a little more neutral."

Chapter 9

685) August 11, 2019-2020 Dems blame Trump, NRA for inaction on guns.
Democratic presidential candidates placed responsibility for inaction on gun violence in the hands of President Donald Trump and the National Rifle Association, in the face of broad national support for some gun control measures. The Democrats largely agreed on the broad contours of the policy debate, emphasizing the need to close background check loopholes, ban assault weapons and fund research into gun violence.

686) August 11, 2019-Trump boosts conspiracy theory about Epstein's death, Clinton link.
President Donald Trump retweeted an unsubstantiated conspiracy theory that former President Bill Clinton was in some way responsible for the death of accused sex trafficker Jeffrey Epstein, hours after reports of the filmmaker's jailhouse suicide.

687) August 13, 2019-Tougher rules for getting a green card.
Trump officials move to restrict immigrants who use public benefits. Legal immigrants who use public benefits, such as Medicaid, food stamps or housing assistance could have a tougher time obtaining a green card under a policy change announced that is at the center of the Trump administrations effort to reduce immigration levels.

688) August 13, 2019-Trump administration weakens application of endangered species act.

The Trump administration moved to weaken how it applies this 45-year-old Endangered Species Act ordering changes that critics say will speed the loss of animals and plants at a time of record global extinctions. The action, which expands the administrations rewrite of U.S. environmental laws, is the latest that targets protections, including the water, air and public lands.

689) August 13, 2019-Greencards become harder to get.

The Trump administration issued a rule that would disqualify legal immigrants from permanent residency if they use certain public assistance programs and block prospective applicants deemed likely to need them. The rule, issued by the Department of Homeland Security, is one of the most sweeping elements of the administrations bid to create what officials described as a tighter more discerning U.S. immigration system. Critics of the regulation said it could hurt poor immigrants and result in widespread confusion in migrant communities. The rule has been a particular priority for top White House aide Stephen Miller.

690) August 13, 2019-Trump's new immigration rule just another way to say, 'send them back'.

Trump famously despised immigrants from Mexico and Central America who are here illegally. He calls them rapists and killers and would like to see them rounded up like cattle. Trump equally well known for his dislike of immigrants who are Muslim. He has singled out for scorn Muslim members of Congress. Now, the Trump administration unveiled a rule that could deny Visa's and permanent residency to hundreds of thousands of other immigrants for the sole crime of being poor.

691) August 14, 2019-Facing pressure, president delays new tariffs plan.

President Trump unexpectedly put off new tariffs on many Chinese goods, including cellphones, laptops computers, and toys, until after the start of the Christmas shopping season, acknowledging the effect that his protracted trade war with Beijing could have on Americans. Mr. Trump pushed a 10 percent tariff on some imports to Dec. 15, and excluded others from it entirely, while facing mounting pressure from businesses and consumer groups over the harm they say the trade conflict is doing.

692) August 14, 2019-Suit contests eased climate rules.

More than 20 states are supping the Trump administration over its rollback of climate change regulations for power plants in what could be a landmark case deciding what the federal government's responsibility is for fighting global warming. The suit is the latest pushback by several Democratic led states that say Trump administration policies are endangering the environment. The Republican administration has been rolling back policies especially climate policy under Democratic President Obama that it says hinder development and push environmental laws beyond their intended use.

693) August 14, 2019-In tariffs delay, Trump concedes consumers may pay more.

President Trump's tariffs in Chinese imports are forcing Americans to pay more for everyday products. Many economists have shown this. If you look at the appropriate inflation data, like the rising price of imported home furnishings, you can see the effect for yourself. Mr. Trump still does not see it, he continues to claim, incorrectly, that China alone is bearing the cost of his trade war with Beijing. But he admitted at least the possibility that he could be wrong about that, conceding that Americans could start paying more for many products if his latest round of tariffs went through as planned. <u>"The only impact has been that we've collected almost 60 billion from China, compliments of China."</u> There were at least a couple of inaccuracies in Mr. Trump's comments, starting with how much money the Treasury had collected as a result of the tariffs. The customs and Border Protection agency put the figure at $24 billion through August 7, less than half of Trump claims.

694) August 15, 2019-Advisors caution president on gun stance.

President Trump's public push for gun control measures is causing consternation among conservatives and some of his advisors, who have privately raised concerns about the political fallout, according to White House officials and people familiar with the discussion.

695) August 16, 2019-Trade warrior facing danger over economy.

Against the backdrop of mounting evidence that the global economy is weakening, President Donald Trump is caught between his desire to pursue the trade war with China he promised to win and his need to keep the economy humming as the 2020 election approaches. The president has insisted that his tariffs on Chinese imports are hurting only China. "The longer the trade war goes on, the weaker China gets and stronger we get." But the economists say the tariffs are causing damage unacknowledged by the administration with slowing growth in China and on economic downturn in Germany, a big exporter to China.

696) August 16, 2019-Trump defends economic record at rally.

Trump seemed particularly attuned to concerns about his handling of the economy, including his decision to impose tariffs on China. He falsely said that action has resulted in billions of dollars coming from China and that American farmers are the "biggest beneficiaries." "I never said China was going to be easy," he said, contradicting his 2018 assertion that "trade wars are good and easy to win."

697) August 16, 2019-Economic risks weigh on Trump 2020 bid.

President Trump has made the strong economy the central selling point of his presidency. But this week's damaging economic developments resulting in fresh warnings of a possible impending recession threatens to complicate the message 14 months before the election. "The economy is phenomenal right now, with a normalized interest rate, we're doing phenomenal." Economic experts say that Mr. Trump's trade war with China has alarmed Americans about the future of trade, and that the changing cost of doing business is causing trepidation.

698) August 16, 2019-Trump eyes U.S. buying Greenland.

President Trump made his name on the world's most famous island. Now he wants to buy the world's biggest. The idea of the U.S. purchasing Greenland captured the former real estate developer's imagination. Mr. Trump has, with varying degrees of seriousness, repeatedly expressed interests in buying the ice-covered autonomous Danish territory. Mr. Trump has asked advisors whether the U.S. can acquire Greenland and according to two of the people, has asked his White House counsel to look into the idea.

699) August 17, 2019-Tariffs will hit wide range of goods.

Consumers will feel the impact starting Sept. 1 despite Trump reprieve for certain categories. President Trump may have scaled back tariffs on Chinese goods to spare holiday shoppers, but consumers are still likely to feel a pinch. An array of apparel, electronics, watches, and sporting goods from China will be hit with levies of 10% starting, Sept.1.

700) August 17, 2019-Immigrants credit data will be considered.

The Trump administration imposed sweeping changes to U.S. immigration policy, including letting the government, apparently for the first time, weigh prospective immigrants credit history when deciding who gets to come to the U.S. and who gets to stay. The Department of Homeland Security tightens the immigration law definition of who is likely to become "public charge", a reason to turn down an applicant. Among other changes, the new rule generally makes it harder for legal immigrants to get permanent residency, or for prospective applicants to enter the U.S., if they rely on social programs like Medicaid or food stamps or deemed likely to need them.

701) August 19, 2019-Feats over shootings grow.

About half of Americans disapprove of President Trump's response to the deadly mass shootings in Texas and Ohio, while broad majorities support Congress moving to expand background checks for all firearm sales, according to a new Wall Street Journal/NBC News poll. The poll, taken in the aftermath of the back-to-back shootings in El Paso, Texas, and Dayton, Ohio portrays an anxious nation uneasy about gun violence. Sixty-eight percent of respondents expressed worry. The U.S. will experience another mass shooting or attack by white nationalists targeting people based on their country of origin, with 55% saying they were "very worried".

702) August 19, 2019-To Trump, economic warning signals are the work of a conspiracy.

President Trump, confronting perhaps the most ominous economic signs of his time in office, has unleashed what is by now a familiar response: lashing out at what he believes is a conspiracy of forces arrayed against him. He has insisted that his own hand-picked Federal Reserve Chair, Jerome H. Powell, is intentionally acting against him. He has said other countries, including allies, are working to hurt American economic interest. And he has accused the news media of trying to create a recession. "The Fake News Media is doing everything they can to crash the economy because they think that will be bad for me and my re-election, the problem they have is that the economy is way too strong and we will soon be winning big on trade, and everyone knows that, including China." The president's broadsides follow a long pattern of conspiratorial thinking. He has claimed, without evidence, that undocumented immigrants cast millions of ballots, costing him the popular vote in the 2016 election. And he has said that reporters are trying to harm him with pictures of empty seats at his rallies.

703) August 21, 2019-Trump retreats on background checks.
President Trump backed further away from calls for stricter background checks for gun purchasers and emphasized mental illness as a prominent factor in mass shootings. "I've said 100 times, it's not the gun that pulls the trigger. These people are sick." Mr. Trump called for sweeping action after the 2018 Parkland school shooting in Florida, then backed off under pressure from the NRA and others.

704) August 21, 2019-Trump say she can cut tax gains on his own.
President Trump said that he was considering giving investors a big tax cut that would primarily benefit the rich, and that he believed he could do it without approval from Congress. "We've been talking about indexing for a long time, and many people like indexing: it can be directly done by me." "I would love to do something with capital gains."

705) August 21, 2019-NRA chat wins convent in Oval Office.
President Donald Trump spent at least 30 minutes on the phone with Wayne LaPierre, the chief executive of the National Rifle

Association. The call ended the way that Mr. LaPierre had hoped it would: with Mr. Trump espousing NRA talking points in the Oval Office and warning of the radical steps he said Democrats wanted to take in violation of the Second Amendment. At the NRA's annual convention in 2017, Mr. Trump assured the group's members: "You came through for me, and I am going to come through for you." And that is what he was doing on his call with Mr. LaPierre, assuring him that even after another round of mass shootings, he was not interested in legislation establishing universal background checks and that his focus would be on the mental health of the gunman, not their guns.

706) August 22, 2019-Trump calls Denmark leaders' comments 'nasty'.

President Donald Trump lashed out at Danish Prime Minister Mette Frederiksen, saying the leader of the U.S. ally had made "nasty" comments about his interest in having the United States purchase Greenland. Trump announced that he was calling off a planned two-day state visit to Copenhagen over Frederiksen' s refusal to entertain sale of Greenland. Frederiksen called the idea of the sale of Greenland "absurd" after news broke of Trumps interest, a characterization that apparently offended him.

707) August 22, 2019-Immigrant families to be held longer.

The Trump administration moved to allow the government to indefinitely detain families crossing the U.S.-Mexican border and supersede a decade old court settlement that both limits how long migrant children can be held in custody and sets standards for their care. The new rules are the Republican administrations latest effort to tighten immigration laws on its own, with Congress long unable to agree on any legal overhauls.

708) August 22, 2019-Trump again calls Jews who back Democrats 'disloyal'.

President Donald Trump's branding on American Jews who vote for Democrats as "disloyal" to their religion and Israel prompted alarms of anti-Semitism. But his ultimate aim appears to be dividing Democrats peeling off Jewish support and shorting up his white evangelical Christian base. Digging in despite widespread criticism, Trump repeated his controversial assertion about Jews who support the Democratic Party.

709) August 23, 2019-Forecast: Trumps tariffs could cost families $1K a year.

More than a year into the U.S.-China trade war, American consumers are about to find themselves squarely in the crosshairs for the first time, with the average household facing up to $1,000 in additional cost each year from tariffs, according to research from JP Morgan. Consumers whose spending fuels about 70 percent of the U.S. economy, have been shielded from previous rounds of tariffs, which have left businesses reeling and up ended global supply chains. But that is about to change with the 10 percent levies on roughly $300 billion in Chinese imports, about a third of which will take effect Sept. 1. Those tariffs will primarily target consumer goods.

710) August 23, 2019-Ending a path to citizenship isn't as easy as Trump says.

The day after his administration unveiled a regulation that would allow it to indefinitely detain migrant families with children, President Trump also revived talk of a much more radical step: abolishing automatic American citizenship for anyone born in the United States. Mr. Trump said the rule, enshrined in the Constitution for more than 150 years and rooted in common law before that, was "looking very, very seriously" at ending a policy that in the past he has called "a magnet for illegal immigration." No, the president cannot amend the Constitution, and an executive order trying to end or restrict the right to citizenship of persons born in the United States would almost certainly be challenged in court as a violation of the 14th Amendment.

711) August 24, 2019-U.S., China ramp up trade war.

"We don't need China," Trump tweets, hitting back with tariffs. President Trump ordered U.S. companies doing business with China to explore relocating their operations and stiffened tariffs on Chinese imports after Beijing unveiled its own new tariffs on U.S. goods, the latest twists in a trade war that showed a new its potency to rattle investors, cofound central bankers and cloud the economy. "We don't need China and frankly, would be far better off without them," Mr. Trump tweeted. "Our great American companies are hereby ordered to immediately start looking for an alternative to China, including bringing your companies HOME."

712) August 24, 2019-On economy, Trump just sees enemies.

President Trump began in a pretty good mood, celebrating the support of Republicans and the strength of the economy. But the president's mood soured quickly as the news rolled in that both China and the Federal Reserve had defied his explicit demands. We'll let Mr. Trump speak for himself: "My only question is: Who is our bigger enemy, Jay Powell or Chairman Xi?" A few minutes later Mr. Trump started tweeting like a potentate, issuing commands to American companies as if he had the power to do so.

713) August 26, 2019-Trumps threats of tariffs worry summit leaders.

President Trump offered deeply contradictory signals about his trade war with China, ending the day by escalating his threats of higher tariffs even as he remained isolated from fellow world leaders on a strategy that has rattled the global economy. Mr. Trump started by conceding that he was having "second thoughts" about a new round of levies on Chinese goods. Within hours, he abruptly reversed himself again, saying that he only regretted not raising tariffs even higher.

714) August 26, 2019-Trump aides temper his remarks.

Kudlow and Mnuchin say president has no plans to take action to force U.S. firms out of China. Aides to President Trump said he has no plans to invoke emergency powers and force companies to relocate operations from China, two days after his tweet that they were "here by ordered" to look for alternative locations. Both Mnuchin and Kudlow said that the president could theoretically force U.S. companies to leave China by invoking a law known as the International Emergency Economic Powers Act of 1977, or IEEPA. The president is required in "every possible instance" to consult with Congress before exercising authorities granted by IEEPA, and to specify in a report to lawmakers why the circumstances constitute a threat.

715) August 26, 2019-As Trump stews, Fed closes ranks.

President Trump characterizes himself as a master deal maker who gets what he wants. But as he tries to pressure the Federal Reserve to lower interest rates, he is contending with a powerful opponent: technocrats! The Fed lowered borrowing costs in July amid mounting trade uncertainties, but it has refused to promise the kind of aggressive rate-cutting campaign that Mr. Trump wants. The central banks unwillingness to bend to the White House's wishes has frustrated Mr. Trump, who implied that the Fed chair be appointed, Jerome H. Powell, was America's enemy. There was no indication that monetary policy thinking was inching any closer to Mr. Trump's, and there were many signs that officials and top economists were closing ranks to protect Mr. Powell and the institution he leads as it came under non-stop attack.

716) August 27, 2019-Will Trump meet with Iran's Rouhani.

President Trump said during the GI Summit there's a "really good chance" he could meet with Iran's leader on their nuclear impasse. French President Emmanuel Macron said he hoped Trump and Iranian President Hassan Rouhani could meet within weeks in hopes of saving the 2015 nuclear deal that Tehran struck with world powers, but which the U.S. unilaterally withdrew from last year.

717) August 27, 2019-Trump softens rhetoric on China and Iran.

President Trump struck a conciliatory tone on the final day of the Group of Seven summit, where he faced pressure from French President Emmanuel Macron to de-escalate the trade war with China and case tensions with Iran. At a joint conference with Mr. Macron, Mr. Trump said he was open to meeting with Iranian President Hassan Rouhani. The remarks came hours after the Iranian leader signaled that he too was open to talks, and Mr. Macron said he hoped the two leaders would speak in the coming weeks. Mr. Trump also sounded a more optimistic note about trade talks with China after having doubled down on his tariff policy only a day ago. "I think they want to make a deal," Mr. Trump said.

718) August 27, 2019-U.S. seeks to enforce rule on asylum.

The Trump administration asked the Supreme Court for authority to immediately begin denying asylum to Central Americans who show up at the U.S. border without first seeking refuge status in Mexico or other countries they traveled through. Federal courts in California had blocked implementation of the administration's interim rule, finding that the Justice and Homeland Security departments skirted federal Administrative Procedure Act requirements that proposed rules published for public notice and comment before taking effect. Four immigrant rights groups had sued to stop the rule. The "ban uplands four decades of unbroken practice and would cause untold harm to families and children if allowed to take effect," said Lee Gelernt, an attorney with the American Civil Liberties Union who represents groups challenging the rule.

719) August 27, 2019-Trump offers his resort as 'Great Place' for GT.

President Trump suggested that the next Group of 7 Summit of World Leaders should be at his own luxury golf resort in Doral, Florida. Mr. Trump said his property is a "great place", was uniquely equipped to handle the Group of 7 meeting in 2020. "It's got tremendous acreage, many hundreds of acres, so we could handle whatever happens. We haven't found anything that could even come close to competing with it."

720) August 28, 2019-Farmer's patience frays as a trade war lingers.

Pepporced with complaints from farmers fed up with President Trump's trade war, Sonny Perdue found his patience wearing thin. Mr. Perdue, the agriculture secretary was the guest of honor of the annual Farm Fest gathering in southern Minnesota. American farmers have become collateral damage in a trade war that Mr. Trump began to help manufactures and other companies that he believes have been hurt by China's "unfair" trade practices. Mr. Trump who regularly brags about an economic boom despite signs of a slowdown, has in some cases made matters worse. He recently dismissed sales of American wheat, suggesting Japan was buying it only as a favor to the United States. And his frequent tweets insisting that "farmers are starting to do great again" have rubbed some agriculture groups the wrong way. "Were not starting to do great again," Brian Thalmann, the president of the Minnesota Corn

Growers Association told Perdue at the event. "Things are going downhill and downhill quickly."

721) August 28, 2019-Bank has tax returns sought by House Panels.

Deutsche Bank AG, for decades President Trump's primary lender, has copies of tax returns sought under a congressional subpoena for the president and his family's financial information, the bank told a federal appeals court. The House Intelligence and Financial Services committees in April subpoenaed Deutsche Bank for documents and financial records, including tax returns related to Mr. Trump, Donald Trump Jr., Eric Trump, Ivanka Trump and various business entities they own the last decade.

722) August 29, 2019-Trump tells aides take the land as impatience grown on border wall.

President Trump's signature campaign promise to build a wall along the southwestern border is far behind schedule. So, he has told his aides to get the job done by whatever means necessary, including by seizing land on the Mexican frontier. The president has repeatedly suggested during meetings an immigration policy that aides "take the land, get it done," according to a person who has heard him say it. Mr. Trump had brought up the land seizures and had floated the idea of offering pardons to aides willing to break the law, a suggestion he has made previously when exploring ways to fulfil his campaign promises.

723) August 29, 2019-Mattis says the U.S. needs allies.

Former Defense Secretary Jim Mattis says he resigned from the Trump administration in late 2018 "When my concrete solutions and strategic advice, especially keeping faith with our allies, no longer resonated." Still without specifically mentioning the president and his feuds with American allies, Mr. Mattis stresses the strategic importance of strong ties with friendly nations. "Nations with allies thrive, and those without them wither." Mr. Mattis left after a disagreement with Mr. Trump over the presidents plans to pull American troops out of Syria. He also said, and made clear, that his view on "treating allies with respect" didn't align with the presidents.

724) August 29, 2019-Trump's mysterious devotion to Putin endures.

President Trump has trouble getting along with leaders from Germany, France, and Japan. His respect for anyone who works for him is often transitory. But when it comes to the Russian President, Trump is a model of loving devotion. Trump's problem was that the preference of Ukrainians did not align with the preferences of Putin, who saw Crimea as rightfully his and had no patience with nonviolent avenues of recourse. Whatever Putin wants, Trump is eager to provide. No president has ever behaved in a more accommodating manor toward. When Trump met with Putin in Helsinki last year, he indicated he believed the Russian leader's denial of meddling in the U.S. election. Maybe its greed. As his attorney Michel Cohen later revealed, Trump was secretly trying for much of 2016 to get approval for a Trump Tower in Moscow, reason enough for him to curry favor with the Kremlin. The president of the United States is supposed to be the servant of the American people.

725) August 29, 2019-Trump pushes limits to build wall.

President Donald Trump is so eager to compete hundreds of miles of border fence ahead of the 2020 presidential election that he has directed aides to fast track billions of dollars' worth of construction contracts aggressively seize private land and disregard environmental rules, according to current and former officials involved with the project. He also told worried subordinates that he will pardon them of any potential wrong doing should they have to break laws to get the barriers built quickly. Trump has repeatedly promised to complete 500 miles of fencing by the time voters go to the polls in November 2020, stirring chants of "Finish the Wall" at his political rallies as he pushes for tighter border controls. The president has told senior aides a failure to deliver on the signature promise of his 2016 campaign would be a letdown to his supporters and an embarrassing defeat.

726) August 30, 2019-Watch: Comey broke FBI rules in handling memos.

Former FBI Director James Comey violated FBI policies in his handling of memos documenting private conversations with President Donald Trump, the Justice Department's inspector general said. But the report denied Trump and his supporters, who have repeatedly accused Comey of leaking classified information, total vindication. It found that none of the information shared by him or his attorneys with anyone in the media was classified, and the Justice Department has declined to prosecute Comey.

727) August 30, 2019-EPA to weaken controls on gas warming planet.

The Trump administration laid out a far-reaching plan to cut back on the regulation of methane emissions, a major contributor to climate change. The Environmental Protection Agency's proposed rule aims to eliminate federal requirements that oil, and gas companies install technology to detect and fix methane leaks from wells, pipelines and storage facilities. It also reopens the question of whether the EPA had the legal authority to regulate methane as a pollutant. Major energy companies have, in fact, spoken out against it, joining utilities and other industrial grants that have opposed other administration initiatives to dismantle climate change and environmental rules.

**728) August 30, 2019-China trade war batters'
American firms.**

More U.S. businesses and farmers say they are suffering amid the prolonged U.S.-China trade war, as they brace for the fallout from a new round of tariffs set to take effect. The latest U.S tariffs will hit a broad range of consumer-goods categories for the first time, raising costs for retailers and consumers. "The most notable affected category, relative to Best Buy are televisions, smart watches and headphones. GOP Senator Pat Toomey said manufacturing in his state of Pennsylvania are finding it difficult to face higher prices on parts the need and it is hurting their ability to be competitive. "Tariffs are painful, and they are a double edge sword" Toomey said. President Trump pushed back hard against Mr. Toomey, <u>"So what does Pat Toomey want me to say, let me put my hands up, China, continue to rip me off."</u>

729) August 31, 2019-President defends China trade policies.

President Trump rejected the notion that his trade policies were having a negative impact on the U.S. economy, instead blaming "badly run and weak companies" for any business setbacks. Mr. Trump said that the U.S. doesn't <u>"have a tariff problem, we have a Fed problem,"</u> he added: <u>"Badly run and weak companies are smartly blaming these small tariffs instead of themselves for bad management, and who could really blame them for doing that? Excuses!"</u>

730) September 1, 2019-Trump falsely claims U.S. never collected 10 cents in tariffs on Chinese goods.

At the August 26 conclusion of the Group of Seven Summit in France, President Trump discussed tariffs, trade, and the relationship between the United States and China. Trump told reporters that the U.S. has "never collected 10 cents" from China before his presidency. But that is incorrect. According to the Washington Post, the U.S. began collecting tariffs on Chinese imports shortly after the Revolutionary War. Tariffs on Chinese goods have brought the U.S. at least $8 billion each year since 2009, according to the Post.

731) September 2, 2019-U.S. sticks new set of tariffs on Chinese goods.

A new wave of tariffs by the Trump administration went into effect rendering the majority of goods imported to the United States from China. A 15% tariff on billions of dollars' worth of Chinese goods as varied as cereal bowls, paint brushes and pajamas are likely to hit American households in the most direct way. About $480 over a year for the average family, according to an analysis from economist. Across the income spectrum, the tariffs may cost up to $970 for America's wealthiest households and as low as $340 for it's poorest.

732) September 3, 2019-Dems to probe presidents alleged role in scheme to keep women quiet.

House Democrats plan to make President Donald Trump's alleged involvement in a 2016 scheme to silence two women who claimed they had affairs with him a major investigative focus this fall, picking up where federal prosecutors left off in a case legal experts say could have led to additional indictments. Democrats say they believe there is already enough evidence to name Trump as a co-conspirator in the episode that resulted in his former attorney Michael Cohen pleading guilty to two campaign finance charges.

733) September 4, 2019-Trump says China will suffer, but data show tariffs hurting U.S.

President Trump said that Chinese manufacturing would "crumble" if the country did not agree to the United States trade terms as newly released data shows his trade war washing back to American shores and hurting the factories that the president has aimed to protect.

734) September 4, 2019-Pentagon will divert billions from projects to pay for wall.

The Pentagon will delay or suspend 127 military construction projects so that $3.6 billion can be diverted to shore up President Trump's border wall, Defense Department officials said. The move is part of President Trump's declaration in February of a national emergency in order to gain access to billions of dollars that Congress refused to give him to build a wall along the border with Mexico. After losing a battle with lawmakers over the funding, a fight that led to a partial government shutdown. The president argued that the flow of drugs, criminals and illegal immigrants from Mexico constitutes a national security threat that justifies using the military without specific approval from lawmakers.

735) September 4, 2019-McConnell says he's waiting for Trump to chart gun path.

Congressional Republicans are waiting for the White House to chart a path forward on gun violence legislation, Senate Majority Leader Mitch McConnell said, effectively putting the border on President Donald Trump to decide the GOP's legislative response to the spate of mass shootings that included another deadly attack in Texas. Trump said that any gun measure must satisfy the competing goals of protecting public safety and the constitutional right to gun ownership. "For the most part, sadly, if you look at the last four or five (shootings) going back even five or six or seven years as strong as you make your background checks, they would not have stopped any of it, so it's a big problem. It's a mental problem. It's a big problem.

736) September 5, 2019-Pentagon lists projects that will be delayed by border wall.

The Pentagon plans to direct funds from military construction projects in nearly half the 50 states, three territories, and 19 countries to the southwestern border wall as part of President Trump's effort to bypass Congress and redirect spending to his signature campaign promise. Nearly every facet of military life, from a concealed dining center in Puerto Rico to a small firing range in Tulsa, OK, to an elementary school in Wiesbaden, Germany will be affected by the transfer of $3.6 billion in congressionally appropriated funds detailed by the Defense Departments. The $3.6 billion, taken from 127 projects across the globe, will go toward 11 projects in Arizona, New Mexico, and Texas.

737) September 5, 2019-Trump covers mistake with doctored hurricane chart.

The White House attempted to retroactively justify a tweet that President Donald Trump issued over the weekend in which he warned erroneously, that Alabama would be in the path of Hurricane Dorian. The National Weather Service office in Birmingham, Alabama, bluntly tweeted 20 minutes later <u>"Alabama will NOT see any impacts from #Dorian."</u>

738) September 5, 2019-Child migrants harmed by detention.

Migrant children separated from their parents last year under the Trump administrations "zero tolerance" immigration enforcement policy didn't receive adequate mental-health care in the government's custody, according to a new report from the Department of Health and Human Services internal watchdog. "According to the program directors and mental health clinicians, separated children exhibited more fear, feelings of abandonment, and post-traumatic stress than did children who were not separated" the report states.

739) September 6, 2019-Trump eyes California on emissions.

The Trump administration is pressing regulators to accelerate the rollout of new tail-pipe-emission rules, an attempt to strike back at California for cutting a side deal with several auto makers to set standards that are tougher than those proposed by the administration. California has a federal waiver to set its own emission rules, which the Trump administration wants to revoke to limit the states influence over the auto industry.

740) September 6, 2019-Aging school loses funding to border wall.

For almost two decades, families at Fort Campbell the sprawling Army base along the Kentucky-Tennessee border, have borne the brunt of the country's war efforts as a steady clip of troops with the 101st Airborne Division and from Special Operations units deployed to Afghanistan and Iraq. This week the families discovered that they would not get the new middle school they were expecting so that President Trump could build his border wall. The Pentagon's decision to divert $62.6 million from the construction of Fort Campbell's middle school means that 552 students in sixth, seventh, and eighth grades will continue to cram themselves, 30 to a classroom in some cases, at the aging Mahaffey Middle school.

741) September 6, 2019-Fallout from spat over storm underscores Trump's mindset.

President Donald Trump doesn't make mistakes. At least according to him. Trump's relentless justifications of his erroneous warnings that Hurricane Dorian was threatening Alabama, which created days of ridicule and skepticism, are just the latest example of the president's lifelong reluctance to admit error, no matter how innocuous. "Great presidents admit when they've screwed up, they fix it, and they move on," said presidential historian John Meacham.

742) September 7, 2019-Trump storm over Alabama keeps raging.

For the sixth straight day, Mr. Trump continued his relentless campaign to prove that he was right when he predicted that Hurricane

Dorian could hit Alabama regardless of what the scientists said, a quest that has come to consume his White House and put his veracity to the test.

743) September 8, 2019-Agency reverses course on Prez's Alabama hurricane claim.

A federal agency reversed course on the question of whether President Donald Trump tweeted stale information about Hurricane Dorian potentially hitting Alabama upsetting meteorologist around the world. Trump had warned that Alabama, along with the Carolina's and Georgia, was "most likely to be hit (much) harder than anticipated." The National Weather Service in Birmingham Alabama tweeted in response: No impacts from Hurricane #Dorian will be felt across Alabama. The system will remain too far east." But the president has been adamant throughout the week that he was correct, and the White House has deployed government resources and staff to back him.

744) September 8, 2019-House panel's first steps toward impeachment.

The House Panel eager to impeach President Donald Trump will adopt rare investigative procedures to bolster its probe, tools used in previous impeachments of American Presidents. The House Panel members and aides have framed it as the first formal step on the road to possibly impeaching Trump.

745) September 9, 2019-Schumer and Pelosi urge Trump to take action on guns in a letter.

The top two Democrats in Congress called on President Trump to defy the National Rifle Association and get behind legislation, already passed by the House but blocked in the Senate, to expand background checks to nearly all gun buyers. Nancy Pelosi and Senator Chuck Schumer, the Democratic leader, sent a joint letter to the president, telling him that his "urgent, personal intervention is needed to stem the endless massacres of our fellow Americans by gun fire" and that he had a "historic opportunity to save lives."

746) September 10, 2019-Mr. Trump backs down, again and again.

President Trump can be pressed to do the wrong thing, as when, at the behest of the gun lobby, and its congressional defenders, he has repeatedly flip-flopped on plans to pursue gun safety measures. He also has a tendency to announce one thing and then reverse himself within days, or hours. It has long been clear that Mr. Trump is not the decisive, resolute leader he imagines himself to be. His presidency is littered with plans and pronouncements that were walked back on abandoned, some good, some not so good.

747) September 10, 2019-U.S. Secretary said to coerce science agency.

The Secretary of Commerce threatened to fire top employees at the federal scientific agency responsible for weather forecast after the agency's Birmingham office contradicted President Trump's claim that Hurricane Dorian might hit Alabama, according to three people familiar with the discussion. That threat lead to an unusual unsigned statement later by the agency, the National Oceanic and Atmospheric Administration, disavowing the National Weather Service's position that Alabama was not at risk. The reversal caused widespread anger within the agency and drew accusations from the scientific community that the National Weather Service, which is part of NOAA, had been bent to political purposes.

748) September 10, 2019-House broadens its investigation of the president.

A planned House Judiciary Committee vote will mark the start of an aggressive new phase of House Democrats oversight of President

Trump, putting new force behind a push to determine whether Mr. Trump's actions during the 2016 presidential campaign and after could form the basis for lawmakers to push him out of office.

749) September 11, 2019-Trump ousts Bolton after clashes.

President Donald Trump abruptly forced out John Bolton, his hawkish National Security Advisor with whom he had strong disagreements on Iran, Afghanistan, and a cascade of other global challenges. The shakeup marked the latest departure of a prominent voice of descent from the president's inner circle, as Trump has grown less accepting of advice contrary to his instincts. Tensions between Bolton, Trump's third national security advisor, and other officials have flared in recent months over influence in the president's orbit and how to manage his desire to negotiate with some of the Worlds' most unsavory actors.

750) September 12, 2019-Trump steps up attacks on Fed to lower interest rates.

President Donald trump upped his attacks on the Federal Reserve, demanding the central banks slash interest rates to zero or even push them into negative territory, claiming that he wants this change to make it cheaper to refinance government debt.

751) September 12, 2019-NOAA backed Trump tweet in his orders.

White House pressed weather agency to support claim storm would hit Alabama. President Donald Trump directed his staff to order the National Oceanic and Atmospheric Administration to prepare a statement that Hurricane Dorian posed a significant threat to Alabama as of September 1st, in contrast to what the agency's forecasters were predicting at the time. Trump instructed chief of staff Mick Mulvaney to direct NOAA's leaders to issue a statement buttressing his contention, according to a senior official who spoke on the condition of anonymity due to the sensitive nature of the matter. Mulvaney then relayed the message to Commerce Secretary Wilbur Ross, this official said, who in turn instructed NOAA officials to put a statement to that effect. Trump told reporters he made no such instructions to Mulvaney.

752) September 12, 2019-Trump calls for ban as vaping concerns deepen.
A 50-year-old Kansan became the sixth person in the USA to die of a vapor-related lung illness, an outbreak that has ramped up health concerns nationwide and prompted President Donald Trump to call for a ban on thousands of e-cigarette flavors. Trump held a policy discussion on vaping and said afterward that he will seek to ban the sale of non-tobacco-flavored products in an effort to get young people to give up e-cigarettes.

753) September 13, 2019-Trump repeals Obama-era rule on clean water.
The Trump administration announced the repeal of a major Obama-era clean water regulation that had placed limits on polluting chemicals that could be used near streams, wetlands and other body of waters. The rollback of the 2015 measure, known as the Waters of the United States rule, adds to a lengthy list of environmental rules the administration has worked to weaken or undo over the past two and a half years. An immediate effect of the clean water repeal is that polluters will no longer need a permit to discharge potentially harmful substances into many streams and wetlands. But the measure, which is expected to take effect in a matter of weeks, has implications far beyond the pollution that will now be allowed to flow freely into waterways.

754) September 13, 2019-U.S. clears a path for drilling in Artic.

The Trump administration said that oil drilling in part of Alaska's Arctic National Wildlife Refuge would have a negligible environmental impact, clearing the way for lease sales to oil companies this year. But environmentalists were quick to react. The National Resources Defense Council said it planned to challenge the environmental assessment. The refuge in Alaska's northeast corner is the country's largest wildlife preserve and may be the country's largest remaining pristine wilderness. It is now closer to widespread drilling than ever before with President Trump and Republicans in Congress pushing to use their power to give oil companies unprecedented access.

755) September 16, 2019-Lawmakers push to limit President's tariff powers.

In Senator Jerry Moran's home state of Kansas, support for President Trump remains high. But so does anxiety among farmers and manufacturers about the economic fallout from the tariffs Mr. Trump has imposed. "This has gone on longer than I think people expected it, and so the financial consequences are increasing," Mr. Moran said. Mr. Moran and some other Republicans-including Senator Chuck Grassley of Iowa, Chairman of the Senate Finance Committee, are searching for ways to team up with Democrats to reassert congressional authority over the levying of tariffs. They aim to curb the type of tariff by tweet policy making that has whip saved markets and stressed U.S. businesses in recent months. The White House did not respond to requests or comments. Mr. Trump has said the U.S. has been taken advantage of by other nations and that comply with U.S. demands.

756) September 17, 2019-Prosecutors subpoena Trump tax returns.

Prosecutors in Manhattan have subpoenaed eight years of President Trump's tax returns from his long-time accounting firm, according to a person familiar with the matter. The subpoena seeks documents including Mr. Trump's personal tax returns and those of his long-time business, the Trump Organization. The probe is examining whether a payment to former adult-film star Stormy Daniels, and the way Trump Organization recorded the reimbursement of the at payment-violated a state law that bars falsifying business records.

757) September 17, 2019-With oil under attack, Trump's deference to Saudis return to the fore.

After oil installations were blown up in Saudi Arabia, President Trump declared that the United States was "locked and loaded" a phrase that seemed to suggest he was ready to strike back. But then he promised to wait for Saudi Arabia to tell him "under what terms we would proceed."

758) September 18, 2019-Trump to scrap California's role on car emissions.

The Trump administration is expected to formally revoke California's authority to set auto emission rules that are stricter than federal standards, taking a major step forward in its wide-ranging attack on government efforts to fight climate change. Lawyers said the action takes the administration into uncharted legal territory in its battle with the state, which has vowed to fight the change all the way to the Supreme Court.

759) September 18, 2019-In confronting Iran, Trump may find the world is wary.

For a president with a loose relationship with the facts and poisonous relationships with allies, the attack on the Saudi oil fields is a challenge. If Mr. Trump tries to gather a coalition to impose diplomatic penalties tighten sanctions to further choke off Iranian oil exports to retaliate with a military or cyber strike, he may discover that, like President George W. Bush heading into Iran 16 years ago, he is largely alone.

760) September 18, 2019-Archaeological in Arizona face a threat: Border wall construction.

The construction of President Trump's wall along the southwestern border will significantly damage or completely destroy more than 20 archaeological sites in a national park in the heart of Arizona's Sonoran Desert, according to a study by the National Park Service. Scientist have found stone tools, rock shelters, artifacts, and ancient engravings in the area, which have been populated for 16,000 years. The National Park Service found 17 archaeological sites that "likely will be wholly or partially destroyed by the forthcoming border fence construction. An additional five sites that park experts want protected under the National Register of Historic Places could also be damaged.

761) September 20, 2019-Standoff over whistleblower escalates.

A whistleblower complaint that prompted a standoff between the U.S. Intelligence community and Democrats in Congress involves President Trump's communications with a foreign leader. The House Intelligence Committee has been gripped in an unusual legal battle with the acting director of National Intelligence, Joseph Maguire, over the complaint. The Intelligence community's inspector general deemed the complaint an urgent matter, and the Democratic chairman of the committee, Adam Schiff, has accused Mr. Maguire of illegally preventing the complaint from being shared with lawmakers to protect the Trump administration. Mr. Schiff issued a subpoena last week to Mr. Maguire over the complaint. Mr. Maguire initially appeared to rebuff the subpoena, but late Wednesday he had agreed to testify at an open hearing next week.

762) September 20, 2019-Trump sues to block latest push for his tax returns.

President Trump filed a lawsuit to block New York prosecutors subpoena for his tax returns, the latest salvo in a continuing battle over the disclosure of the president's financial information. The suit filed in federal court in Manhattan against Manhattan District Attorney Cyrus Vance Jr. and accountant firm Mazars USA LLP, comes in response to a subpoena, state prosecutors sent last month to the accounting firm requesting eight years of personal and business tax returns. State prosecutors are examining whether a payment to former adult film star Stormy Daniels, and how the reimbursements of that payment was recorded that could violate a state law against falsifying business records.

763) September 20, 2019-Whistleblower sets off battle involving Trump.

President denies having improper talks with any world leader. A potentially explosive complaint by a whistle-blower in the intelligence community said to involve President Trump emerged as the latest front in a continuing oversight dispute between administration officials and House Democrats. It involves at last one instance of Mr. Trump making an unspecified commitment to a foreign leader and includes other actions. At least part of the allegation deals with Ukraine.

764) September 20, 2019-Blocked complaint centers on Ukraine.

A whistleblower complaint about President Donald Trump made by an intelligence official centers on Ukraine, according to two people familiar with the matter, which has set off a struggle between Congress and the executive branch. The complaint involved communications with a foreign leader and a "promise" that Trump made, which was so alarming that a U.S. intelligence official who had worked at the White House went to the inspector general at the intelligence community, two former officials said.

765) September 21, 2019-President asked Ukraine's leader for Biden inquiry.

President Donald Trump pressed the Ukrainian president in a July call to investigate former Vice President Joseph R. Biden Jr.'s son, according to a person familiar with the conversation, an apparently blatant mixture of foreign policy with his 2020 re-election campaign. Mr. Trump also repeatedly told President Volodymyr Zelensky of Ukraine to talk with his personal lawyer Rudolph W. Giuliani, who had been urging the government in Kier for months to investigate Mr. Biden and his family, according to other people briefed on the call.

766) September 21, 2019-Trump calls China a "threat to the world" ahead of his talks.

President Trump said that China was a "threat to the world" and suggested Beijing was eager to make a trade deal because his tariffs were hurting the Chinese economy, coarsening his tone as the two countries prepared to resume negotiations.

767) September 22, 2019-Trump brings unfinished deals to U.N.

President Donald Trump, a self-described deal maker, is saddled with a long list of unresolved foreign policy deals he has yet to close heading into his U.N. visit. There are challenges with Iran, North Korea, the Afghan Taliban, Israel, and the Palestinians, not to mention a number of trade pacts. Some are inching forward, some have stalled. Trump has said repeatedly that he is in "no rush to wrap up deals."

768) September 23, 2019-Trump suggests he mentioned Biden to Ukraine's president.
President Donald Trump suggested that he raised former Vice President Joe Biden and Biden's son in a summer phone call with Ukraine's new leader, as Democrats pressed for investigations into whether Trump improperly used his office to try to dig up damaging information about a political rival.

769) September 23, 2019-Trump says Biden came up on call.
President Trump confirmed that he discussed Joe Biden with Ukraine's president during a July call, a conversation that has prompted Democrats to accuse the president of wrongfully pres-suring a foreign leader to investigate a political opponent. Mr. Trump defended his call with Mr. Zelensky as routine while again suggesting Mr. Biden, a potential opponent in 2020, and his son should be investigated, though neither have been accuse of wrong doing over their work in Ukraine. "The conversation I had was largely congratulatory, was largely the fact that we don't want our people like Vice President Biden and his son (contributing) to the corruption already in the Ukraine," Mr. Trump said. Mr. Trump had declined to say what the two leaders had discussed, saying "It doesn't matter."

770) September 24, 2019-Mantra shift: 'No collusion' to 'so what?'
The last time he was accused of collaborating with a foreign power to influence an election, he denied it and traveled the country prac-tically chanting, "No Collusion!" This time, he is saying in effect, so what if I did. Even for a leader who has audaciously disregarded many of the boundaries that restrained his predecessors, President

Trump's appeal to a foreign power for dirt on former Vice President Joseph R. Biden Jr. is an astonishing breach of the norms governing the American presidency.

771) September 24, 2019-Trump is defiant as House presses for Ukraine files.

Leading congressional Democrats demanded that the Trump administration turn over documentation about allegations that President Trump sought to pressure the Ukrainian president to dig up dirt on a leading political rival, as a growing number of their colleagues said his actions could warrant impeachment. Mr. Trump buffeted by questions about his conduct, denied accusations that he had withheld $391 million in security aid from Ukraine in an attempt to press President Volodymyr Zelensky to do his bidding. The president also continued to insist he acted appropriately.

772) September 25, 2019-Pelosi opens formal impeachment probe.

Speaker calls Trump's actions over Ukraine a 'betrayal of our national security.' House Speaker Nancy Pelosi announced a formal impeachment inquiry into President Donald Trump, a dramatic turnaround by the Democratic leader that sets up a constitutional and political clash pitting Congress against the nation's chief executive. "The actions of the Trump presidency have revealed the dishonorable fact of the president's betrayal of his oath of office, betrayal of our national security and betrayal of the integrity of our elections." Pelosi said in brief remarks. "Therefore, today, I am announcing the House of Representatives is moving forward with an official impeachment inquiry."

773) September 25, 2019-Pelosi: No one is above the law.

The House will begin a formal impeachment inquiry into President Donald Trump, House Speaker Pelosi announced, the culmination of a month's long investigative battle between Democrats and the White House that finally came to a head over the president's efforts to get Ukraine to go after Joe Biden. "The president must be held accountable. No one is above the law," said Pelosi, who accused Trump of betraying his oath of office and endangering National Security. "The actions taken to date by the president have seriously violated the Constitution, especially when the president says, "I can do whatever I want!"

774) September 25, 2019-Trump rejects Dem's efforts as 'garbage'

President Donald Trump dismissed House Democrats decision to launch an impeachment inquiry as "Witch hunt garbage." "Such an important day at the United Nations, so much work and so much success, and the Democrats purposely had to ruin and demean it with more breaking news witch hunt garbage, so bad for our country," Trump tweeted.

775) September 26, 2019-Witnesses bolster whistle-blower complaint.

The intelligence officer who filed a whistle-blower complaint about President Trump's interactions with the leader of Ukraine raised alarms not only about what the two men said in a phone call, but also about how the White House handled records of the conversation, according to two people briefed on the complaint. The whistle-blower, moreover, identified multiple White House officials as witnesses to potential presidential misconduct who could corroborate the complaint the people said-adding that the inspector general for the intelligence community, Michael Atkinson, interviewed witnesses. Mr. Atkinson eventually concluded that there was reason to believe that the president may have illegally solicited a foreign campaign contribution, and that his potential misconduct created a national security risk, according to a newly disclosed Justice Department memo.

776) September 27, 2019-White House officials accused of cover-up.

Whistle-blower says aides his Trump's abuse of his office. White House officials took extraordinary steps to "lock down" information about President Donald Trump's summertime phone call with the president of Ukraine, even moving the transcript to a secret computer system, a whistle-blower alleges in a politically explosive complaint that accuses the administration of a wide-ranging cover-up. The whistleblower's official complaint alleges a concerted White House effort to suppress the transcript of the call and describes a shadow campaign of diplomacy by the president's personal lawyer Rudy Giuliani that worried some senior administrator officials.

777) September 28, 2019-Trump envoy for Ukraine steps down.

Kurt Volker, President Donald Trump's special envoy to Ukraine has stepped down, according to two people familiar with the matter, a day after he was named in a whistleblower's complaint over Trump's telephone call with Ukrainian President Volodymyr Zelensky. According to the whistleblower, Volker visited Ukrainian Capital of Kier the day after Trump spoke with Zelensky on July 25, and he provided advice about how to "navigate" the American president's request for an investigation of former Vice President Joe Biden and his son Hunter.

778) September 28, 2019-Democrats seek Pompeo's papers in investigation.

House Democrats, moving quickly to escalate their impeachment inquiry into President Trumps, subpoenaed Secretary of State

Mike Pompeo, demanding that he promptly produce a trance of documents and a slate of witnesses that could shed light on the president's attempts to pressure Ukraine to help tarnish a leading political rival.

779) September 29, 2019-Clinton email probe back.
The Trump administration is investigating the email records of dozens of current and former senior State Department officials who sent messages to then-Secretary of State Hillary Clinton's private email, reviving a politically toxic matter that overshadowed the 2016 election, current and former officials said.

780) September 30, 2019-Whistleblower to testify soon, Schiff says.
Trump aide Miller says president is real whistleblower. House Intelligence Committee Chairman Adam Schiff said that he expects the whistleblower at the heart of impeachment proceedings against President Donald Trump to testify "very soon."

781) September 30, 2019-Trump embraced Ukraine conspiracy theory; former advisor says.
President Trump was repeatedly warned by his own staff that the Ukraine conspiracy theory that he and his lawyers were pursuing was "completely debunked" long before the president pressed Ukraine this summer to investigate his Democratic rivals, a former top advisor said. Thomas P. Bossert, who served as Mr. Trumps first homeland security advisor, said he told the president there was no basis to the theory that Ukraine not Russia, intervened in the 2016 election and did so on behalf of the Democrats. Speaking out for the first time, Mr. Bossert said he was "deeply disturbed" that Mr. Trump nonetheless tried to get Ukraine's president to produce damaging information on Democrats.

Acknowledgements

Journalists and Newspaper Sources

Chapter 1

1)   July 21, 2016-Tina Sfondeles-Chicago Sun Times
2)   July 22, 2016-Marena Garcia-Chicago Sun Times
3)   July 22, 2016-Tina Sfondeles Chicago Sun Times
4)   August 1, 2016-Jill Colvin & Lois Alonso Lugo-Chicago Daily Herold
5)   August 10, 2016-Chicago Sun Times
6)   August 10, 2016-Facts-Chicago Daily Herald
7)   August 11, 2016-Josh Lederman-Associated Press
8)   August 11, 2016-Evan Vucune-Chicago Sun Times
9)   August 14, 2016-Steven Peoples, Jill Colvin, Josh Lederman-Chicago Daily Herald
10)   August 15, 2016-David Jackson-USA Today
11)   August 18, 2016-David Jackson-USA Today
12)   August 21, 2016-Mona Charen-Chicago Sun Times
13)   August 22, 2016-Brion Bennett-Los Angeles Times
14)   August 23, 2016-Rosalind S. Helderman, Spenser S. Hsu, Tom Hamburger-Chicago Daily Herald
15)   August 24, 2016-Roger Simon-Chicago Sun Times
16)   August 25, 2016-S.E. Cupp-Chicago Sun Times
17)   August 26, 2016-Lisa Maschild- Washington Bureau
18)   August 29, 2016-Sean Sullivan-The Washington Post

19) September 1, 2016-Noah Bierman, Tracy Wilkinson, Kate Linthicum-Washington Bureau

20) September 2, 2016-David Lauter, Brian Bennett, Lisa Mascaro, Contributor

21) September 3, 2016-Jill Colvin, Corey Williams-Los Angeles Times

22) September 10, 2016-Gene Lyons-Chicago Sun Times

23) September 18, 2016-Peter Suderman-Chicago Sun Times

24) September 21, 2016-Roger Simon-Chicago Sun Times

25) September 24, 2016-Glenn Kessler

26) October 1, 2016-Chicago Daily Herald-Associated Press

27) October 2, 2016-David Jackson-USA Today

28) October 4, 2016-David Fehrenthold-The Washington Post

29) November 19, 2016-Doug Stanglin-USA Today

30) November 19, 2016- Heidi M. Przybyla, Elizabeth Collins-USA Today

31) November 28, 2016-Steve Peoples, Calvin Woodward-Chicago Sun Times, Associated Press

32) November 28, 2016-Tom Minnerick-Chicago Daily Herald

33) November 29, 2016-Editorial-Chicago Sun Times

34) December 1, 2016-David Jackson-USA Today

35) December 2, 2016-Dan Lamothe-The Washington Post

36) December 5, 2016-David Jackson-USA Today

37) December 8, 2016-Steve Chapman-Chicago Tribune

38) December 8, 2016-Lynn Sweet, Fran Spielman-Chicago Sun Times

39) December 8, 2016-Chicago Tribune

40) December 10, 2016-Adam Entous, Ellen Nakashima, Greg Miller-The Washington Post

41) December 11, 2016-Julie Pace-Associated Press

42) December 12, 2016-Sarah D. Wire-Los Angeles Times

43) December 13, 2016-Henry Meyer, Ilya Arkhipov-Bloomberg

44) December 15, 2016-Craig Whitlock, Greg Miller-The Washington Post

45) December 16, 2016-Bradlye Klapper, Jack Lederman-Associated Press

46) December 16, 2016-Associated Press

47) December 17, 2016-Chicago Daily Herald

48) December 17, 2016-Josh Lederman, Julie Pace-Associated Press

49) December 19, 2016-Richard Wolf-USA Today

50) January 3, 2017-Lisa Macard-The Washington Post

51) January 3, 2017-Philip Rucker-The Washington Post

52) January 5, 2017-Alan Fram-Associated Press

53) January 5, 2017-Associated Press

54) January 6, 2017-Ellen Nakashima, Kevin Demirtian, Philip Rucker-Associated Press

55) January 7, 2017-Brian Bennett-Washington Bureau

56) January 7, 2017-David Jackson-USA Today

57) January 7, 2017-Gregory Korte-USA Today

58) January 9, 2017-Noah Bierman-Washington Bureau

59) January 12, 2017-Joseph Tanfani, Jim Puzzanghera

60) January 12, 2017-John Bierman, Brian Bennett-Washington Bureau

61) January 18, 2017-Vladimir Isachenkov-Associated Press

Chapter 2

62) January 20, 2017-Matthew Rosenberg, Adam Goldman, Matt Apuzzo-The New York Times

63) January 21, 2017-Don Bale, Noah Bierman-The Washington Post

64) January 23, 2017-John Wagner-The Washington Post

65) January 24, 2017-Donavan Slack-USA Today

66) January 25, 2017-Noah Bierman-Washington Bureau

67) January 25, 2017-David Jackson-USA Today

68) January 26, 2017-Brain Bennett, Noah Bierman-Washington Bureau
69) January 26, 2017-David Jackson, Kevin Johnson-USA Today
70) January 27, 2017-Erin Kelly-USA Today
71) January 30, 2017-Susan Page-USA Today
72) February 3, 2017-Kevin Freking, Matthew Daly-Associated Press
73) February 6, 2017- David Jackson-USA Today
74) February 10, 2017-Maura Dolan-Los Angeles Times
75) February 14, 2017-Lisa Mascaro-Washington Bureau
76) February 14, 2017-Ellen Wakashima, Philip Rucker-The Washington Post
77) February 15, 2017-Julie Pace, Vivian Salama-Associated Press
78) February 16, 2017-Oren Dorell-USA Today
79) February 17, 2017-Donavan Slack-USA Today
80) February 25, 2017-Gene Lyons-Chicago Sun Times
81) February 28, 2017-David Jackson-USA Today
82) March 1, 2017-Julie Pace-Associated Press White House
83) March 3, 2017-The Washington Post
84) March 6, 2017-B.D. Sullivan, Keith Johnson, David Jackson-USA Today
85) March 10, 2017-Associated Press
86) March 10, 2017-Erin Kelly-USA Today
87) March 11, 2017-Ledyard King-USA Today
88) March 13, 2017-Deb Riechmann-Associated Press
89) March 16, 2017-Donavan Slack, Gregory Korte-USA Today
90) March 19, 2017-Mark Phelan-Detroit Free Press
91) March 19, 2017-David S. Cloud, Del Quentin-The Washington Post
92) March 25, 2017-Erica Werner, Alan Fram-Associated Press
93) March 28, 2017-Evan Halper-Washington Bureau, Los Angeles Times

94)   March 28, 2017-Gregory Korte-USA Today

95)   March 29, 2017-Jennifer Robin-The Washington Post

96)   March 30, 2017-David Lauter, David S. Cloud-The Washington Post

Chapter 3

97)   April 6, 2017-David Jackson, Jim Michaels, Tom Vanden Brook-USA Today

98)   April 7, 2017-W.J. Hennigan, Tracy Wilkinson-Washington Bureau

99)   April 10, 2017-Robert Reich-Chicago Sun Times

100)   April 12, 2017-Tracy Wilkinson, Brian Bennett-Washington Bureau, Los Angeles Times

101)   April 12, 2017-Ellen Wakashima, Devlin Barrett, Adam Entous-The Washington Post

102)   April 22, 2017-Julie Pace-Associated Press

103)   April 24, 2017-Susan Page-USA Today

104)   April 26, 2017-Stephen Ohlemacher, Josh Boak-Associated Press

105)   April 27, 2017-Joseph Tanfoni-Washington Bureau

106)   April 28, 2017-Fredreka Schouten-USA Today

107)   May 10, 2017-David Lauter, Michaela A. Memoli-Washington Bureau, Los Angeles Times

108)   May 12, 2017-David Jackson-USA Today

109)   May 17, 2017-Eric Tucker-Associated Press

110)   May 18, 2017-Joseph Tanfoni, Noah Bierman, Brian Bennett-The Washington Post

111)   May 19, 2017-Joseph Tanfoni, Lisa Mascaro, Evan Halper-Washington Bureau

112)   May 19, 2017-David Jackson-USA Today

113)   May 20, 2017-Erica Werner, Eileen Sullivan-Associated Press

114)   May 23, 2017-Chad Day, Stephen Braun-Associated Press

115) June 2, 2017-Sabrea Ayers-Los Angeles Times

116) June 3, 2017-Sadie Gurman, Eric Tucker, Jeff Horowitz-Associated Press

117) June 8, 2017-David S. Cloud, Joseph Tanfoni-Washington Bureau

118) June 9, 2017-David S. Cloud, Joseph Tanfoni-The Washington Post

119) June 10, 2017-Jill Colvin, Calvin Woodward-Associated Press

120) June 16, 2017-Brian Bennett, Noah Bierman-Washington Bureau

121) June 28, 2017-Erica Werner, Alan Fram-Associated Press

122) June 28, 2017-John Flesher, Michael Biesecker-Associated Press

123) July 4, 2017-Michael Biesecker-Associated Press

124) July 5, 2017-Trevor Hughes-USA Today

125) July 7, 2017-Brian Bennett, Michael A. Memoli-Washington Bureau, Los Angeles Times

126) July 10, 2017-Laura King-Washington Bureau

127) July 11, 2017-Chad Day, Wakesa Mumbi-Associated Press

128) July 12, 2017-David S. Cloud-Washington Bureau, Los Angeles Times

129) July 13, 2017-Fredreka Schouten-USA Today

130) July 13, 2017-Brian Bennett-Associated Press, Los Angeles Times

131) July 19, 2017-Erica Werner, Alan Fram-Associated Press

132) July 20, 2017-Laura Rosenblatt-Washington Bureau

133) July 23, 2017-Doug Stanglin-USA Today

134) July 26, 2017-Tracy Wilkinson-Washington Bureau

135) July 27, 2017-Lynn Sweet-Chicago Sun Times

136) July 29, 2017-Allan From, Erica Werner-Associated Press

137) July 29, 2017-Eric Talmadge, Mary Yamaguchi-Associated Press

138) August 1, 2017-Ashley Parker, Carol D. Leonnig, Philip Rucker, Tom Hamburger-The Washington Post
139) August 4, 2017-David S. Cloud-Washington Bureau
140) August 9, 2017-John Bacon-USA Today
141) August 11, 2017-Joseph Tanfoni-Washington Bureau
142) August 25, 2017-Erin Kelly-USA Today
143) August 28, 2017-Carol D. Leonnig, David Hamburger, Rosalind S. Helderman-The Washington Post
144) August 31, 2017-Alan Gomez-USA Today
145) September 4, 2017-Robert Burns, Catherine Lucey-Associated Press

Chapter 4

146) September 5, 2017-Jill Colvin-Associated Press
147) September 6, 2017-Brian Bennett, Joseph Tanfoni-Washington Bureau
148) September 14, 2017-Erica Werner, Jill Colvin-Associated Press
149) September 15, 2017-Gregory Korte-USA Today
150) September 16, 2017-Jason Meisner, John Byrne-Chicago Tribune
151) September 28, 2017-Marcy Gordon, Andrew Taylor-Associated Press
152) September 28, 2017-Evan Halper-Washington Bureau
153) October 8, 2017-Noah Bierman-Washington Bureau
154) October 13, 2017-Ken Thomas, Andrew Taylor-Associated Press
155) October 25, 2017-Lisa Mascaro-Washington Bureau
156) October 31, 2017-Joseph Tanfoni-Washington Bureau
157) November 1, 2017-Stephen Braun, Steve Peoples-Associated Press
158) November 4, 2017-Philip Rucker, Matt Zapotosky-The Washington Post

159) November 12, 2017-Jill Colvin, Jonathan Lemire-Associated Press

160) November 16, 2017-Kevin Freking-Associated Press

161) November 21, 2017-Sudhin Thanawala-Associated Press

162) December 2, 2017-Chris Megerian, David S. Cloud, David Willman-Washington Bureau

163) December 4, 2017-Laura King-Washington Bureau

164) December 5, 2017-Chris Megerian, Joseph Tanfoni-Chicago Tribune

165) December 12, 2017-Rex W. Huppke-Chicago Tribune

166) December 13, 2017-John Wagner, Ed O'Keefe, Ashley Parker- Daily Herald

167) December 16, 2017-Joseph Tanfoni-Washington Bureau

168) December 18, 2017-Laura King-Washington Bureau

169) December 19, 2017-Brian Bennett-Washington Bureau

170) December 21, 2017-Lisa Mascaro-Contributor Herb Jackson-The Washington Post

171) December 27, 2017-David Jackson-USA Today

172) December 30, 2017-Ryan W. Miller-USA Today

173) January 4, 2018-Jill Colvin, John Hanna-Associated Press

174) January 6, 2018-Gene Lyons-Opinion-Chicago Sun Times

175) January 9, 2018-Caorl D. Leonnig-The Washington Post

176) January 14, 2018-Clarence Page-Perspective-Chicago Tribune

177) January 14, 2018-Calvin Woodward, Jill Colvin-Associated Press

178) January 16, 2018-Don Lee-Washington Press

179) January 17, 2018-Richard Wolf-USA Today

180) January 18, 2018-Clarence Page-Perspective-Chicago Tribune

181) January 21, 2018-Glenn Kessler, Meg Kelly- The Washington Post

182) January 23, 2018-Lisa Mascaro-Washington Bureau

183) January 25, 2018-Erick Tucker, Chad Day-Associated Press

184) January 29, 2018-Dahleen Glanton-Chicago Tribune

185) January 30, 2018-Jesse Jackson-Chicago Sun Times

186) January 31, 2018-Chicago Tribune "Address"

187) February 1, 2018-Joseph Tanfoni, Chris Megerian-Washington Bureau

188) February 5, 2018-Laura King-Washington Bureau

189) February 7, 2018-Lisa Mascaro-Washington Bureau

190) February 13, 2018-Andrew Taylor-Associated Press

191) February 14, 2018-Lisa Mascaro-Washington Bureau

192) February 16, 2018-Elizabeth Collins, Deirdre Shesgreen-USA Today

193) February 17, 2018-Sari Horwitz, Devlin Barrett, Craig Timber-The Washington Post

194) February 17, 2018-Mark Landler, Michael D. Shear-The New York Times

195) February 19, 2018-Jason Dearen, Terry Spencer, Allen G. Breed-Associated Press

196) February 21, 2018-Assoicated Press, Daily Herald

197) February 22, 2018-Chirsti Parsons-Washington Bureau-Contributing

198) February 23, 2018-Chicago Tribune-Christi Parsons

199) February 25, 2018-Richard Lardner, Nicholas Riccardi-Associated Press

200) February 26, 2018-Lisa Mascaro, Matthew Daly-Associated Press

201) February 26, 2018-Laura King, Washington Bureau

202) February 28, 2018-Len Goodman-Opinion-Guest Column

203) March 1, 2018-Christi Parsons-Washington Bureau

204) March 5, 2018-Laura King-Washington Bureau

205) March 8, 2018-Ken Thomas-Associated Press

206) March 9, 2018-Anna Fifield-The Washington Post

207) March 9, 2018-David Jackson-USA Today

208) March 14, 2018-Josh Lederman, Zeke Miller-Associated Press
209) March 15, 2018-Associated Press, Chicago Tribune
210) March 19, 2018-Laura King-Washington Bureau
211) March 21, 2018-Carol D. Leonnig, David Nakamura, Josh Dawsey, -The Washington Post
212) March 23, 2018-Ken Thomas, Paul Wiseman-Associated Press
213) March 24, 2018-Ken Thomas-Associated Press
214) March 29, 2018-Byron York-Daily Herald

Chapter 5

215) April 2, 2018-Philip Rucker, David Weigel- The Washington Post
216) April 4, 2018-Seung Min Kim-The Washington Post
217) April 4, 2018-Samantha Schmidt-The Washington Post
218) April 4, 2018-Lynn Sweet-Chicago Sun Times
219) April 11, 2018-Chicago Tribune
220) April 14, 2018-Daily Herald, Associated Press
221) April 16, 2018-Catherine Lucey, Eric Tucker-Associated Press
222) April 20, 2018-Mary Clare Jalonick, Eric Tucker, Chad Day-Associated Press
223) April 20, 2018-Chad Day-Associated Press
224) April 25, 2018-Chicago Sun Times-Associated Press
225) May 1, 2018-Michel Finnegan-Los Angeles Times
226) May 3, 2018-Devlin Barrett, Philip Bump, John Dawsey-The Washington Post
227) May 4, 2018-John Wagner-The Washington Post
228) May 4, 2018-Noah Bierman, Michael Finnegan, Joseph Tankini-Washington Bureau
229) May 5, 2018-Noah Bierman-Washington Bureau
230) May 5, 2018-Catherine Lucey-Associated Press

231) May 6, 2018-Joe Heim-The Washington Post

232) May 7, 2018-Laura King-Washington Bureau

233) May 8, 2018-Zeke Miller, Catherine Lucey-Associated Press

234) May 9, 2018-Noah Bierman, Tracy Wilkinson-Washington Bureau

235) May 17, 2018-Mary Clare Jalonick, Eric Tucker, Chad Day-Associated Press

236) May 18, 2018-Philip Rucker, Robert Costa, Josh Dawsey-The Washington Post

237) May 20, 2018-Connie Hassett-Walker-The Washington Post

238) May 22, 2018-Martin Crutsinger, Paul Wiseman-Associated Press

239) May 23, 2018-Eli Stokols-Washington Bureau

240) June 1, 2018-Ashley Thomas, Chad Day-Associated Press

241) June 1, 2018-Don Lee, Kate Linthicum-Washington Bureau

242) June 1, 2018-David J. Lynch, Josh Dawsey, Damian Paletta-The Washington Post

243) June 2, 2018-Matthew Daly-Associated Press

244) June 5, 2018-Eli Stokols-Washington Bureau

245) June 14, 2018-Alan Gomez-USA Today

246) June 15, 2018-Ken Thomas, Paul Wiseman-Associated Press

247) June 16, 2018-Joe McDonald-Associated Press

248) June 17, 2018-Carol D. Leonnig, Robert Costa-The Washington Post

249) June 18, 2018-Mitch Dudek-Staff Reporter-Chicago Sun Times

250) June 19, 2018-Eli Stokols, Noah Bierman-Washington Bureau

251) June 20, 2018-Garlance Burke, Marsha Mendoza-Associated Press

252) June 21, 2018-Editorial-Chicago Tribune

253) June 21, 2018-Jill Colvin, Colleen Long-Associated Press

254) June 25, 2018-Neil Steinberg-Chicago Sun Times

255) June 25, 2018-Philip Rucker, David Weigel-The Washington Post

256) June 26, 2018-Elliot Spagat, Morgan Lee

257) June 27, 2018-Opinion Editorial-Chicago Sun Times

258) June 30, 2018-Tiffany HSU-The New York Times

259) July 4, 2018-Anne Gearan-The Washington Post

260) July 5, 2018-Joe McDonald-Associated Press

261) July 6, 2018-Alan Gomez-USA Today

262) July 11, 2018-Brittny Mejia-Los Angeles Times

263) July 12, 2018-Eli Stokols-Washington Bureau

264) July 14, 2018-Mark Mazzetti, Katie Benner- The New York Times

265) July 15, 2018-Matthew Lee-Associated Press

266) July 16, 2018-Jill Colvin- Associated Press

267) July 17, 2018-Julie Hirschfeld Davis

268) July 17, 2018-Sarah D. Wire-Washington Bureau

269) July 18, 2018-Zeke Miller, Lisa Mascaro-Associated Press

270) July 18,2018-Kevin Freking-Associated Press

271) July 19, 2018-Chris Megerian-Washington Bureau

272) July 23, 2018-Zeke Miller-Associated Press

273) August 2, 2018-Chris Megerian, Noah Bierman, Eliza Fawcett-Washington Bureau

274) August 3, 2018-Brady Dennis, Michael Laris, Juliet Eilperin-The Washington Post

275) August 4, 2018-Emily Rauhala-The Washington Post

276) August 6, 2018-Laura King-Washington Bureau

277) August 15, 2018-John Wagner-The Washington Press

278) August 17, 2018-Jill Colvin, Catherine Lucey-Associated Press

279) August 17, 2018-Kurtis Less-Los Angeles Times

280) August 17, 2018- David Nakamura, John Dawsey-The Washington Post

281) August 21, 2018-Evan Halper-Washington Bureau

282) August 22, 2018-Fredreka Schouten, John Friter- USA Today

283) August 24, 2018-Devlin Barrett, John Wagner, Seung Min Kim-The Washington Post

284) August 29, 2018-Associated Press-World & Nation

285) September 1, 2018-Jennifer Jacobs, Shawn Donnan, Andrew Mayeda, Salena Mohsin-Bloomberg News

286) September 6, 2018-Zeke Miller, Catherine Lucey-Associated Press

287) September 7, 2018-Jonathan Lemire-Associated Press

288) September 7, 2018-Zeke Miller, Johnathan Lemire-Associated Press

289) September 8, 2018-Juana Summers, Sara Burnett-Associated Press

290) September 9, 2018-Calvin Woodward, Nancy Benac-Associated Press

291) September 11, 2018-Cokie, Steve Roberts-Opinion-Daily Herald

292) September 14, 2018-Catherine Lucey, Zeke Miller, Jonathan Lemire-Associated Press

293) September 15, 2018-Spencer S. Hsu, Devlin Barrett, Justin Jouvenal-The Washington Post

294) September 16, 2018-David S. Cloud-Los Angeles Times

295) September 20, 2018-John Wagner, Matt Zapotosky-The Washington Post

296) September 21, 2018-Matthew Daily- Associated Press

297) September 27, 2018-Zeke Miller, Jonathan Lemire – Associated Press

298) October 2, 2018-Damian Paletta, Erica Werner-The Washington Post

299) October 3, 2018-Joe Palazzolo, Michael Rothfeld-The Wall Street Journal

300) October 3, 2018-David Barstow, Susanne Craig, Russ Buettner-The New York Times

301) October 9, 2018-Eric Tucker, Jonathan Lemire-Associated Press

302) October 12, 2018-Matthew Pennington, Catherine Lucey-Associated Press

303) October 14, 2018-Philip Rucker-The Washington Post

304) October 16, 2018-Kareem Fahim, John Wagner, Souad Mekhennet- The Washington Post

305) October 17, 2018-Jay Abuelgasim, Suzan Fraser, Jon Gambrell-Associated Press

306) October 19, 2018- John Wagner, Alex Horton-The Washington Post

307) October 26, 2018-Aya Batrawy, Christopher Torchia-Associated Press

308) October 30, 2018-Catherine Lucey-Associated Press

309) October 30, 2018-Robert Burns, Colleen Long, Jill Colvin-Associated Press

310) October 31, 2018-Maggie Haberman, Benjamin Weiser-The New York Times

311) November 2, 2018-Nathan Bomey-USA Today

312) November 2, 2018-Jill Colvin, Colleen Long-Associated Press

313) November 4, 2018-David S. Cloud-Los Angeles Times

314) November 8, 2018-Eric Tucker, Michael Balsamo-Associated Press

315) November 8, 2018-David Jackson, John Fritze-USA Today

316) November 8, 2018-Peter Baker, Michael D. Shear-The New York Times

317) November 9, 2018-Richard Wolf, Alan Gomez-USA Today

318) November 10, 2018-Eric Tucker, Jonathan Lemire-Associated Press

319) November 17, 2018-Chicago Daily Herald Wire Reports

320) November 18, 2018-Ben Poston, Angel Jennings, Joseph Serna, Javier Panzar- Los Angeles Times, Associated Press Contributing

321) November 19, 2018-Felicia Sonmez, Karen DeYong-The Washington Post

322) November 19, 2018-Felicia Sonmez-The Washington Post

323) November 20, 2018-Robert Burns-Associated Press

324) November 20, 2018-Carol D. Leonnig, Josh Dawsey-The Washington Post

325) November 21, 2018-Josh Dawsey, Shane Harris, Karen DeYoung-The Washington Post

326) November 21, 2018-Rebecca Ballhaus, Vivian Salama-The Wall Street Journal

327) November 21, 2018-Mark Landler-The New York Times

328) November 22, 2018-Deb Riechmann-Associated Press

329) November 22, 2018-Felicia Sonmez-The Washington Post

330) November 23, 2018-John Dawsey-The Washington Post

331) November 23, 2018-Jill Colvin-Associated Press

332) November 24, 2018-Brady Dennis, Chris Mooney-The Washington Post

333) November 25, 2018-Opinion Editorial-Chicago Sun Times

334) November 26, 2018-Karoun Demirjian-The Washington Post

Chapter 6

335) November 27, 2018-Sharon LaFraniere-The New York Times

336) November 28, 2018-Philip Rucker, Josh Dawsey, Damian Paletta-The Washington Post

337) November 29, 2018-Felicia Sonmez-The Washington Post

338) November 29, 2018-Mary Clare Jalonick, Susannah George-Associated Press

339) November 30, 2018-Eric Tucker, Larry Neumeister, Chad Day-Associated Press

340)   November 30, 2018-Kevin Johnson, Bart Jansen-USA Today
341)   December 3, 2018-Julian E. Barnes, Eric Schmitt-The New York Times
342)   December 6, 2018-Rex W. Huppke-Chicago Tribune
343)   December 9, 2018-Josh Dawsey, Seung Min Kim, Philip Rucker-The Washington Post
344)   December 10, 2018-Hope Yen-Associated Press
345)   December 12, 2018-The Washington Post
346)   December 13, 2018-Matt Zapotosky, Devin Barrett-The Washington Post
347)   December 14, 2018-Jim Mustian-Associated Press
348)   December 14, 2018-John Wagner-The Washington Post
349)   December 17, 2018-Craig Timberg, Tony Romm-The Washington Post
350)   December 18, 2018-Mary Clare Jalonick-Associated Press
351)   December 19, 2018-Matt Zapotosky, Carol D. Leonnig-The Washington Post
352)   December 19, 2018- Michael M. Sisar-Associated Press
353)   December 20, 2018-Tom Vanden Brook, David Jackson-USA Today
354)   December 21, 2018-Erica Werner, Damian Paletta, Mike DeBonis-The Washington Post
355)   December 21, 2018-David S. Cloud-Los Angeles Times
356)   December 24, 2018-Philip Rucker, Dan Lamothe, Josh Dawsey-The Washington Post
357)   December 24, 2018-Binyamin Appelbaum-The New York Times
358)   December 24, 2018-Michael R. Gordon, Nancy A. Youssef, Jessica Donati-The Wall Street Journal
359)   December 26, 2018-Sadie Gurman, Jess Bravin-The Wall Street Journal
360)   December 26, 2018-Norman Merchant-Associated Press

361) December 27, 2018-Annie Karni, Mark Landler, Thomas Gibbons-Neff-The New York Times
362) December 28, 2018-Mark Landler-The New York Times
363) December 28, 2018-Mona Charen-Chicago Sun Times
364) December 29, 2018-Felicia Sonmez-The Washington Post
365) December 31, 2018-Ian Talley-The Wall Street Journal
366) December 31, 2018-Peter Nickolas-The Wall Street Journal
367) January 1, 2019-Eric Schmitt, Maggie Haberman-The New York Times
368) January 2, 2019-Anne Gearan-The Washington Post
369) January 3, 2019-Damian Paletta, Erica Werner-The Washington Post
370) January 4, 2019-The Washington Post
371) January 5, 2019-David Nakamura, Josh Dawsey-The Washington Post
372) January 5, 2019-Sheryl Gay Stolberg, Michael Tackett-The New York Times
373) January 8, 2019-Jim Tankersley, Matthew Goldstein, Glenn Thrush-The New York Times
374) January 9, 2019-Rebecca Ballhaus, Kristina A. Peterson, Michael C. Bender-The Wall Street Journal
375) January 9, 2019-Catherine Lucey, Jill Colvin, Lisa Mascaro-Associated Press
376) January 9, 2019-Sharon LaFraniere, Kenneth P. Vogel, Maggie Haberman
377) January 11, 2019-Eli Stokols, Molly Hennessy-Fiske-Los Angeles Times
378) January 11, 2019-Mary Clare Jalonick, Eric Tucker, Chad Day-Associated Press
379) January 12, 2019-The Washington Post
380) January 14, 2019-Peter Baker-The New York Times
381) January 14, 2019-Vivian Salama, Rebecca Ballhaus, Andrew Duehren-The Wall Street Journal

382) January 15, 2019-Julian E. Barnes, Helene Cooper-The New York Times
383) January 17, 2019-Lisa Friedman-The New York Times
384) January 19, 2019-Delvin Barrett, Matt Zapotosky, Karoun Demirjian-The Washington Post
385) January 19, 2019-Rebecca Ballhaus, Natalie Andrews
386) January 20, 2019-Jill Colvin, Catherine Lucey, Zeke Miller-Associated Press
387) January 21, 2019-Paige Cunningham-The Washington Post
388) January 21, 2019-Mark Mazzetti, Maggie Haberman, Michael S. Schmidt- The New York Times
389) January 23, 2019-Sheryl Gay Stolberg, Julie Hirschfeld Davis-The New York Times
390) January 26, 2019-Peter Baker-The New York Times
391) January 26, 2019-Rosalind S. Helderman, Devlin Barrett, John Wagner-The Washington Post
392) January 27, 2019-Joshua Partlow, David A. Fahrenthold-The Washington Post
393) January 28, 2019-Jay Reeves-Associated Press
394) January 28, 2019-Felicia Sonmez-The Washington Post
395) January 29, 2019-Michael Sneed-Chicago Sun Times
396) January 30, 2019-David E. Sanger, Julian E. Barnes-The New York Times
397) January 30, 2019-Aruna Viswanatha, Sadie Gurman-The Wall Street Journal
398) January 31, 2019-Mark Landler-The New York Times
399) February 2, 2019-Anne Gearan, Carol Morello, Paul Sonne-The Washington Post
400) February 3, 2019-Associated Press
401) February 6, 2019-Rebecca Ballhaus, Peter Nicholas-The Wall Street Journal
402) February 8, 2019-Marcy Gordon-Associated Press

403) February 15, 2019-Peter Baker, Emily Cochrane-The New York Times

404) February 16, 2019-Peter Baker-The New York Times

405) February 17, 2019-Damian Paletta, Mike DeBonis, John Wagner, Amy B. Want, Missy Ryan-
The Washington Post

406) February 19, 2019-Amy Goldstein-The Washington Post

407) February 20, 2019-John Wagner-The Washington Post

408) February 23, 2019-Emily Cochrane-The New York Times

409) February 23, 2019-Mark Landler, Helena Cooper-The New York Times

410) February 25, 2019-Emily Cochrane-The New York Times

411) February 26, 2019-Dustin Volz, Courtney McBride-The Wall Street Journal

412) February 26, 2019-Assoicated Press

413) February 27, 2019-The Washington Post

414) February 27, 2019-Rebecca Ballhaus, Warren P. Strobel-The Washington Post

415) February 28, 2019-Rebecca Ballhaus, Joe Palazzolo-The Wall Street Journal

416) February 28, 2019-Peter Baker, Nicholas Fandos-The New York Times

417) March 1, 2019-Deb Reichmann, Hyung-Jin Kim, Catherine Lucey-Associated Press

418) March 1, 2019-John Dawsey, Philip Rucker-The Washington Post

419) March 1, 2019-Alan Fram, Andrew Taylor-Associated Press

420) March 1, 2019-Andrew Duehren, Rebecca Ballhaus-The Wall Street Journal

421) March 1, 2019-Natalie Andrews, Kristina Peterson-The Wall Street Journal

422) March 4, 2019-Rebecca Ballhaus, Dustin Volz-The Washington Post

423) March 5, 2019-Dustin Volz-The Wall Street Journal

424) March 5, 2019-Iliana Magra-The New York Times

425) March 6, 2019-Rebecca Ballhaus-The Wall Street Journal

426) March 6, 2019-Damian Paletta, Erica Werner-The Washington Post

427) March 6, 2019-Marc Fisher-The Washington Post

428) March 6, 2019-Josh Zumbrun-The Wall Street Journal

429) March 7, 2019-Josh Boak-Associated Press

430) March 8, 2019-Aruna Viswanatha-The Wall Street Journal

431) March 8, 2019-Felicia Sonmez, Associated Press Contributed, The Washington Post

432) March 9, 2019-Lingling Wei, Jeremy Page, Bob Davis-The Wall Street Journal

433) March 10, 2019-The Washington Post

434) March 11, 2019-Lisa Mascaro-The Associated Press

435) March 11, 2019-Lisa Mascaro-The Associated Press

436) March 13, 2019-Catie Edmondson-The New York Times

437) March 14, 2019-Katie Rogers-The New York Times

438) March 15, 2019-Spencer S. Hsu, Rachel Weiner, Anne E. Marimow-The Washington Post

439) March 15, 2019-Catie Edmondson-The New York Times

Chapter 7

440) March 16, 2019-Kristina Peterson, Natalie Andrews-The New York Times

441) March 16, 2019-Alex Leary, Kristina Peterson-The Wall Street Journal

442) March 18, 2019-Richard Wolf-USA Today

443) March 18, 2019-Felicia Sonmez-The Washington Post

444) March 18, 2019-Darlene Superville-Associated Press

445) March 19, 2019-Neal E. Boudette, Tiffany Hsu-The New York Times

446) March 20, 2019-Jim Tankersley-The New York Times

447) March 20, 2019-Catherine Lucey-Associated Press
448) March 21, 2019-Maggie Haberman, Annie Karni, Michael Tuckett-The New York Times
449) March 21, 2019-Alan Rappaport-The New York Times
450) March 21, 2019-Jill Colvin-Associated Press
451) March 22, 2019-James Comey-The New York Times
452) March 22, 2019-Jonathan Lemire, Mary Clare Jalonick-Associate Press
453) March 23, 2019-Aruna Viswanatha, Sadie Gurman-The Wall Street Journal
454) March 23, 2019-Michael R. Gordon, Ian Talley-The Wall Street Journal
455) March 24, 2019-Ben Protess, William K. Rashbaum, Benjamin Weiser, Maggie Haberman-The Washington Post
456) March 24, 2019-Philip Rucker, Robert Costa, Josh Dawsey, Ashley Parker-The Washington Post
457) March 24, 2019-Mark Mazzetti, Katie Benner-The New York Times
458) March 25, 2019-Delvon Barrett, Matt Zapotosky-The Washington Post
459) March 26, 2019-Peter Baker, Nicholas Fandos-The New York Times
460) March 26, 2019-Mary Clare Jalonick-Associated Press
461) March 27, 2019-Sheryl Gay Stolberg, Roberta Pear-The New York Times
462) March 27, 2019-Michael Collins, David Jackson, Maureen Groppe-USA Today
463) March 28, 2019-Stephen Castle, Richard Perez-Peña-The New York Times
464) March 29, 2019-Jim Tankersley-The New York Times
465) March 29, 2019-Natalie Andrews, Warren P. Strobel, Byron Tau-The Wall Street Journal

466) March 29, 2019-Matthew Townsend, Eric Martin-Bloomberg News

467) March 29, 2019-Lisa Mascaro, Laurie Kellman, Mary Clare Jalonick-Associated Press

468) March 30, 2019-Nomaan Merchant, Jonathan Lemire-Associated Press

469) March 31, 2019-David A. Fahrenthold, Jonathan O'Connell-The Washington Post

470) March 31, 2019-Lisa Mascaro, Catherine Lucey-Associated Press

471) March 31, 2019-Jonathan Lemire, Nomaan Merchant, Colleen Long-Associated Press

472) April 1, 2019-Joel Achenbach, David J. Lynch, Marybeth Sheridan-The Washington Post

473) April 1, 2019-Felicia Sonmez-The Washington Post

474) April 1, 2019-Katie Rogers-The New York Times

475) April 2, 2019-Siobhan Hughes, Byron Tau-The Wall Street Journal

476) April 2, 2019-Nicholas Fandos, Maggie Haberman-The New York Times

477) April 2, 2019-David E. Sanger-The New York Times

478) April 3, 2019-Jim Tankersley, Ana Swanson-The New York Times

479) April 3, 2019-Rober Pear, Maggie Haberman-The New York Times

480) April 3, 2019-Stephanie Armour, Kristina Peterson-The Wall Street Journal

481) April 3, 2019-Jill Colvin, Colleen Long-Associated Press

482) April 4, 2019-Rebecca Davis O'Brien, Rebecca Ballhaus-The Wall Street Journal

483) April 4, 2019-Richard Rubin-The Wall Street Journal

484) April 4, 2019-Rachael Bade-The Washington Post

485) April 5, 2019-Ellen Nakashima, Carol D. Leonnig, Rosalind Helderman-The Washington Post

486) April 5, 2019-David Nakamura, Felicia Sonmez-The Washington Post

487) April 6, 2019-Zeke Miller, Jonathan Lemire-Associated Press

488) April 9, 2019-Rebecca Ballhaus, Vivian Salama-The Wall Street Journal

489) April 9, 2019-Brent Kendall, Louise Radnofsky-The Wall Street Journal

490) April 10, 2019-Sadie Gurman, Byron Tau-The Wall Street Journal

491) April 11, 2019-Nicholas Fandos, Adam Goldman-The New York Times

492) April 11, 2019-Alan Rappaport-The New York Times

493) April 12, 2019-Jonathan Lemire, Eric Tucker-Associated Press

494) April 12, 2019-Rachael Bade, Nick Miroff-The Washington Post

495) April 13, 2019-Maggie Haberman, Annie Karni, Eric Schmitt-The New York Times

496) April 13, 2019-Louise Radnofsky, Rebecca Ballhaus- The Wall Street Journal

497) April 14, 2019-Andrew Taylor- Associated Press

498) April 15, 2019-Mike DeBonis, Rachel Bade, Felicia Sonmez- The Washington Post

499) April 15, 2019-Annie Karni, Maggie Haberman- The New York Times

500) April 15, 2019-Felicia Sonmez, Mike DeBonis-The Washington Post

501) April 16, 2019-Devlin Barrett-The Washington Post

502) April 17, 2019-Vivian Salama-The Wall Street Journal

503) April 17, 2019-Michel D. Shear, Katie Benner-The New York Times

504) April 18, 2019-Chad Day, Eric Tucker, Michael Balsamo-Associated Press

505) April 19, 2019-Devlin Barrett, Matt Zapotosky-The Washington Post

506) April 19, 2019-Opinion-Chicago Sun Times

507) April 19, 2019-Sadie Gurman-The Wall Street Journal

508) April 20, 2019-Rebecca Ballhaus, Vivian Salama, Natalie Andrews-The Washington Post

509) April 20, 2019-Peter Baker, Nicholas Fandos-The New York Times

510) April 22, 2019-Tim Tankersley-The New York Times Business

511) April 22, 2019-Tom Nichols-USA Today-Opinion

512) April 23, 2019-Karoun Demirjian-The Washington Post

513) April 23, 2019-David A. Fahrenthold, Rachael Bade, John Wagner-The Washington Post

514) April 23, 2019-Michael S. Schmidt-The New York Times

515) April 23, 2019-Assoicated Press, Daily Herald

516) April 24, 2019-Damian Paletta, Erica Werner-The Washington Post

517) April 24, 2019-Adam Liptak-The New York Times

518) April 25, 2019-Charlie Savage-The New York Times

519) April 26, 2019-Rebecca Ballhaus, Alex Leary-The Wall Street Journal

520) April 27, 2019-Alex Leary-The Wall Street Journal

521) April 28, 2019-Laurie Kellman-Associated Press

522) April 29, 2019-The Washington Post

523) April 30, 2019-Michelle Goldberg-The Washington Post

524) April 30, 2019-Byron Tau-The Wall Street Journal

525) May 1, 2019-Mark Mazzetti, Michael S. Schmidt-The New York Times

526) May 2, 2019-Sadie Gurman, Byron Tau, Christina Peterson-The Wall Street Journal

527) May 3, 2019-Byron Tau, Natalie Andrews, Rebecca Ballhaus-The Wall Street Journal

528) May 4, 2019-Mark Landler-The New York Times

529) May 5, 2019-Glenn Thrush-The New York Times

530) May 5, 2019-The Washington Post

531) May 5, 2019-Carol D. Leonnig-The Washington Post

532) May 6, 2019-Bob Davis, Rebecca Ballhaus-The Washington Post

533) May 6, 2019-Micheal Tackett, Maggie Haberman-The New York Times

534) May 7, 2019-Nicholas Fandos, Alan Rappaport-The New York Times

535) May 8, 2019-World Nation-Associated Press

536) May 9, 2019-Mark Mazzetti, Maggie Haberman-The New York Times

537) May 9, 2019-Byron Tau, Rebecca Ballhaus-The Wall Street Journal

538) May 11, 2019-Bob Davis-The Wall Street Journal

539) May 12, 2019-Rachael Bade, Seung Min Kim-The Washington Post

540) May 12, 2019-Andrew Taylor-Associated Press

541) May 12, 2019-Catherine Lucey, Robert Burns-Associated Press

542) May 13, 2019-Jeanna Smialek, Jim Tankersley, Mark Landler-The New York Times

543) May 14, 2019-David J. Lynch, Taylor Telford, Damian Paletta, Gerry Shih-The Washington Post

544) May 15, 2019-Damian Paletta, Erica Werner, Taylor Telford-The Washington Post

545) May 15, 2019-Spencer S. Hsu-The Washington Post

546) May 16, 2019-Michael D. Shear-The New York Times

547) May 17, 2019-Jill Colvin, Zeke Miller, Lisa Mascaro-Associated Press

548) May 17, 2019-Opinion-The New York Times
549) May 18, 2019-Ana Swanson-The New York Times
550) May 18, 2019-Rebecca Ballhaus-The Wall Street Journal
551) May 19, 2019-Coley Itkowitz-The Washington Post
552) May 20, 2019-David Enrich-The New York Times
553) May 21, 2019-Rebecca Ballhaus-The Wall Street Journal
554) May 21, 2019-Spencer S. Hsu-The Washington Post
555) May 21, 2019-Charlie Savage, Nicholas Fandos-The New York Times
556) May 22, 2019-Mary Clare Jalonick, Lisa Mascaro-Associated Press
557) May 23, 2019-Rebecca Ballhaus, Michael C. Bender-The Wall Street Journal
558) May 23, 2019-Emily Flitter, Jesse McKinley, David Enrich, Nicholas Fandos
The New York Times
559) May 23, 2019-Michael Collins, John Fritze, Eliza Collins-USA Today
560) May 24, 2019-Ana Swanson-The New York Times
561) May 24, 2019-Michel Collins, John Fritze-USA Today
562) May 24, 2019-Gordon Lubold, Dion Nissenbaum-The Wall Street Journal
563) May 24, 2019-Michael C. Bender, Rebecca Ballhaus-The Wall Street Journal
564) May 25, 2019-Julian E. Barnes, David E. Sanger-The New York Times
565) May 25, 2019-Helene Cooper, Edward Wong, Catie Edmondson-The New York Times
566) May 25, 2019-Deb Riechmann-Associated Press
567) May 26, 2019-Daisy Nguyen, Elliot Spagat-Associated Press
568) May 27, 2019-Felicia Sonmez-The Washington Post
569) May 28, 2019-Coral Davenport, Mark Landler-The New York Times

570) May 29, 2019-Peter Baker, Maggie Haberman-The New York Times
571) May 30, 2019-Sharon LaFraniere-The New York Times
572) May 30, 2019-Byron Tau, Aruna Viswanatha, Sadie Gurman-The Wall Street Journal
573) May 31, 2019-Louise Radnofsky, William Mauldin, David Luhnow-The Wall Street Journal
574) May 31, 2019-Peter Baker, Eileen Sullivan-The New York Times
575) May 31, 2019-Deb Riechmann-Associated Press
576) June 1, 2019-The Washington Post
577) June 1, 2019-Ana Swanson-The New York Times
578) June 1, 2019-Jim Tankersley-The New York Times
579) June 3, 2019-Santiago Perez-The Wall Street Journal
580) June 4, 2019-Luis Alonso Lugo, Lisa Mascaro, Hope Yen-Associated Press
581) June 5, 2019-Erica Werner, Seung Min Kim, Damian Paletta, Marybeth Sheridan
The Washington Post
582) June 5, 2019-Catie Edmondson, Maggie Haberman-The New York Times
583) June 6, 2019-Michael D. Shear, Zolan Kanno-Youngs, Ana Swanson-The New York Times
584) June 6, 2019-Maria Sacchetti-The Washington Post
585) June 7, 2019-Colby Itkowitz-The Washington Post

Chapter 8

586) June 7, 2019-John Wagner-The Washington Post
587) June 8, 2019-Michel Laforgia, Walt Bogdanich-The New York Times
588) June 8, 2019-David Nakamura, Nick Miroff, John Wagner-The Washington Post
589) June 10, 2019-Rebecca Ballhaus-The Wall Street Journal

590)   June 10, 2019-Peter Baker-The New York Times

591)   June 11, 2019-Anna Swanson, Jeanna Smialek-The New York Times

592)   June 11, 2019-Martin Crutsinger-AP Economic Writer

593)   June 11, 2019-Jill Colvin, Colleen Long, Maria Verza-Associated Press

594)   June 11, 2019-Damian Paletta-The Washington Post

595)   June 12, 2019-Michel D. Shear-The New York Times

596)   June 12, 2019-Mike DeBonis-The Washington Post

597)   June 13, 2019-Bart Janson-USA Today

598)   June 13, 2019-Alex Leary-The Wall Street Journal

599)   June 14, 2019-Natalie Andrews, Siobhan Hughes-The Wall Street Journal

600)   June 15, 2019-Peter Baker-The New York Times

601)   June 15, 2019-Peter Baker-The New York Times

602)   June 16, 2019-Ros Krasny-Bloomberg News

603)   June 19, 2019-Nick Miroff, Maria Sacchetti, Abigail Hauslohner, Josh Dawsey-The Washington Post

604)   June 19, 2019-Jill Colvin, Jonathan Lemire, Michael Schneider-Associated Press

605)   June 20, 2019-Lisa Friedman-The New York Times

606)   June 20, 2019-A.G. Sulzberger-The Wall Street Journal

607)   June 20, 2019-Ledyard King-USA Today

608)   June 20, 2019-Ellen Knickmeyer-Associated Press

609)   June 21, 2019-Karoun Demirjian-The Washington Post

610)   June 23, 2019-Colleen Long, Lisa Mascaro-Associated Press

611)   June 24, 2019-Michael D. Shear-The New York Times

612)   June 25, 2019-Jeanna Smialek-The New York Times

613)   June 26, 2019-Rachael Bade, Matt Zapotosky-The Washington Post

614)   June 27, 2019-Martin Crutsinger-Associated Press

615)   June 27, 2019-Ann E. Marimow, Jonathan O'Connell, Carol O. Leonnig-The Washington Post

616) June 28, 2019-Brent Kendall, Jess Bravin, Janet Adamy-The Wall Street Journal

617) June 28, 2019-Richard Wolf-USA Today

618) June 29, 2019-Peter Baker-The New York Times

619) June 29, 2019- Michel D. Shear, Adam Liptak-The New York Times

620) July 3, 2019-Richard Rubin-The Wall Street Journal

621) July 3, 2019-Jeff Bravin, Janet Adamy-The Wall Street Journal

622) July 4, 2019-Zolan Kanno-Youngs-The New York Times

623) July 4, 2019-Michael Wines, Maggie Haberman, Alan Rappaport-The New York Times

624) July 5, 2019-Joseph Holt-Chicago Tribune (Professor Notre Dame)

625) July 5, 2019-Paul Krugman-Op-Ed-The New York Times

626) July 6, 2019-Peter Baker, Maggie Haberman-The New York Times

627) July 6, 2019-Michael Wines, Adam Liptak-The New York Times

628) July 6, 2019-Colby Itkowitz-The Washington Post

629) July 7, 2019-The Washington Post

630) July 8, 2019-Emily Cochrane-The New York Times

631) July 8, 2019-Aruna Viswanatha-The Wall Street Journal

632) July 10, 2019-Byron Tau-The Wall Street Journal

633) July 11, 2019-Ann E. Marimow, Jonathan O'Connell-The Washington Post

634) July 12, 2019-Katie Rogers, Adam Liptak, Michael Crowley, Michael Wines- The New York Times

635) July 12, 2019-Sydney Ember, Katie Glueck-The New York Times

636) July 13, 2019-Abigail Hauslohner, Maria Sacchetti, Colby Itkowitz-The Washington Post

637) July 15, 2019-Yan Zhang-USA Today

638) July 15, 2019-William Cummings-USA Today
639) July 16, 2019-Ashley Parker, Rachael Bade, John Wagner-The Washington Post
640) July 16, 2019-David Jackson, Alan Gomez-USA Today
641) July 16, 2019-Sadie Gurman, Santiago Perez-The Wall Street Journal
642) July 16, 2019-Juie Hirschfield Davis-The New York Times
643) July 17, 2019-Alisha A. Caldwell, Brent Kendall-The Wall Street Journal
644) July 17, 2019-John Wagner, Mike DeBonis, Colby Itkowitz-The Washington Post
645) July 18, 2019-Andrew Duehren, Dian Nissenbaum-The Wall Street Journal
646) July 18, 2019-Alan Fram, Mary Clare Jalonick-Associated Press
647) July 19, 2019-Alan Fram, Darlene Superville-Associated Press
648) July 21, 2019-Reid J. Epstein, Linda Qiu-The New York Times
649) July 21, 2019-Peter Baker, Michael M. Grynbaum, Maggie Haberman, Ann Karni, Russ Buettner-New York Times
650) July 21, 2019-Mary Clare Jalonick-Associated Press
651) July 22, 2019-Alan Rappaport-The New York Times
652) July 22, 2019-Tarini Parti-The New York Times
653) July 23, 2019-Elliot Spagat-Associated Press
654) July 24, 2019-Michael J. Stern-USA Today
655) July 24, 2019-Nicholas Fandos, Jesse McKinley-The New York Times
656) July 25, 2019-Eric Tucker, Mary Clare Jalonick, Michael Balsamo-Associated Press
657) July 25, 2019–Carol Giacomo-Editorial Observer-The New York Times

658) July 25, 2019–Sadie Gurman, Aruna Viswanatha-The Wall Street Journal

659) July 26, 2019–Associated Press-Daily Herald

660) July 27, 2019–Adam Liptak-The New York Times

661) July 27, 2019–Ana Swanson-The New York Times

662) July 28, 2019–Zeke Miller-Associated Press

663) July 29, 2019–Zeke Miller, Hope Yen-Associated Press

664) July 30, 2019–Warren P. Strobel-The Wall Street Journal

665) July 30, 2019–Ana Swanson, Keith Bradsher-The New York Times

666) July 30, 2019–Sheryl Gay Stolberg-The New York Times

667) July 30, 2019–Catie Edmondson-The New York Times

668) July 31, 2019–Alicia A. Caldwell-The Wall Street Journal

669) July 31, 2019–David Jackson-USA Today

670) August 1, 2019–Laura Reiley-The Washington Post

671) August 2, 2019–Alan Rappaport-The New York Times

672) August 2, 2019–Thomas Gibbons-Neff, Edward Wong-The New York Times

673) August 2, 2019–William Mauldin, Vivian Salama-The Wall Street Journal

674) August 3, 2019–Paul Kiernan, Anthony DeBarros-The Wall Street Journal

675) August 5, 2019–Vivian Salama-Josh Zumbrun-The Wall Street Journal

676) August 6, 2019–Peter Baker, Michael D. Shear-The New York Times

677) August 7, 2019–John Wagner, Felicia Sonmez-The Washington Post

678) August 7, 2019–Karla K. Johnson-Associated Press

679) August 7, 2019–Editorial-Chicago Tribune

680) August 7, 2019–Matthew Daly-Associated Press

681) August 7, 2019–Annie Karni-The New York Times

682) August 8, 2019–Opinion-The New York Times

683) August 8, 2019–Ellen Nakashima, Karoun Demirjian-The Washington Post

684) August 10, 2019–Sheryl Gay Stolberg, Maggie Haberman, Jonathan Martin-The New York Times

Chapter 9

685) August 11, 2019–Andrew Restuccia-The Wall Street Journal

686) August 11, 2019–Alexandra Jaffe-Associated Press

687) August 13, 2019–Daily Herald-Bloomberg News

688) August 13, 2019–Abigail Hauslohner, Nick Miroff, Maria Sacchetti, Tracy Jan-The Washington Post

689) August 13, 2019–Ellen Knickmeyer-Associated Press

690) August 13, 2019–Andrew Restuccia, Louise Radnofsky-The Wall Street Journal

691) August 14, 2019–Editorial-Opinion-Chicago Sun Times

692) August 14, 2019–Ana Swanson-The New York Times

693) August 14, 2019–Timothy Puko-The Wall Street Journal

694) August 15, 2019–Jim Tankersley-The New York Times

695) August 16, 2019–Rebecca Ballhaus, Andrew Restuccia, Natalie Andrews-The Wall Street Journal

696) August 16, 2019–Jim Tankersley, Jeanna Falk, Ana Swanson-The New York Times

697) August 16, 2019–Josh Dawsey, Coley Itkowitz, Laura Hughes-The Washington Post

698) August 16, 2019–Andrew Restuccia, Rebecca Ballhaus-The Wall Street Journal

699) August 17, 2019–Vivian Salama, Rebecca Ballhaus, Andrew Restuccia, Michael C. Bender-The Wall Street Journal

700) August 17, 2019–Anthony DeBarros, John Zumbrun-The Wall Street Journal

701) August 17, 2019–Anna Marie Andriotis-The Wall Street Journal

702) August 19, 2019–Ken Thomas-The Wall Street Journal

703) August 21, 2019–Maggie Haberman-The New York Times

704) August 21, 2019–Alex Leary-The Wall Street Journal

705) August 21, 2019–Alan Rappaport-The New York Times

706) August 22, 2019–Maggie Haberman, Annie Karni, Danny Hakim-The New York Times

707) August 22, 2019–Daily Herald-The Washington Post

708) August 22, 2019–Michelle Hackman-The Wall Street Journal

709) August 23, 2019–Jill Colvin, Elana Schor-Associated Press

710) August 23, 2019–Taylor Telford-The Washington Post

711) August 24, 2019–Patrick J. Lyons-The New York Times

712) August 24, 2019–William Mauldin, Alex Leary-The Wall Street Journal

713) August 26, 2019–Opinion-The New York Times

714) August 26, 2019–Michael D. Shear-The New York Times

715) August 26, 2019–Jessica Donati-The Wall Street Journal

716) August 27, 2019–Jeanna Smialek-The New York Times

717) August 27, 2019–Lori Hinnant, Sylvie Corbet, Zeke Miller-Associated Press

718) August 27, 2019–Rebecca Ballhaus, Stacy Meichtry, Noemie Bisserbe-The Washington Post

719) August 27, 2019–Jess Bravin-The Wall Street Journal

720) August 28, 2019–Patricia Mazzei, Michael D. Shear, Eric Lipton-The New York Times

721) August 28, 2019–Allan Rappaport-The New York Times

722) August 29, 2019–Rebecca Ballhaus, Corinne Ramey-The Wall Street Journal

723) August 29, 2019–Katie Roger, Zolan Kanno-Youngs-The New York Times

724) August 29, 2019–Gerald F. Seib-The Wall Street Journal

725) August 29, 2019–Steve Chapman-Chicago Tribune Perspective

726) August 30, 2019–Nick Miroff, Josh Dawsey-The Washington Post

727) August 30, 209–Eric Tucker-Associated Press

728) August 30, 2019–Lisa Friedman, Coral Davenport-The New York Times

729) August 31, 2019–Chad Deng, William Mauldin (Natalie Andrews, Katy Stech Ferek, Lin Zhu-Contributors) The Wall Street Journal

730) September 1, 2019–Bob Oswald-Chicago Journalist-Daily Herald

731) September 2, 2019–Quoctrung Bui-The New York Times

732) September 3, 2019–Rachael Bade, Tom Hamburger-The Washington Post

733) September 4, 2019–Ana Swanson-The New York Times

734) September 4, 2019–Helene Cooper, Emily Cochrane-The New York Times

735) September 4, 2019–Matthew Daly-Associated Press

736) September 5, 2019–Emily Cochrane, Helene Cooper-The New York Times

737) September 5, 2019–World & Nation-Daily Herald-The Washington Post

738) September 5, 2019–Michael Hackman-The Wall Street Journal

739) September 6, 2019–Timothy Puko, Ben Foldy, Mike Collins (contributing)

The Wall Street Journal

740) September 6, 2019–Helene Cooper-The New York Times

741) September 6, 2019–Jonathan Lemire-Associated Press

742) September 7, 2019–Peter Baker, Sarah Mervosh-The New York Times

743) September 8, 2019–Seth Borenstein, Kevin Freking-Associated Press

744) September 8, 2019–Rachael Bade-The Washington Post

745) September 9, 2019–Sheryl Gay Stolberg-The New York Times

746) September 10, 2019–Michelle Cottle (Editorial Observer)-The New York Times

747) September 10, 2019– Christopher Flavelle, Lisa Friedman, Peter Baker-The New York Times

748) September 10, 2019–Siobhan Hughes, Natalie Andrews-The Wall Street Journal

749) September 11, 2019–Zeke Miller, Deb Riechmann-Associated Press

750) September 12, 2019–Taylor Telford, David J. Lynch-The Washington Post

751) September 12, 2019–Andrew Freedman, John Dawsey, Juliet Eilperin, Jason Samenow

752) The Washington Post

753) September 12, 2019–Doug Stanglin-USA Today

754) September 13, 2019–Lisa Friedman, Coral Davenport-The New York Times

755) September 13, 2019–Timothy Puko-The Wall Street Journal

756) September 16, 2019–Lindsey Wise-The Wall Street Journal

757) September 17, 2019–Corinne Ramey, Rebecca Ballhaus-The Wall Street Journal

758) September 17, 2019–Peter Baker, David E. Sanger-The New York Times

759) September 18, 2019–Coral Davenport-The New York Times

760) September 18, 2019–David E. Sanger-The New York Times

761) September 18, 2019–Zolan Kanno-Youngs-The New York Times

762) September 20, 2019–Dustin Vole, Siobhan Hughes-The Wall Street Journal

763) September 20, 2019–Corinne Ramey-The Wall Street Journal

764) September 20, 2019–Julianne E. Barnes, Nicholas Fandos, Michael S. Schmidt, Matthew Rosenberg-The New York Times

765) September 20, 2019–Ellen Nakashima, Shane Harris, Greg Miller, Carol D. Leonnig-The Washington Post

766) September 21, 2019-Julian E. Barnes, Michael S. Schmidt, Kenneth P. Vogel, Adam Goldman, Maggie Haberman-The New York Times

767) September 21, 2019–Alan Rappaport-The New York Times

768) September 22, 2019–Deb Riechmann-Associated Press

769) September 23, 2019–Darlene Superville-Associated Press

770) September 23, 2019–Dustin Vole, Rebecca Ballhaus-The Wall Street Journal

771) September 24, 2019–Peter Baker-The New York Times

772) September 24, 2019–Nicholas Fandos, Michael Crowley-The New York Times

773) September 25, 2019–Rachael Bade, Mike DeBonis-The Washington Post

774) September 25, 2019–Bart Jansen, Christal Hayes-USA Today

775) September 25, 2019–John Fritze, David Jackson-USA Today

776) September 26, 2019–Charlie Savage, Michael S. Schmidt, Julian E. Barnes-The New York Times

777) September 27, 2019–Eric Tucker, Mary Clare Jalonick-Associated Press

778) September 28, 2019–Nick Wadhams-Bloomberg

779) September 28, 2019–Nicholas Fandos, Sheryl Gay Stolberg-The New York Times

780) September 29, 2019–Greg Miller, Greg Jaffe, Karen Demir J. Fan-The Washington Post

781) September 30, 2019–Laurie Kellman-Associated Press

782) September 30, 2019–Sheryl Gay Stoleberg, Maggie Haberman, Peter Baker The New York Times

Afterword

This book doesn't end here, it is like outer space, endless. Soon there will be an ending that journalist around the world will be able to express their thoughts truthfully without prejudice, an ending that will surprise many around the world. I give praise to the many journalists who have performed their jobs in an honest presentation to the world. President Donald Trump has not given the many journalists credit for stating the news media as it actually happens, especially if the written media does not agree with his performance. It is difficult to see or predict what will happen from this point on, so this book will continue soon. This book opens with the July 2016 Republican convention and follows President Donald Trump through September 2019. President Donald Trump describes journalism as "**the enemy of the people**" and that **FAKE** news doesn't tell the truth. So, follow him through his journey to the White House, and you will see there will be an ending that will, like Paul Harvey said: "Wait just a little bit longer for the rest of the story."

CPSIA information can be obtained
at www.ICGtesting.com
Printed in the USA
LVHW031552100220
646431LV00001B/64